THE RENAISSANCE DRAMA
OF KNOWLEDGE

IORDANI
BRVNI ·NOLANI
DE MONADE NVMERO ET
Figura liber Consequens Quin-
que DE MINIMO MAGNO
& Mensura.

Item

DE INNVMERABILIBVS, IM-
menso, & Infigurabili; seu De Vniuerso
& Mundis libri octo

AD ILLVSTRISSIMVM ET RE-
uerendiss. Principem HENRICVM IV-
LIVM Brunsuicensium & Lunebur-
gensium ducem, Halberstaden-
sium Episcopum, &c.

FRANCOFVRTI,
Apud IOAN. Wechelum & PETRVM
Fischerum consortes. 1591.

THE RENAISSANCE DRAMA OF KNOWLEDGE

Giordano Bruno in England

Hilary Gatti

ROUTLEDGE
LONDON AND NEW YORK

First published 1989
by Routledge
11 New Fetter Lane, London EC4P 4EE
29 West 35th Street, New York, NY 10001

Printed in Great Britain
by T. J. Press (Padstow) Ltd., Padstow, Cornwall

British Library Cataloguing in Publication Data

Gatti, Hilary
The Renaissance drama of knowledge.
1. Italian philosophy. Bruno, Giordano
I. Title
195
ISBN 0-415-03207-5

Library of Congress Cataloging in Publication
Data
also available

To the memory
of
Donald J. Gordon

CONTENTS

ILLUSTRATIONS

ix

PREFACE

The Nolan . . . has freed the human soul and its faculty of
knowing which was closed up in the suffocating prison of the
turbulent air whence it could only glimpse the distant stars as
if through narrow chinks. For its wings were clipped so that it
could not fly and pierce the veil of those clouds and see what
really lies up there. Nor could it free itself from the monstrous
fantasies created by those, risen from the mud and caves of the
earth, . . . who with impostures of all kinds have filled the
world with infinite forms of madness, bestiality and vice, as if
they were so many virtues, divinities, and disciplines. And it is
they who have dimmed the light which made the souls of our
ancient fathers heroic and divine, while approving and
confirming the sooty shadows of sophists and fools.

(Giordano Bruno, *Cena delle Ceneri*, Dialogue I)

It was the chance event of happening to discover Bruno's *Cena
delle Ceneri* ('Ash Wednesday supper'), while at the same time
teaching a course on Shakespeare's *Hamlet*, that gave rise to this
book. The Brunian impetus towards a new 'faculty of knowing',
linked to the bitter attack against forces of vice and obscurity
whose impostures have taken them to power, seemed to project
directly into the world of *Hamlet*. There was the same profuse
architecture of dramatic metaphor and image, the same urgency
in the writing. There was the concern with deciphering the
language of a new and larger cosmos; the revolt against
prevailing cultural modes in the name of a more heroic past
symbolized in the figure of a lost father: not just Hamlet's father
but all ideal fathers, the collective ghosts, 'nostri padri antichi'.

The initial reading left no room for doubt: surely Shakespeare
had passed through those pages written and published in

xi

London less than twenty years before the composition of *Hamlet*. Later on it took little enquiry to realize that the subject was a demanding one with a long and contradictory critical history. The first debt I have to acknowledge is to the Faculty of Letters and Philosophy of the University of Rome ('La Sapienza') which allowed me a year's study-leave to begin research in 1981/2. I was able to pass that year at the Warburg Institute which previously I knew only indirectly through the work of my one-time professor at Reading University, D.J. Gordon. It is to his memory as a fine Renaissance scholar and a remarkable teacher that this book is dedicated. Through the link with Gordon, and my interest in the work of Bruno, I came to know the Director of the Warburg Institute, Professor J. B. Trapp, whose constant concern for my work has been one of the most valuable benefits which this study has brought me. In a brief preliminary visit to London, I had the opportunity of meeting Dame Frances Yates who sadly died a few months later. Bruno studies were still represented at the Warburg Institute during my period of research there in the distinguished figure of Professor D.P. Walker, whose quiet and courteous availability was a source of frequent advice and information. At a later stage of my work, I came into contact with Dr Charles Schmitt, whose study of Aristotle in the Renaissance was opening up some new and interesting prospects. The recent deaths of both these scholars (Schmitt far too young) is a severe loss for Renaissance studies.

My gratitude towards the Warburg Institute is all the greater as my interpretation of Bruno tended, from the beginning, to differ from that associated with the names of Walker and above all Yates. The Bruno presented here is not primarily a Hermetic magus involved in a religious reform which may have led to the formation of secret, esoteric societies, but rather a Renaissance philosopher who declared throughout the Europe of his times his conviction that the human mind was capable of attaining forms of knowledge of the universe so far undreamt of and unrealized. I was comforted in this conviction by the work of Professor Giovanni Aquilecchia of London University who has frequently made available to me, throughout my work on this book, his wide knowledge of Bruno and Bruno studies.

An emphasis on Bruno's natural philosophy tends inevitably to revalue his Copernicanism and to consider important his contribution to the development of modern science. For a time my concern with the Shakespeare relationship gave way to a study of the more scientific minds of Elizabethan England. The divide between disciplines was not then the abyss it has become today; and it was clear to me from the start that Bruno would lead into multiple spheres of enquiry. My concern with the more documented, scientific forms of Elizabethan thought yielded concrete results with the discovery of a substantial collection of Bruno texts in the library of the Ninth Earl of Northumberland. I am grateful to the present Duke of Northumberland and to Lord Egremont for allowing me to examine these texts at Alnwick Castle and Petworth House where they are now held.

The discovery led me to a study of the cultural activities of the so-called Wizard Earl (in my mind a misnomer for a man essentially involved in a philosophical-scientific enquiry) who appears to have spent much of his imprisonment in the Tower learning Italian and reading and annotating Bruno's *Heroici furori*. His figure led directly to those of his associates such as Thomas Harriot and Walter Warner whose private papers yielded clear signs of a direct influence of Bruno. In this phase of my work, I was much indebted to Professor G. Batho and Dr C. Tanner, whose invitation to speak at the Thomas Harriot Seminar held at the University of Durham in December 1983 led to an evaluation of Bruno's influence on this exciting group of philosophical and scientific enquirers. The studies of the Ninth Earl himself and of the Northumberland circle are presented here among the early chapters of this book.

My interest in the Elizabethan drama had far from waned. It became clear at this point that the study of Bruno in late Elizabethan England had led me to isolate a crisis of knowledge which was not limited to the development of the new science. I became particularly concerned with the early Elizabethan tragedies: the emergence in tragic terms of a new intellectual hero. Bruno himself, as well as being a philosopher, was a dramatist and a poet who visualized his search for new forms of knowledge as a dramatic clash with the cultural and religious orthodoxies of his times. Close to the Northumberland circle, I glimpsed the doomed figure of the young Christopher Marlowe conversing daily with Harriot (according to a well-known testimony of Thomas Kyd) in St Paul's Churchyard. I began to think of Marlowe's treatment of the Faust figure as closely connected with the new forms of enquiry I had been studying. The development on the Elizabethan stage of this European myth in the form of a tragic failure of an alternative metaphysic which would allow new forms of human knowledge stands at the centre of this book.

My articles on the Northumberland circle were followed by an invitation from Professor E. Garin to contribute to *Rinascimento*, where my study of *Dr Faustus* first appeared. To acknowledge and thank Eugenio Garin publicly for his life-long work on Renaissance culture, to which all students of the period owe so much, is a pleasure I have long looked forward to. Through contact with him, I learnt of the recent Italian research on Bruno which is confirming the vision of him as an ever more controlled and conscious philosophical intelligence whose work is proving to have had an unsuspected diffusion throughout the Europe of his times.

It was in the light of these various experiences that I came back, as the final stage of my study of Bruno's influence on late Elizabethan England – by no means an exhaustive one – to the Shakespeare of *Hamlet*. I wanted to see how far the theme which had started me out on the subject of this book, and which has enthralled or angered so many critics for a century or more, would stand up to treatment in the context of the most recent research and critical developments. Shakespeare seldom, if ever, disappoints: he as often exasperates by his extraordinary originality which seems to make all his subjects his own, by his enigmatic silences, and his often oblique treatment of multiple themes. Added to the almost total lack of documentary evidence, these are the characteristics which make the search for his sources such a difficult one. Nevertheless *Hamlet* proved, in Brunian terms (as well as so many others), a richly rewarding text, for it shows Shakespeare to have been aware of, and sensitive to, the contemporary crisis in a new search for knowledge about man and the universe. In *Hamlet*, as in Marlowe's *Dr Faustus*, that crisis is acted out on the Elizabethan stage in terms of tragedy: the archetypal tragedy of a meditative hero who claims new spheres of knowledge and power for the aspiring mind. That was Bruno's story and his message.

Some parts of this book have already been published in slightly different form. I am grateful to the editors of the following journals for permission to reproduce: 'Giordano Bruno: the texts in the library of the Ninth Earl of Northumberland', *Journal of the Warburg and Courtauld Institutes*, 46, 1983; 'Minimum and maximum, finite and infinite: Bruno and the Northumberland circle', *Journal of the Warburg and Courtauld Institutes*, 48, 1985; 'Bruno's heroic searcher and Marlowe's *Dr Faustus*', *Rinascimento*, XXVI, 1986.

ABBREVIATIONS

Bib. Salvestrini	V. Salvestrini, *Bibliografia di Giordano Bruno (1582–1960)*, seconda edizione postuma a cura di Luigi Firpo, Florence, 1958.
Bib. Sturlese	R. Sturlese, *Bibliografia, censimento e storia delle antiche stampe di Giordano Bruno*, Quaderni di Rinascimento VI, Florence, 1987.
BL	British Library.
Dial. ital.	Giordano Bruno, *Dialoghi italiani*, con note di Giovanni Gentile, terza edizione a cura di Giovanni Aquilecchia (1957), seconda ristampa, 2 vols, Florence, 1985.
Documenti	*Documenti della vita di Giordano Bruno*, a cura di Vincenzo Spampanato, Florence, 1933.
Il processo	L. Firpo, *Il processo di Giordano Bruno*, Quaderni della rivista storica italiana, I, Naples, 1949.
JWCI	*Journal of the Warburg and Courtauld Institutes*, London.
Op. lat.	Giordano Bruno, *Opera latine conscripta publicis sumptibus edita*, ed F. Fiorentino, V. Imbriani, C.M. Tallarigo, F. Tocco, V. Vitelli, Naples-Florence, 1879–91, 3 vols, 8 parts. Facsimile reprint by Friedrich Fromman Verlag Gunther Holzboog, Stuttgart-Bad Cannstatt, 1962.
Rinasc.	*Rinascimento*, Rivista dell'Istituto Nazionale di studi sul Rinascimento, Florence.

THE BRUNIAN SETTING

BRUNO IN EUROPE

Perhaps no writer more than Giordano Bruno has made such large claims for the extraordinary value of his own work. It is enough to remember the opening of his letter to the Vice-Chancellor of the University of Oxford, written in 1583, where he presents himself as a philosopher whose work is applauded by all noble minds;[1] or the pages of the first dialogue of the *Cena delle Ceneri* in which he praises his own work glowingly between references to Copernicus as the discoverer of a new cosmology and Columbus as the discoverer of a new geography.[2] Eight years later, after a long and often unquiet period in Germany, Bruno dedicates his Latin trilogy containing the final expression of his philosophical vision to Prince Henry Julius of Brunswick. Here he claims, in the first work of the trilogy, the *De triplici minimo*, to have reached through erudition and science an understanding of the primary elements; in the second, the *De monade*, to have penetrated through to the foundations or footsteps of imaginings, opinions, and common assumptions; but it is above all in the third work, the *De immenso*, that his vein of self-assertion is stimulated; for here, he assures his reader, he presents unequivocal, certain, and incontestable demonstrations such as those on the disposition of the worlds in the universe, on the unity of the infinite universe governed by a single principle, and on the manner in which implicitly or explicitly the natural order is revealed.[3] These claims are more circumstantial and clearly defined than those in the letter to the University of Oxford, or in the *Cena*; but they are no less large, and above all they show no mitigation of Bruno's confidence in his own erudition and intellectual powers.

It is easy enough, and has been an almost constant characteristic of Bruno criticism, to declaim against this aspect of his work, dismissing it as eccentric or in strident bad taste. It is more important to understand the intimate motives which led Bruno throughout his life to place himself in such an unusual posture towards his own figure and intellectual enquiry. Undoubtedly the answer is to be found in his sense of the cultural crisis which had developed at the end of the sixteenth century as a consequence of the ferocious tensions in the religious sphere linked to a decadence in the humanistic movement which was beginning to codify in tired and pedantic formulas experiences which had long animated a cultural awakening throughout Europe. In feeling the force of that crisis, Bruno was only one of a number of sensitive European intellects of the final decades of the century. What gives his work its particular power and impetus both within his own times and more generally within the modern world is the nature of his response. For Bruno, placed in front of a newly entrenched and often obscure rigidity on the part of the traditional cultural institutions, both academic and religious, takes upon his own individual intellect the task of repudiating an old and worn-out world order and of opening up new vistas of knowledge and understanding.

His constant reference to his erudition as a primary factor of his intellectual enquiry does not allow accusations of an excessive individualism; for Bruno is always profoundly aware of a centuries-old, internationally wide and immensely rich body of wisdom and knowledge to which the modern intellect must refer and within which it will choose its own essential sources.[4] There is, then, no question with Bruno of disregarding tradition. Rather, his distinctive note is sounded where he claims an unlimited autonomy in operating his cultural choices, and in developing from them his own vision of the truth and order of the universe: it is only to the criterion of a natural principle of truth which lies both within the order of the universe and within the light of reason which illuminates the individual mind that Bruno will declare his adherence:

> He who desires to philosophize will first doubt all things, refusing to assume any position in a debate before having

heard the contrasting points of view, and after having well
considered the arguments for and against he will judge and
take up his position not on the basis of hearsay or according to
the opinion of the majority or their age, merits, or prestige,
but according to the persuasiveness of an organic doctrine
which adheres to reality as well as to a truth which is
comprehensible according to the light of reason.[5]

Traditional schools of thought, of whatever origin or kind,
tend to require some form of submission to criteria of collective
doctrine. The humanist movement had already done much to
accentuate the autonomy of the individual intellect with respect
to the claims of church, corporation, or civic authority which
had had such a dominating influence on the medieval mind. But
Bruno's uncompromising position sounds a new and forward-
looking note which inevitably brought him to clash with the
authorities of his times which had little idea as yet of protecting
any rights to protest or dissent. These were primarily the
churches as religious authorities, the universities as cultural
authorities, and the courts of the Renaissance princes as political
authorities. Bruno's story with all of them is one of tension and
drama.

The break with the churches was the first stage of his life story
in these terms, and had already been completed by the time he
reached Paris in 1581.[6] First, in 1576, came his flight from the
Monastery of St Domenic in Naples and then, soon afterwards,
from a monastery of the same order in Rome, after enquiries
into his religious beliefs had established that he had sympathies
with Arian doctrine and consequently that he may not have
accepted orthodox belief in the Trinity. In his convent years
Bruno is also known to have destroyed his images of the saints
leaving only his crucifix intact and to have advised his fellow
monks to pay more attention to the early Fathers of the Church:
positions which would inevitably be interpreted as moving
dangerously near to Protestant doctrine. It may well have been
sympathies of this kind which drew Bruno, on his journey north
after his escape from Rome, to the Geneva of Calvin. But his stay
there in 1579 lasted only a brief space of months; for he was
soon arrested for printing a notice objecting to twenty errors
contained in the lessons of one of the chief pastors, M. de la
Faye. The surviving documents relating to this episode do not

specify the nature of these objections but only that Bruno called all the ministers of the Church of Geneva 'pedagogues', adding that he had further erred 'blasonnant les ministres en plusieurs et diversses façons'.[7] By the time he reached London, Bruno's position was one of anti-Christian polemic with both sides of the religious divide.

This position of equidistant refusal of Christian orthodoxies is clearly illustrated in the final image of the Explanatory Epistle prefixed to the *Spaccio della bestia trionfante* ('Expulsion of the triumphant beast'), a text which has recently been at the centre of research into the terms of Bruno's quarrel with Christianity.[8] Here, after describing the rejection of the ancient astrological images which he will carry out in his work envisaging their replacement by moral virtues, Bruno leads his reader to the altar on which he intends to celebrate his own idea of true religion, piety, and faith. This idea corresponds with the substance of his philosophical vision of an infinite, divinely animated universe which becomes the only proper object of contemplation both in the religious and in the philosophical spheres. Such contemplation implies a severe refusal of 'iniquous Impiety' and 'insane Atheism', which Bruno visualizes as falling down an ignominious precipice on the west side of his heavenly altar. On the east side of the altar are attached the Christian religions of both sorts.[9] The first of these is presented by Bruno as an 'iniquous Credulity' linked to 'so many forms of madness'. These expressions refer to his polemic, which became particularly virulent at that stage of his stay in England, with the Protestant doctrine of salvation by faith alone, with its corresponding rejection of human works as able to save the believer's soul: doctrines which he thought (in not very original terms, for here he is merely repeating, for his own different ends, the main terms of much Catholic abuse of the Protestant movement) were leading to moral hypocrisy and degeneration as well as to cultural laziness and stagnation. The other form of Christianity, the Catholic faith, is rejected by Bruno with equal decision. This he sees (again without great originality, for here he is repeating a widespread Protestant objection to Catholicism) as based on superstition rather than true faith, and as surrounded by what he calls 'Cose, coselle e coselline' – *nugae*, small insignificant things – by which he means the various objects and appurten-

4

ances, such as images and relics, which play such an important part in Catholic worship. Both forms of Christian religion are then seen as falling together from the east side of Bruno's altar, leaving him free to celebrate what he presents to the reader as the only object of a correctly conceived worship: the Infinite and Universal One as expressed in the Infinite Universe. Bruno believes, with what are clearly Epicurean echoes, that such a form of worship, which is identifiable with philosophical contemplation of the divine principle of order within the infinite universe, will fill the mind with a 'voluptuous torrent of joy and delight'.[10]

Bruno was not the unrealistic mystic and visionary which he has been made so often to appear. Even after the definition of his own religious position, which is expressed so clearly in this page of the *Spaccio*, he continued to be deeply interested in the various forms of Christianity and their relations with each other, aware as he was that they were not going to fall away in historical terms as easily as in his vision of his ideal altar. But I do not believe that he was primarily interested in a religious reform for its own sake, or that he thought of himself as carrying out a religious mission. Rather he was interested in, and appealed continually in his works for, a movement towards tolerance and religious compromise which would leave the way free for the development of intellectual enquiry into the divine order and harmonies which regulate the universe. It was not his philosophy which modulated continually into a religious message, but his idea of the divinity which governed his conception of the universe as the eternal reflection in terms of multiplicity, movement, and continual process of the infinite One: the scattering into an infinite number of mobile fragments of the single, divine ray of light and truth. The nature of the order governing that multiplicity, in Bruno's opinion, had to be defined by a philosophical enquiry which, in its turn, had to be free to develop according to the impetus of the affections and the light of reason.[11]

It was in these terms that Bruno searched throughout his life for an academic institution within which he could develop his thought and teach it to others. But the universities of the sixteenth century were closely linked to the ecclesiastical authorities of the part of Europe in which they operated, and were unlikely to offer Bruno a comfortable haven. What he was searching for amounts to an early ideal vision of a lay university of European culture rather than to any institution existing at that time. His claim in his letter to the Vice-Chancellor of the University of Oxford that he had been approved and welcomed throughout the principal universities of Europe is far from the truth. In fact, in his journey north, Bruno had taught at Toulouse between 1579 and 1581, but had then been forced to leave because of rising religious tensions between the Catholics and the Huguenots. In Paris he was unable to hold an official position at the Sorbonne where fidelity to the Catholic religion was required, although he became one of the public 'royal' lecturers due to the influence of Henry III who was interested in his doctrine of memory and patronized him between 1581 and 1583. His celebrated clash in the summer of 1583 with the Oxford dons over the Copernican question was brief and violent, arising as it did from religious rather than philosophical or, even less, scientific objections.[12] On his return to Paris in 1585, religious tension was far more acute than during his previous visit, with Henry III much weakened by the increasing power and fervour of the Guise faction and the Catholic League which would soon depose him. Henry III's assassination in 1589, followed by the emergence of Henry of Navarre as the new heir to the throne and his conversion to Catholicism in 1593, and finally the achievement of the Edict of Nantes in 1598, which at last conceded liberty of conscience and worship to the French Calvinists, were developments in the history of France which Bruno would only follow from an ever greater distance. The tense and fanatical Paris of 1585–6 was no safe place as yet for a mind like Bruno's, and in the summer of 1586 he left France for Germany. It was Wittemberg which eventually offered him the nearest approach to an academic haven, with a regular teaching post which he covered from 1586 to 1588.

Bruno's arrival in Wittemberg was preceded by a significant interlude at the University of Marburg, where he matriculated on 25 July 1586. He at once petitioned the Rector, Nigidius, a professor of moral philosophy, to be permitted to hold public disputations on philosophy, but this permission was denied him on the grounds of what the Rector, in a personal account of the episode, defined as 'weighty reasons'. The following scene between Bruno and the Rector, narrated by the latter himself, is often taken as a testimony of Bruno's irascible, southern temperament. But, as the Rector himself seems to have been aware, it is far more telling in its expression of intense disappointment with respect to an ideal academic institution which Bruno was evidently convinced, at this point, he could find in Germany alone:

> he fell into a passion of anger and he insulted me in my house, as though I had acted in this matter against the rights of man and the usages of all the German universities, and against all zeal in learning; and, therefore, he desired not to continue a member of the academy, to which desire we agreed gladly, and his name was cancelled by me on the rolls of the university.[13]

Fortunately the Marburg episode failed to influence Bruno's reception at Wittemberg, where he matriculated on 20 August of the same year. Bruno's arrival at Wittemberg was marked by a stroke of extraordinary good luck and a stroke of equally extraordinary bad luck. His good luck was to find there, in a position of prestige and respect, his fellow countryman Alberigo Gentile, who had probably heard Bruno speak at Oxford where the patronage of Leicester had installed him in a good position and where he would return to be awarded a Chair in 1589. Gentile was a highly respected student of law, who is recognized as having founded the important concept of international law. His influence may perhaps be traced in Bruno's concept of the true law as not only international but universal, as he defines it in the *Spaccio* where the Law, in the reformed universal order, reigns in the heavens beside Prudence and Truth. Gentile had left Italy on account of his Protestant sympathies, and he professed Calvinism during his Oxford years. At Wittemberg he was attached to the English Embassy at the Court of Saxony. It was Gentile's direct influence which obtained for Bruno at Wittemberg a post for teaching the *Organon* of Aristotle and other philosophical subjects. But the stroke of ill luck which marked out Bruno's Wittemberg experience as necessarily brief was not long in making itself felt. The Elector of Saxony, Augustus I, who had favoured religious peace and tolerance, died on 11 February of the year of Bruno's arrival in Wittemberg. His place was taken by his weak and degenerate son Christian who came rapidly under extreme Calvinist influence. The tolerant effects of religious compromise which had been arduously achieved through conventions such as the Treaty of Passau (1552) and the Peace of Augsburg (1555) began to give way within the University of Wittemberg itself; and by 1588 the influence of rigorous Calvinist doctrine was making itself felt. Bruno decided to leave, but not before he had expressed his gratitude to the university in which he was most fully and generously welcomed, in spite of the fact that he taught there doctrines which conceded little to the tastes and canons of the times.

Bruno's public recognition of Wittemberg as a place of culture approaching his ideal of an academic institution was expressed in two separate moments. The first of these was a dedication which he added to his work *De lampade combinatoria Lulliana* published in Wittemberg in 1587. The dedication is addressed to the Senate of the university and it expresses grateful praise for the 'liberty of philosophy' which Bruno found there. Bruno underlines his appearance in Wittemberg as a stranger 'not distinguished by any royal commendation, bearing no ensigns of honour'. Yet he was never questioned in religion, but allowed to proceed in his own enquiry which he describes as one of 'universal philanthropy'. In this dedication Bruno further describes Wittemberg as 'the Athens of Germany, the daughter of Minerva, and the Queen of German schools'. It is the reference to Minerva which he takes up and develops in his *Oratio valedictoria* pronounced to the professors and assembly of the university on 8 March 1588, shortly before his departure from Wittemberg.[14] The oration takes the form of a redefinition of the myth of the golden apple awarded by Paris to Venus on Mount Ida: Bruno's choice goes to Minerva who 'drew me to her, and fettered me'(see Plate 1). In the remarkable celebration of Minerva which follows, Bruno mixes elements of classical myth with the language of the psalms and prophetic vision to create an image of wisdom which expresses itself both as the divine unity, inscrutable to man, and as the richness and abundance of universal variety which it is given to man to approach and comprehend through dedicated search and enquiry. The complexity of Minerva's wisdom is expressed through a number of her attributes, foremost among them her

Plate 1 Images of Minerva issuing from the head of Jupiter, and Minerva with Mercury in Vincenzo Cartari's *Le Imagini de i Dei de gli Antichi*, 1556. Reproduced by courtesy of the Biblioteca Nazionale Centrale, Vittorio Emanuele II, Rome.

helmet. This is crested to signify that we are not to put our trust in strength alone, but to show a courteous and quiet spirit. But above Minerva's crest is a cock with outspread wings which represents the swiftness, vigilance and foresight of the combatant; her keen-edged lance is her intelligence, ready for offence and for defence; while to them who oppose her she shows the Gorgon's head, for her formidable and admirable qualities are such as strike the beholder dumb with awe. Bruno has approached the throne of Minerva which stands on a pillar of clouds:

> On the outer part of the throne I beheld engraven an owl, which is her emblem; for night is not darkness to her, and for her night shines with the light of day, and my countenance is not hidden from her.

The key to this approach to the throne lies in the design on its surface which is the work of Vulcan; for here

> was a wondrous representation of the universe, which is the work of the gods, a plastic picture, and underneath was written, 'He bestowed upon me the knowledge of all living things, so that to me the disposition of the sphere of the earth is laid bare, the powers of the elements, the beginning, the end, and the midst of time, the sway of fate, the changes of custom, the course and lapse of years, the order of the stars, the nature of the animals, the deadly rage of beasts, the powers of the winds, the thoughts of men, the variety of plants, the virtue of roots; for that which is hid from others lies open for ever before me'.

Gradually the sense of Bruno's amalgam of classical myth, the language of prophecy, and mystical vision becomes clear; although, as he had warned his audience at the beginning of the oration, 'fate decrees we shall deal in words with that which is unspeakable'. The question which he poses is whether words, which are the signs and tokens of things, can do more than specify the presence and evidence of objects. He answers his own question when he declares that he is attempting to use words to specify all three modes of perceiving the sun of intelligence which manifests itself in essence, in substance, and in activity. It is where Bruno considers that manifestation in its incomprehensible essence that he adopts cabbalistic imagery and arcane myths expressing mystical concepts of varying traditions. In the second mode, Wisdom is apparent in substance in the shape and body of all things and takes the name of Minerva: 'it calls upon man with a thousand voices, and in all parts of the earth'. Here all the varieties of language are necessary to express the richness and plenitude of the universal being. In the third mode, Wisdom is implanted within the spirit, in the profound thoughts of mankind. In this expression Wisdom as activity may be seen as having built a house of reason and design in the individual soul from which man can glimpse the image of the first archetypal house which is before the world as well as of the second house, according to the senses and to nature, which is the world.

In Bruno's universe as thus defined time is eternal, and his concept of wisdom looks back to the arcane mysteries which were a form of participation in the divine essence, as well as forward to a more rational and organized enquiry into the order of the universal whole. Bruno's work derives its substance and value from his awareness of the necessity for the individual intellect to hold in harmonious tension these various stages of wisdom: imaginative myth combines with rational discourse; mystical aspiration to absorption into the divine essence is accompanied by a stand in favour of man's historical autonomy and free will; a sense of the magic and occult powers which vivify the universe coexists with an intellect projected towards the rational discovery and revelation of nature's secrets. At this point one wonders how, and in what terms, Bruno will manage to introduce the figure of Luther, who could hardly be left out of a celebration of wisdom pronounced in sixteenth-century Wittemberg; for Bruno has so far defined a complex and coherent philosophical concept of wisdom in terms which include no reference to the Christian faith on which Luther had erected the whole structure of his religious reform.

Bruno's answer to this conundrum is a brilliant one. It ignores any reference to the Lutheran doctrines of justification by faith alone and the refusal of human works which Bruno had opposed so bitterly in his dialogues written in England, but rather it introduces Luther in his heroic stance as the opponent of papal power and authority: 'that vicar of the princes of hell, who by cunning and violence polluted the world', writes Bruno, taking over in mass the familiar terms of Protestant anti-papal polemic. The really significant phrase, however, is that which defines Luther as a 'mighty hero, armed to the teeth with club and sword'. Here Luther is clearly identified with Hercules and thus with the profound significance of the virtue of 'fortezza' (strength) as Bruno had defined it in the *Spaccio*. Although Bruno would remain convinced to the end that Luther's reform was not the right one, it is clear that his welcome in Wittemberg had led him to a revaluation of the reformer's stature as well as of some of the effects, in terms of liberty and tolerance, which his insistence on the divine light which illuminates the individual intellect was leading to. Like Bruno himself, Luther had opposed his own vision of things to the whole weight of an immensely powerful and entrenched prevailing culture. He is accorded the status of a hero in Bruno's scheme of things; and it is even suggested, although in not very precise terms, that the Nolan philosophy, by which Bruno means his own thought, 'is not altogether alien' to the philosophy of contemporary Lutheran Germany. It could be interesting to speculate how far Bruno's reading of Luther, which led to the clear and reasoned refusal of so much of the doctrine of the Reformation in his Italian dialogues written in England, had influenced some of his own way of expressing himself in his most polemical moments. Consider, for example, Luther's angry cry against Erasmus for his defence of the freedom of the will:

> Away, now, with Sceptics and Academics from the company of us Christians; let us have men who will assert, men twice as inflexible as very Stoics! Take the Apostle Paul – how often does he call for that 'full assurance' which is, simply, an assertion of conscience, of the highest degree of certainty and conviction.[15]

Here Bruno is undoubtedly closer to Erasmus's undogmatic humanism on the level of ideas. Yet Bruno's own voice, in his moments of indignation and refusal, often sounds with notes that are reminiscent of Luther's decided and uncompromising tones. It is significant that Bruno concludes his praise of Luther with a reference to what he managed to do 'through the power of the Word'. It is that power which formed Luther's 'Herculean club' (see Plate 2); and it is through words (his own words

Plate 2   A sixteenth-century engraving of Hercules by Adamo Scultori (*c.* 1530–85). Reproduced by courtesy of the Istituto Nazionale per la Grafica, Rome, cat. no. F.C. 50610.

rather than those of the Scriptures) that Bruno too is trying to bring about a cultural reawakening.

Wittemberg listened to that message in spite of the fact that it was very different from what its own reformer had preached. Bruno's farewell to Wittemberg was also a farewell to the academic life of his times which was not yet ready for spirits such as his. He left for Prague, but appears to have ignored the university there; and when later he went to Helmstedt, attracted by the Academia Julia founded by Duke Julius of Brunswick, he took no regular academic post. He appears to have been more interested in seeking the patronage of Emperor Rudolf II at Prague, or of Duke Julius at Brunswick, in the hope, perhaps, that the protection of an enlightened Prince might offer him more security than the academic halls had done.

The third dimension of Bruno's story with the authorities of his times is in fact represented by his relationship with the Princes and their Courts. Here too we have the continually renewed search for an ideal, although in this case the search is less solitary and projects us less into the modern world. Rather it represents a precise moment in the history of political power in Europe linked to the widespread realization, which is such a marked characteristic of the humanist movement in the sixteenth century, that any renovation in the society of the time involved a rethinking of the role of the Prince from whom, wrote Thomas More, all evils and benefits flow as if from a bounteous fountain.[16] More in his *Utopia* proposed a solution well in advance of his times, and certainly uncongenial to his own Tudor monarch Henry VIII, when he saw the necessity of abolishing the hereditary principle and establishing a mechanism of regular elections to positions of power. Machiavelli was equally projected into the modern world where his uncompromising realism left the Prince naked of ambiguous and often imaginary ideal attributes, and offered him instead a manual of instructions in the harsh realities of political virtue. But the solution most widely accepted by the humanists of the period was rather that of Erasmus, which went back through the Middle Ages to Plato's concept of the Philosopher-Prince, developed in a Christian dimension with a primary emphasis on his religious and intellectual education to power.[17] This profound desire to see the Prince absorb into himself the humanist

14

ideal of special forms of wisdom and culture, combining them, in some unspecified, if not miraculous, way, with the active political virtues, seems to have become more widespread and deeply felt as the century progressed. It is clearly linked to the increasing sense of crisis which was beginning to invest the concept of monarchy itself as we see it explored with increasing scepticism in dramatic representations of the weak or incompetent Prince such as Marlowe's *Edward II* or Shakespeare's *Richard II*. It was not the solution which the modern world would adopt, with its progressive emargination of the figure of the monarch and its development of a parliamentary principle. And given that one of the main leads in that direction would so soon be offered by the England of the following century, it remains a curious cultural phenomenon that so meagre a meditation on the parliamentary alternative was developed by the culture of the sixteenth century, in England as elsewhere. Shakespeare, together with his fellow dramatists, remains deeply immersed in a meditation on the figure of the Prince himself. The crisis which was growing around him is clearly felt where the ideal Princes, in the Erasmian sense of the specially wise and cultured princely mind, are deposed or deprived of their rights, as both Hamlet and Prospero are, by more ignorant but wily and unscrupulous rivals. Nevertheless, the solution to the crisis is always proposed in the form of a return of just (at least hypothetically) princely rule, with the arrival of Fortinbras or the return to power of Prospero himself. The extreme limit which Shakespeare achieved, or possibly was able to achieve as a dramatist whose plays were represented at Court, is the doubt and ambiguity which he allows to surround his solution. For it is far from certain that Fortinbras, who leads armies of ignorant soldiers to lose their lives for new territories whose real worth is less than an eggshell, will in fact prove to be the gentle and promising ruler that Hamlet hopefully imagines in his dying speech. As for Prospero, his return to power coincides clearly with his own (or according to another critical tradition, Shakespeare's) setting aside of his magician's cloak with its special forms of secret wisdom and power.

Much Italian and French meditation on the figure of the Prince was based on a far more intense monarchical idealism than is found in the Elizabethan dramatists, who, by the very fact of dramatizing the history of Princes in problematical terms, have been seen as partially subverting their sacred and inviolable authority.[18] The French and Italian tradition, instead, was more concerned with celebrating an ideal of monarchy which was projected towards expanding that authority in terms of empire which looked back to the example of ancient Rome. Bruno has been seen as participating in what was a widespread Italian as well as French reference to the monarchy of France in these terms; for looking back to the figure of Charlemagne, it was possible to see the French kings as inheriting a mission to install a form of Roman-imperialistic rule which would bring back peace and justice to a divided and bloodstained Europe.[19] The tribute to Henry III in the closing pages of the *Spaccio* undoubtedly participates in this tradition, creating of the French king a mythical figure who ascends to the heavens to take the place of the constellation of the Southern Crown, symbolizing with his ascent the opening of the new era of universal peace and tranquillity which Bruno, together with so many of the intellects of his age, ardently desired: 'he loves peace, keeps his loved subjects as far as possible in tranquillity and devotion; he is not pleased by the noise, clashes and fanfares of martial instruments which lead to the blind conquering of unstable tyrannies.'[20]

It is in similar terms that Bruno treats the figure of Elizabeth I, whom he praises above all for the era of peace she had brought to her island kingdom, but also for her culture and intellectual powers which confer on her a status of exceptional authority and standing among the Princes of the time:

> her judgement, wisdom, political virtue, and art of government are next to none who carries a sceptre on earth: in her knowledge of the arts, scientific notions, expertise and practice of all those languages which the educated in Europe are accustomed to speaking, I leave the whole world to judge what rank she holds among her fellow princes.[21]

Bruno treats her in mythological terms as Amphitrite declaring that her rule should ideally extend not just to England but to the world, if not to the universal whole.[22] There is an obvious dose of rhetoric and favour-seeking here, but even so it remains a fact that Bruno's virulent attacks against so many aspects of

English life and society never extended to the figure of the Queen even after he had left England and had no further need of her protection. It is a stand which the Inquisitors during his trial would be quick to pick up, accusing him of undue praise of a heretical and excommunicated monarch.[23]

It would appear that Bruno's participation in the cult of the English monarchy in its new imperialistic aspirations was known in the early years of the seventeenth century when the Stuarts, aided by the myth-making art of Rubens and the celebratory masques of Ben Jonson and Inigo Jones, made their dramatic but disastrous attempt to imitate French models of absolute, imperialistic power. For among the Stuart masques, we find the curious work of Carew, *Coelum Britannicum*, in which parts of the *Spaccio*, and in particular the monarchical-imperialistic vision of the closing pages, are used as a source, to be applied, inevitably, to the Stuart rather than to the French monarchy.[24] But it is far from clear that Bruno would have approved of Stuart rule which opposed so many of his desires for religious, political, and cultural tolerance and peace. It was precisely these virtues, which the Stuart kings would so sadly lack, that Bruno extols in the crucially important pages of his dedication to Emperor Rudolf II of the *Articuli centum et sexaginta* published in Prague in 1588.[25]

Bruno's dedication to Rudolf II addresses that monarch as *Divo Rodolpho II Romanorum Imperatori semper Augusto*: a form of address which is not just empty flattery. For Bruno defines human knowledge itself, and the philosopher who pursues it, in terms of a universal brotherhood of intellectual searchers over which Rudolf, in his capacity as Holy Roman Emperor, is seen as presiding. It is in terms of this concept of the universal value which is to be attributed to all true forms of knowledge that Bruno launches into a bitter attack against all those sects and religions which persist in asserting that God has conceded them some particular form of revelation: a conviction which leads them to believe 'that only they dwell in the house of truth (outside which the blind and erring legions wander lost and aimless)'. In his refusal of this concept, Bruno not only urges the necessity of a search for truth based on a spirit of universal love which sees God as the father of all men, 'good and bad, just and unjust', but he makes it clear that he repudiates entirely the whole concept of divine revelation. God has not revealed any sacred truths to any privileged sects, religions, or peoples. He has done something far more valuable and challenging, giving to every man the 'eyes' of sense and intelligence with which to pursue truth on his own account. What derives from this concept is a vision of knowledge as necessarily multiform and conflicting, but at the same time active and assertive: knowledge which, when a man has acquired it through dedicated and rigorous intellectual endeavour, will give him the capacity not only to judge but to 'direct the cause'.

Hermetic elements stressing the autonomy of man within the universal whole amalgamate with what is already a Baconian concept of organized research into the forces regulating the universe which will lead man to an ever greater dominion over the natural world. But above all Bruno is concerned with clarifying here what he sees as the fundamental and necessary condition for such a pursuit of knowledge: a degree of freedom of enquiry which in his time was clearly unrealizable, and which may still be considered as advanced even today. For it is correct to speak of a 'religion of freedom' in Bruno, which goes far beyond an illuministic plea for rational and judicious tolerance and intellectual harmony. Rather, the idea of liberty and autonomy of enquiry becomes the defining characteristic of the truly philosophical spirit: a sign of a fully mature humanity which relegates to the status of beasts (the asses, sheep, etc. of his *Cantus Circaeus*) all those unable or unwilling to carry intellectual enquiry to its greatest possible limits or heights. Although, in the closing passage of his dedication, Bruno admits that the pressures of social cohesion may, in some circumstances, oblige the wise man to hide his wisdom with humility, nevertheless such wisdom must be nourished as the occult sign of God's light which hides within man. When he is occupied with philosophical speculation (which Bruno here formally declares is the sphere of activity to which he has dedicated his life and intellectual powers) the wise man will only agree to listen to those masters who exhort him to open his eyes and not to close them.

Rudolf II had succeeded in the year 1576 to the throne of Maximilian II, the worldly and tolerant emperor who in 1574–5 had given the young Philip Sidney the welcome to his Court remembered in the opening page of his *Defence of Poetry*. Rudolf was a more melancholic figure, something of a recluse with an interest in esoteric studies and enquiries. He had shown rather too keen and ingenuous an interest in the spiritualistic magic of John Dee and his spurious companion Edward Kelley, who had both been entertained at his Court from 1584: Kelley was still there when Bruno arrived from Wittemberg.[26] Bruno clearly hoped that he too would find favour with the eccentric Rudolf II; but he was disappointed. He received only a modest payment for his dedication of the *Articuli centum et sexaginta*, and in August of 1588 he left Prague without having obtained any official post either at the university or the Court. His new journey took him to Helmstedt where he was attracted by the university which had been founded in 1575 by Duke Julius of Brunswick. But Bruno seems to have moved on the outskirts of the Duke's Court rather than the university, in which he held no official position. It was, nevertheless, at the university that he spoke on 1 July 1589, when he pronounced a highly formal and rhetorical *Oratio consolatoria* as part of the funeral rites following Duke Julius's death.[27]

Underneath the elaborate praise Bruno heaps on the dead Duke, it is possible to trace a further meditation on the figure of the Prince, above all in his function of guardian of the intellectual life of his small community. The Duke is pictured as gathered into the heavenly regions from where he looks down on to his academy, guiding it towards new vistas of divine knowledge. It is a concern with this same aspect of the princely role which appears with particular clarity and force in the dedication of his major philosophical work, the so-called Frankfurt Trilogy, which Bruno published in that town in 1591, to the son of Duke Julius, the new Duke Henry Julius of Brunswick.[28] This dedication develops a meditation on the figure of the Prince of a different order from that applied to Henry III of France or to Elizabeth I or to Emperor Rudolf II. It is no longer imperial dominion seen as a universal force of cohesion and unity which constitutes the primary element of Bruno's interest here, but rather the aspect of exceptional wisdom and intellectual power which certain Princes are seen as achieving, in part at least due to their divinely consecrated status. Such wisdom gives them particular authority and power within the confines of their kingdom, creating at the same time a special relationship between them and the philosophers among their subjects. This is the concept which lies behind Shakespeare's creation of Prospero, and it appears to constitute an extreme form of meditation on the figure of the Prince. For either he represents an exceptionally potent form of wisdom, with special insight into divine truths, or he has no right to exert his power and dominion over those who dedicate themselves to obtaining similar wisdom through intellectual enquiry.

It is the nature of the relationship which links the figure of the Princely sage to the philosophical enquirer which Bruno is anxious to define in his dedication. Princes who are also sages and seers deserve the name of Trismegisti, which means 'three times great' in virtue of their knowledge, power, and authority: the number three, as Bruno had underlined in the *De monade*, possessing special significance, made up as it is of the first even number added to the first odd number, and so containing within itself potentially all numbers and being.[29] It was among the Trismegisti, the wisest of men, that the ancient Egyptians, Persians, and Romans chose their kings. Constructing his meditation around a complex series of trinities which takes as its starting-point the Trismegistus-Prince and ends with the 'gift' to this Prince of his philosophical trilogy, Bruno sees such Princes as the authorities who decide and defend the laws, religions, and cults to be practised by the community. Such Princes guarantee stability within the state, seen as a necessary condition for philosophical enquiry to proceed and develop. The authority of the Prince, however, cannot extend to an interference with the enquiries of the true philosophers 'who must never suppress the light of reason for fear of those in power, showing themselves insensible to the voice of nature, nor hypocritically hide the truth in order to receive the consent of men of the church'.

Bruno's development of his final meditation on the figure of the Prince in these terms, in a work which is generally considered to contain his most advanced speculations on subjects connected with the development of a new science, is of particular interest if we compare it with Francis Bacon's dedication of *The Advancement of Learning* to James I in 1605.[30] Bacon too was interested in the Prince in so far as he acted, in his special wisdom and power, to guarantee the free advancement of the new scientific philosophy. Bacon's praise of James in these terms echoes so closely Bruno's dedication to the Duke of Brunswick as to make it seem that he is modelling his text on it. For Bacon too uses the term of Trismegistus, applied by the ancient Greeks to the god Hermes, to celebrate the figure of James as sage and seer: 'your Majesty standeth invested of that triplicity which in great veneration was ascribed to the ancient Hermes, the power and fortune of a King, the knowledge and illumination of a Priest, and the learning and universality of a Philosopher'.

Both Bruno and Bacon consider the wisdom of the Trismegistus-Prince in part as a divine gift, and in part as acquired through study and meditation: Bruno praises the Duke of Brunswick as possessing 'all virtue, grace and ornament... as innate gifts magnified by a superior, interior Genius'; while Bacon says of James, 'there seemeth to be no less contention between the excellency of your Majesty's gifts of nature and the universality and perfection of your learning'. It is to the Prince who reveals himself in these terms as the example and defender of arcane, semi-divine forms of wisdom and learning, that both men are prepared to offer their works as gifts which, in Bacon's words, constitute 'a fixed memorial, and immortal monument, bearing a character or signature both of the power of a King and the difference and perfection of such a King'.

It was, as we can now see, an impossible ideal which led both men to inevitable disappointment. James I would do almost nothing to further Bacon's project for a new scientific community, which he would be later forced to outline in terms of a Utopia in his *New Atlantis*. As for Bruno, he wrote his dedication after he had left Helmstedt which he would never see again. History would show that the advancement of learning in terms of new and free enquiry into the order of the universe would develop most fully where monarchical absolutism was overcome. But Bruno and Bacon were in many respects in advance of their times, which were still dominated on a political level by the Renaissance Princes and their Courts. This imaginative construction of a figure of the Prince as seer and sage was not so much a question of monarchical faith or political principle as an extreme effort to visualize the form of princely rule which would, they both hoped, offer the maximum guarantee for the development of the new learning. In so far as their image of the

Prince as possessing special forms of wisdom projected them clearly into an ideal region outside the process of modern history (recalling a long-lost concept of the Prince as priestly demi-god rooted in the dawning centuries of mankind), they can be seen as contributing, even if obliquely, to the critical meditation on the figure and role of the Prince which would eventually culminate in disillusion, leading to the decline of the monarchical principle itself.

The most important event in Bruno's final period of freedom was the publication in Frankfurt of his Latin trilogy containing the dedication to Duke Henry Julius of Brunswick. He supervised the publication himself in spite of the fact that the Senate of the city refused his request, made on 2 July 1590, to lodge with the publisher Wechel. Through Wechel's influence, however, he was allowed to stay in the Carmelite convent where he worked on his publication until February 1591 when he received an order of expulsion from the city. He was thus obliged to leave Frankfurt before the appearance of his final and most ambitious philosophical work which was published during the autumn book fair of that year together with his final work on memory, the *De imaginum, signorum et idearum compositione*.

It was at this point that Bruno, having received an invitation from the Venetian nobleman Giovanni Mocenigo to stay with him in Venice and teach him the 'secrets of memory', decided to return to Italy. He passed through Zurich where he lectured to private groups of students.[31] At the end of August 1591, he reached Venice; and the last act of his story began.

The decision to return to Italy has been the subject of much and various comment. Apart from the enticement offered by Mocenigo's invitation, there was a historical context of a particular moment of optimism which, as the documents relating to Bruno's trial clarify, he had carefully considered: the accession to the French throne of Henry of Navarre and the rumours of his imminent conversion to Catholicism, which seemed to presage a slackening of the wars of religion; the accession to the papal throne of Clement III who, in 1592, called Francesco Patrizi to Rome and gave him a Chair there in what appeared to be a gesture of goodwill towards the new philosophers. The choice of Venice as a starting-point for the return to Italy clearly related not only to the invitation from Mocenigo but also to the tolerant religious policy of the independent city-state which had strenuously opposed the efforts of the Catholic church, after the Council of Trent, to exert a much greater control over secular affairs throughout southern Europe. This was a period in which many Protestant visitors to Italy, such as Philip Sidney and his companions in the 1570s, chose to stay only within the Venetian dominions, where they felt safe from religious persecution; while the University at Padua, which was part of Venetian territory, was attracting an ever greater number of celebrated teachers due to the relative freedom of thought and enquiry permitted there. The appointment of Galileo to the Chair of mathematics in 1592 may be considered as symbolic of the standing of the Paduan University at that time; while the final years of the century and the beginning of the new one would see the emergence in Venice itself of the figure of Paolo Sarpi, whose critical *History of the Council of Trent* was to be so deeply admired and studied throughout Protestant Europe. What, then, was so particular about Bruno's position that made his return to Italy end in tragic failure, in spite of the carefully chosen geographical setting and historical moment in which he attempted it?

It is here that opinions diverge. One thesis, which has had several supporters, sees Bruno as planning to initiate in Italy some form of religious 'mission' which, so the thesis goes, with an almost insane recklessness he thought of starting from the very heart of Christianity, that is Rome itself. The Hermetic interpretation of Bruno adopts this thesis, lending it support by pointing out that in Padua, where he went before taking up his final residence in Mocenigo's house in Venice, he dictated to a group of pupils his final works on magic thus defining his 'mission' as a magic-Hermetic one which would inevitably clash with any form of Christian authority.[32] This answer to the problem has recently been rigorously contested and replaced by the thesis that Bruno's real aim in Italy was to obtain an academic position as Patrizi had done, and that he went to Padua attracted by the still vacant Chair of mathematics. This thesis is supported by the recent discovery of two new texts related to his logical-mathematical enquiry which Bruno dictated to private pupils in Padua; thus he was not completely immersed in his magical-Hermetic studies there as had previously been thought.[33] It is a thesis which has the merit of bringing Bruno back from the borders of insanity, and allowing him a greater measure of rational and judicious behaviour. Even so, there is no precise documentary evidence to support the thesis that he was looking for an academic appointment (he had not held one anywhere since his departure from Wittemberg); and if that was the case, it is obvious that he had miscalculated his chances, for after only a brief stay in Padua he went to Venice and took up Mocenigo's invitation. In the end, it is only possible to speculate on the exact reasons which led Bruno to return to Italy; and perhaps there is no need to create hypothetical religious missions or academic programmes to justify them. Bruno had been an exile since his flight from Italy in 1579, and it is natural that he should have wished to return to a country which was not only his by birth, language, and traditions, but which had created and guided the Renaissance culture of which he must be considered still, in many respects, an intimate part. His decision was made in a moment which appeared, in objective historical terms, to be particularly propitious. Furthermore, it is important to understand that the cultural policy of the Counter-Reformation, particularly with respect to the new philosophy, did not become clear at once even to the ecclesiastical authorities themselves. It was only over a long period of discussion and debate, with frequent changes of attitude on both sides, that Bruno's imprisonment, trial, and death at the stake became a symbolic moment in the definition of a rigorously severe policy towards heretical thinking at whatever level. The decision to put Copernicus's *De revolutionibus orbium* on the Index of forbidden books, which was only taken in 1616, has been seen as a direct result of the final outcome of Bruno's trial.[34] According to this interpretation, both events lead directly to the trial and punishment of Galileo, 'grown old', as Milton would write, 'a prisner to the Inquisition, for thinking in Astronomy otherwise than the Franciscan and Dominican licencers thought'.[35] But such severe rigour with respect to the new philosophy and science was only slowly defined, as the hesitations over the case of Copernicus show; and Bruno's trial, rather than the inevitable result of an already rigorously entrenched policy, should properly be seen as one of the main moments through which that policy was gradually defined. The very rigour of his sentence was clearly intended to underline its symbolic character; for Bruno was not only burnt at the stake but carried to his death with his tongue tied to signify the silence imposed on the particularly dangerous and impenitent heretic. Such was the end to the battle with the authorities which Bruno had waged throughout his life in the name of what he called a 'universal philanthropy'. Fortunately history is not made only by the authorities in power. As Milton would write not many years later: 'Many a man lives a burden to the Earth; but a good Booke is the pretious life-blood of a master-spirit, imbalm'd and treasur'd up on purpose to a life beyond life.'[36]

BRUNO IN ENGLAND

Along the spine of Europe, the Tiber runs angrily, the Po menacingly, the Rhone is violent, the Seine stained with blood; the waters of the Garonne are muddy, the Ebro and the Tagus rage furiously, the Moselle is uneasy, and the Danube unquiet.[37]

With these words, in the opening dialogue of his *De la causa, principio et uno* ('Of the cause, the beginning and the one'), Bruno expressed his sense of the crisis of Europe as a convulsed century moved to its close: a century which had opened with high hopes for a new affirmation of mankind in its dignity and autonomy inspired by the Florentine Neoplatonic movement to be wrenched in opposite and opposing directions first by the ruthless political realism of the Renaissance Princes, rigorously exposed and theorized by Machiavelli, then by the religious contest between the often violent ardours of the Protestant Reformation and the uncompromising reactions of a Counter-Reformation slowly but mercilessly evolved in the lengthy sittings of the Council of Trent. In the ensuing conflicts of a bitterly divided Europe, the brilliant Copernican proposal of a radically modified vision of the traditionally conceived earth-centred cosmic order (one of the few concepts tenaciously held on to by both sides of the Christian divide) appeared to most as yet another element of disturbance and confusion in an already bloodstained world. Within such a conflicting historical situation, the England of Elizabeth I appeared to many exiled visitors to her shores, as well as to many of her subjects, as an oasis of relative tolerance and peace, ruled by the Astraea of a new order of justice and harmony. Bruno was among the first to pay homage to this England, bringing his river imagery to a close with a finely idealized vision of the Thames presided over by its Virgin Queen whom he praises as superior to any male ruler of the times: 'with the splendour of her eyes, for five lustres and more she has brought peace to the Ocean which, with its continual ebb and flow, gathers her beloved Thames happily and quietly into its ample breast'.

Yet Bruno's overall vision of England, although always admiring of the figure of Elizabeth herself, contains ominous shadows which often contradict this idyllic picture, involving England too in the crisis of the times. The terms of his attack on the culture of Elizabethan England are already clearly outlined in his letter to the Vice-Chancellor of the University of Oxford which he published at the beginning of the *Ars reminiscendi*. This was the first of Bruno's books to appear in London in 1583 and constitutes one of his central texts on the subject of memory and cabbalistic magic. Yet the letter which he prefaced to it, or at least to some but not all the copies, is an expression of rather different concerns. It is now thought to have been written between Bruno's first visit to Oxford in June 1583, when he is known to have been involved in a violent debate with the theologian John Underhill, who was soon to become Vice-Chancellor, and his later visit in the same summer when his lectures were interrupted in the well-known terms later described by George Abbot, a future Archbishop of Canterbury, at that time a fellow of Balliol College. If this thesis is correct, the letter becomes not only a presentation by Bruno to the university of his own figure and intellectual enquiry, but also an attempt to clarify the terms in which he could, without intellectual incoherence, develop a fruitful debate with the Oxford dons. This attempt to prepare the territory for what, in the first place, Bruno obviously hoped was going to be an academic activity in England, proved a disastrous failure which would lead to his violent attack on the Oxford 'pedants' and 'grammarians' in his later Italian dialogues written in London. Nevertheless, this failure does nothing to diminish the importance of the letter, which clearly defines the terms in which Bruno conceived, from the beginning, his intellectual enquiry in England: a conception to which he would remain faithful in spite of the conflicts and opposition which he met with even on the banks of the 'quiet and happy Thames'.[38]

Bruno opens his letter with a presentation of himself and his intellectual enquiry which is generally described as pompous and self-opinionated, but which is above all a declaration of the fact that he is going to oppose his own theology, which he describes as 'better elaborated', and his own concept of knowledge which he describes as 'more innocent and pure', to the prevailing Christian culture of the times. Bruno then proceeds to distinguish himself from his fellow philosophers in highly significant terms: he allows no nationalistic prejudices which distinguish between Italian and English, no sexual prejudices which distinguish between man and woman, no social prejudices which distinguish the crowned head from the mitred one, or the man in a toga from a military man. He concedes no importance to external signs of distinction: to ritual acts of ordination such as the anointed head, the forehead signed with a cross, the washed hands, or the circumcised penis. The true man of culture is defined in quite different terms from these: by the intimate nature of his soul and the refinement of his intellect. There are probably Epicurean influences behind this refusal of public and external marks of honour, and the radical interiorization of the true cultural enquiry; and Bruno is fully aware of the liberation which can derive from such an interiorization. The essential point of happiness, according to Epicurean philosophy, is an intimate disposition of the mind of which we ourselves are masters.

It is in a development of this plea for a free and individual intellectual enquiry that Bruno launches one of the first of his attacks against the doctrines of the Reformation. It is an attack carried out with subtle irony through multiple quotations from the biblical texts which the Reformation was using to justify its sense of the special kinds of illumination open to the faithful who trust in Christ. Bruno's attack is clearly directed above all against the Calvinists, who were beginning to acquire a strong influence in England in the 1580s. In particular, Bruno is severe in his criticisms of the Calvinistic doctrine of election. Knowledge acquired through such processes of special illumination appears to him no knowledge worth the name: 'all of a sudden, without studying, they become knowledgeable'. Such men are furthermore made dangerous by their unshakeable conviction that only they are the pure, the elect, the true priests and demigods; and Bruno fears them 'more than death itself'. Against their doctrines he places those of Pythagoras, Parmenides, Anaxagoras, and 'the best philosophers', in a revaluation of the pagan, pre-Socratic philosophy which could only be anathema to an Aristotelian and Reformed Oxford. Yet Bruno tries to open a space for debate by declaring that his own ideas are not put forward as absolute truths but rather as enquiry in progress; and by saying that if the dons would assume the same attitude, they could dispute together, 'experimenting the measure of each other's forces'.

It was precisely this attitude that the Oxford dons showed themselves incapable of assuming. Disregarding Bruno's call for internationalism, Abbot in his description of Bruno's performance at Oxford calls him an Italian didapper and sneers at his pronunciation of Latin. He goes on to make two principal accusations against him: that his lectures were no more than a cribbing of Ficino's *De vita coelitis comparanda* (1489), and that Bruno undertook to 'set on foote' the opinion of Copernicus. It is the first accusation which is offered as the official reason for the interruption of the lectures, while Bruno's Copernicanism only appears to Abbot to prove his madness. But it seems likely that it was the Copernicanism, which Abbot mentions first, which was the real cause of the quarrel. Abbot appears unaware that his arguments are contradictory; for if Bruno discussed the Copernican question at Oxford, then he was not simply cribbing from Ficino's pre-Copernican book.

Bruno often cribbed, not from one but from a remarkably wide choice of authors. The habit is part of his eclecticism, which was assumed by him consciously and coherently as a method; for he saw himself involved in a slow and arduous process of progression towards ever fuller knowledge of the universal whole which linked him to all the true philosophers of both ancient and modern culture. This concept of knowledge has been discussed in some recent comment on Bruno's London period in terms of the radical contrast with the idea of knowledge proposed by the Reformation.[39] But it has also been acutely pointed out that Bruno's anti-Calvinism, which dated

28

from his misfortunes at Geneva, was based on a partial mis-understanding; for his idea of philosophical method was not altogether divorced from the doctrines being developed by the Reformation.[40] The insistence on the individual mind as a source of illumination, a lamp which irradiates the light of divine truth, was common to Bruno and the reformers. They differed where they posited the source of that illumination and its ultimate point of reference which, for Bruno, was divorced from Christian faith and found no privileged source of truth in the Scriptures, although some of the biblical books, such as Job and the Song of Solomon, were highly esteemed by him. The internal lamp, or light of reason, for Bruno, could only be put in relation to the One principle and divine cause. In his distance, on this plane, from the Christian zeal of the reformers, he failed to recognize similarities which led him on a path not different from some of the greatest reformers, such as Milton for example, towards a plea for free thought and expression for the individual enquirer, necessarily in possession of only a part of the truth, in his arduous progression towards a total divine illumination. It was only at Wittemberg, and in relation to the more tolerant and imaginative doctrines of Luther, that Bruno seems to have realized that some of the intellectual aspects of the Reformation were not totally divorced from his own philosophical doctrine.

Another aspect of Bruno's dialogues written in London which has attracted much recent attention, particularly on the part of Italian scholars, is the attack against the diminished importance which the reformers conceded to human works. There can be no doubt that the obsessive concern of the reformed churches of all kinds with problems of faith and spiritual salvation was an aspect of the culture of the Reformation which Bruno, through-out his work, repudiated with eloquent indignation; and recent readings of the *Spaccio*, which is central in this context, have led to some excellent comment on the precise terms in which Bruno developed this theme.[41] What he saw as the essential passivity of the new believers, in reference to a divine will which invaded the individual mind in already preordained terms, was contrasted by his vision of a new cycle of history in which the concern for worldly justice and civil living became the primary and proper centre of attention of mankind in his social dimension.[42] The necessity for re-establishing the laws of a civilized society involved the possibility of using force against the blindness and distorted reasoning of fools and pedants, such as the reformers themselves, who undervalued the laws of social living in this world in their concern with achieving salvation in the next. Hence the necessary return of Hercules to the world, which Bruno posited as a condition for the re-establishment of a fully civilized society.

The terms of Bruno's argument in this sense can be said now to have been fully acquired by recent research, which has also shown how he includes lengthy passages from Luther's *Bondage of the Will* into the *Spaccio* in order to reverse the Lutheran scheme of values by claiming the primary importance of worldly concerns with law and social cohesion.[43] What has appeared with less clarity is a certain simplification of Bruno's reading of the Reformation. If in the 1580s his reasoning was still anchored to the Erasmus-Luther polemic over the problem of free will, then much of the development of Reformation thinking, particularly in Calvin, had been lost on him. Was he, for example, aware of the terms in which Calvin tried to reintroduce the concept of law into the formation of a Christian community? Or did he understand the intimate contradiction in the thinking of the Reformation which made the doctrine of election, which apparently led to passivity and stasis, a spring of industry and action in so far as the believer felt continually obliged to prove, through his dedication to the good life, the always basically unascertained fact of his election? The concept of the Reformation which Bruno developed is to some extent denied, in historical terms, by the cultural aggressiveness and political awareness of the reformed parts of Europe, from Calvin's Geneva to Elizabethan England, and even more by the later departure of the Pilgrim Fathers to conquer a new continent. It is probable that Bruno would not have approved of the terms in which these developments took place. What appears less clearly from recent readings of his comments on the Reformation is any awareness on Bruno's part of the complexities of a movement which could stimulate such developments. A full consideration of Bruno's relation to the Reformation as a whole must, I think, at least in the present state of our knowledge, arrive at the conclusion that his reading of this aspect of sixteenth-century culture, though extremely acute and articulate in some of its criticism, was nevertheless based on an imperfect knowledge and understanding of its full character and implications.

It must in fact be recognized that Elizabethan London – together with Wittemberg – was the social and intellectual context in which Bruno found most stimulus for the development of his intellectual message. After his débâcle at Oxford, he knew that London too would supply its share of surly pedants unwilling to pass their Ash Wednesday supper listening to his advanced development of the Copernican theory. Yet it represented a far more varied and articulate cultural environment than the contemporary Oxford. In London debate was possible, particularly within the free-thinking aristocratic elites with whom Bruno came into contact through his position at the French Embassy; and it is significant that in London his work assumes throughout the form of dialogue, bordering at times on drama in its clashes and contrasts of opinions. It is a London dominated by two figures who rapidly assume in Bruno's eyes mythical status: the Queen on the one hand, and on the other her elegant and learned courtier Philip Sidney 'whose brilliant intelligence (as well as his praise-worthy behaviour) are so rare and singular that neither in Italy herself nor outside is it easy to find such another'.[44] Both the Queen and Sidney are thus assumed, in Bruno's scheme of things, as humanist aristocrats to be opposed to the ranks of dull and obtuse pedants who represented in his eyes the official Anglican–Aristotelian culture: another simplification, one could argue, but in this case pervaded with fertile insights which explain the ambivalent attitude towards English culture which Bruno assumed throughout his visit.

Sidney's defence of poetry against the heavy moralistic attacks of intransigent puritans such as Stephen Gosson in the *Anatomy of Abuse* was based on his evaluation of the 'idea' in the human mind which, although fallen and corrupt, projects itself in the creative, poetic impulse towards spheres of divine knowledge. It is clearly no coincidence that it is in the *Heroici furori* ('Heroic fury'), dedicated to Sidney, that Bruno gives the richest poetic expression to his philosophical message using specifically the form of the sonnet. On the other hand, he was also aware of the London which was developing new forms of scientific enquiry, to a large extent stimulated and patronized by the aristocratic humanists such as Sidney himself, Ralegh, and the Ninth Earl of Northumberland. It is in this complex cultural context that Bruno developed his first meditation on the Copernican theory, expanding it to the concept of an infinite universe populated by an infinite number of worlds:

> Now behold the man who has fended the air, pierced the sky, journeyed amongst the stars, travelled beyond the margins of the world, dissolved the imaginary barriers of the first, eighth, ninth, tenth, and other spheres, if it had been possible to add others through the reports of vain mathematicians, and the blind visions of false philosophers. Thus using every sense and reason, with the key of passionate enquiry, he has opened those cloisters of truth which it is in our power to open, laid bare veiled and hidden nature: he has given eyes to the moles, illuminated the blind who are unable to fix their eyes and focus her image in the many mirrors which on all sides reflect it to him.[45]

This celebrated passage of the *Cena* merits to be quoted once again for it is here that we find the essence of Bruno's most original and passionate thinking, which most deserves to be remembered; and not only for the daring extension of the Copernican theory to the vision of an infinitely extended and infinitely rich material universe. For what is equally important here is the sense that with the new vision of the infinite universe, new territories of exploration and understanding are opened up for the human mind. To the infinite number of worlds which make up the whole, Bruno adds the image of the infinite number of mirrors which reflect the divine abundance and order, making gradually available to the enquiring mind an ever fuller and more coherent sense of the true nature of the universal whole.

Such is the complex of dangerous yet stimulating ideas which Bruno passes on to the English figures who will be examined in the next chapters: figures, all of them, projected towards new, and as yet largely undefined forms of intellectual enquiry; and all of them, like Bruno himself, tragically cut off from the possibility of carrying those enquiries to full, public completion. At the heart of the following chapters, in just these terms, lies a crucial European myth: that of Faustus in his tragic ambiguities and failures but also in his essential intellectual vitality and unfailing curiosity for new enquiries and truths. It is Faustus, too, in Marlowe's great dramatization of his story (the first great English tragedy) who links together the two aspects of this book: the new science and the new drama; a science which is not yet fully 'rationalistic', not yet expressed in the cool, clear brevity of the Baconian aphorism or the Newtonian 'law', but surrounded and penetrated by areas of shadow and mystery, 'Delphic' secrets which call into action the techniques and obscure symbolism of the magician or the astrologer; a scientist who is not yet a 'specialist', distant and revered in his Salomon's House of advanced equipment and research techniques, but a philosopher, something too of a theologian, at times a poet, concerned as much with defining the mind and its workings in its new activity of daring and dangerous discovery of the universe as with codifying the discoveries themselves. To have perceived that in the emergence of this new, and as yet largely 'forbidden' science, lay one of the central historical dramas of the times is one of the major achievements of the Elizabethan dramatists. Faustus, the Wittemberg scholar, leads on directly to Hamlet, the ex-Wittemberg student, different from Faustus primarily in his lucid awareness that the new universe he wishes to study must remain undefined until a new social order has been established.

Knowledge as a drama: the drama of the new philosophy. From the start, the barriers are never clearly defined. The Renaissance propagated the idea of the essential unity of all knowledge, and Bruno as a philosopher/poet deeply concerned with new forms of knowledge of the universe appears as a major representative of the Renaissance in this sense, as do those who were influenced by him. Northumberland meditating on his dilemma as a courtier bound to established modes of courtly love, and attempting to define the precise moment of his repudiation of his early life and his dedication to new forms of enquiry echoes Faustus in his first monologue which is also an intellectual biography: the repudiation of orthodox forms of knowledge and belief in favour of a new 'metaphysic of magitians'. Thomas Harriot meditating on the implications of the new cosmological enquiries into an infinite universe ('Maximum: that which will press men to death') echoes Faustus's lucid awareness of the impossibility of pursuing his new studies ('I'le burne my bookes'). Hamlet's thoughts are of the same order as he expresses them to his ex-fellow students of Wittemberg become his gaolers and spies ('Oh God, I could be bounded in a nutshell and count myself a king of infinite space – were it not that I have bad dreams'). In a letter to Kepler written in the first years of the new century, in the reign of James I, Harriot writes significantly: 'I cannot philosophize freely, for here we still stick in the mud'.[46] The sentence is an eloquent comment on Bruno's river imagery of twenty years before. The waters of the Thames, too, like those of the other rivers of Europe, have become muddy; and much water stained with blood will run into the ocean in the slow working out of a more tolerant, democratic social order in which the new enquiries may develop.

Bruno lived in the moment of major conflict and represented that conflict in its most extreme and dramatic form. In his Utopian vision of a 'purged' and reformed universe developed in the *Spaccio*, the first of his moral dialogues, it is the status of truth which lies at the dramatic centre of his attention: a truth which he visualizes as finally triumphant and pure, protected in a place

> where the finger-nails of detraction cannot scratch, the pallor of envy cannot poison, the shadows of error are unable to gather; where she will be stable and firm, undisturbed by the waves and tempests, a secure guide to those who wander in this stormy pool of errors; there revealing herself as the bright unsullied mirror of contemplation.[47]

In his belief that the modern mind was moving towards new and as yet undreamt-of forms of knowledge, and in his vision of a new figure of man capable of dominating that knowledge, Bruno expressed the high hopes of a still humanistic culture, while the violent end of his story struck a warning note to all who followed those hopes too ardently. It was precisely here, in his awareness of a crisis centred on the possibility of conquering new forms of knowledge and truth, that Bruno offered one of his major lessons to history; and from the seeds of that awareness came the dark but unforgettable flowering of the first great English tragedies.

2

THE NORTHUMBERLAND TEXTS

HENRY PERCY, THE NINTH EARL

The Ninth Earl of Northumberland (1564–1632) is chiefly remembered today for his patronage of scholars and scientists, which a study of the Northumberland papers reveals to have been generous and which links him to a circle of men such as Thomas Harriot, Walter Warner, and Robert Hues, increasingly recognized for their contribution to the development of Renaissance science.[1] However, contemporary references indicate that Northumberland was considered in his time as more than the aristocratic patron of such men, and that he was himself widely admired for his studies in natural philosophy. The most-quoted text is Chapman's dedication of *The Shadow of Night* to Mathew Roydon, where 'deep searching Northumberland' is mentioned in a passage in praise of those men who 'had most profitably entertained learning in themselves, to the vitall warmth of freezing science, & to the admirable luster of their true Nobilitie'.[2] Even more telling than such public and formal praise is Francis Bacon's note written in a private memorandum of July 1608, which mentions Northumberland, together with Ralegh and Harriot, as possible allies in his great project for the development of experimental science 'themselves being already inclined to experim[en]ts'.[3] Such testimonies indicate that Northumberland is to be considered as an active and lucid focal point of his circle, consciously promoting and stimulating a cultural activity of a quite precise and definable nature: the development of scientific enquiry within a broadly humanistic and aristocratic cultural framework.

Northumberland's own writings are limited to brief compositions after the manner of the aristocratic society of the period. Some of these remain unpublished, while the *Advice to his Son* and the 'Essay on Love' were published and discussed with critical interest in the first half of this century.[4] The *Advice* is particularly revealing, for it indicates the limits and merits of Northumberland's cultural stance. To a great extent it is composed of traditional social and practical advice which will fit his son for the aristocratic role he has been born to, and at times it is anything but progressive, in particular as regards the advice about women, praised only in their role as breeders of men, to be kept as far as possible out of every other activity, including the administration and organization of the family and household. There are, however, passages of the greatest interest on the cultural activity which the father wishes his son to undertake. For example, his choice of scholars to patronize is to be based on a perception of the true and disinterested desire for knowledge in a man, as against the desire for gain; while even among those men who may fairly be defined as scholars, a distinction is to be drawn between those who are truly pursuing new knowledge and those who are offering nothing of original worth:

> Yet are there again of [scholars] of many kinds, of many professions, that will desire to make you the bridge to go over to their conclusions. Amongst which there are impostures in all kinds of learnings – I will not call them mountebanks – whoever have more wares laid out than they have to sell.[5]

Such passages suggest that it was no mere chance that Northumberland surrounded himself with men of the stature of Harriot, Warner, Hues, or the philosopher Nicolas Hill. Indeed the direction that the pursuit of knowledge should take in his time is as clearly defined in the *Advice* as the kind of man best suited to pursue it most earnestly. Northumberland, having urged his son to use his travels primarily to learn new languages, 'whereby a possibility to understand all authors is gained', then advises

> deeper contemplations, as Arithmetic, Geometry, Logic, Grammar Universal, Metaphysics, the Doctrine of Motion of the Optics, Astronomy, the Doctrine of Generation and

Corruption, Cosmography, the Doctrine *de Anima*, Moral, Politics, Economics, the Art Nautical and Military.[6]

Each of these disciplines is then explained and its function in the spectrum of desirable knowledge defined, in terms which make clear Northumberland's lucid commitment to the surge of scientific enquiry and activity which characterizes European culture in the early seventeenth century.

Of these definitions, one is of particular interest, for it demonstrates Northumberland's awareness of the new philosophy, and particularly of the atomism which Bruno had revived as part of his theory of matter, his vision of an infinite universe, unchangeable and incorruptible, in which 'vi son moti ed alterazioni innumerabili e infiniti, perfetti e compiti' (there is an infinite number of perfectly concluded processes of change).[7] And Northumberland is further aware of how such a philosophy can stimulate and facilitate many branches of scientific investigation:

The Doctrine of Generation and Corruption unfoldeth to our understandings the method general of all atomical combinations possible in homogeneal substances, together with the ways possible of generating of the same substance, as by semination, vegetation, putrefaction, congelation, concoction, etc., with all the accidents and qualities rising from those generated substances, as hardness, softness, heaviness, lightness, tenacity, frangibility, fusibility, ductibility, sound, colour, taste, smell, etc. The application of which doctrine satisfieth the mind in the generation and corruption, as also for the qualities of all substances actually existent, as air, water, earth, stones, wood, metals, and the homogeneal parts of animals and vegetals, etc., which part of philosophy the practice of Alchemy does much further, and in itself is incredibly enlarged, being a mere mechanical broiling trade without this philosophical project.[8]

This passage raises the question of Northumberland's reading in the new philosophy, and particularly of his knowledge of the philosophy and cosmology of Bruno which was stimulating advanced thinking on scientific matters. Northumberland himself makes no mention of Bruno, although concrete proof of Bruno's influence on his associates is offered by their papers, which will be discussed in the following chapter. However, even in these there are few direct references to Bruno's work, and the precise measure of his influence has proved difficult to assess.[9]

It was in relation to this problem that an investigation into the library of the Ninth Earl proved rewarding; for it established what Bruno texts were in his possession and available not only to him but to his circle. Part of the Ninth Earl's collection of books is still extant, divided between the libraries at Petworth House, Sussex, and Alnwick Castle, Northumberland. Among the Ninth Earl's books held in these libraries are six of Bruno's works (seven texts), including a copy of *De gl'heroici furori* annotated by the Earl himself: a collection of Bruno texts which had so far remained unknown.[10]

In chronological order, the Northumberland group of Bruno texts is composed as follows:

1 *De gl'heroici furori* (Paris [=London], 1585)
2 *De progressu et lampade venatoria logicorum* (Wittemberg, 1587)
3 *De specierum scrutinio et lampade combinatoria Raymundi Lulli (Prague, 1588)*
4 *De triplici minimo et mensura* (Frankfurt, 1591)
5 *De monade numero et figura, de minimo magno & mensura,* together with *De innumerabilibus, immenso, & infigurabili; seu de universo & mundis* (Frankfurt, 1591)
6 *De imaginum, signorum, & idearum compositione* (Frankfurt, 1591)

The presence of these poems in the Northumberland library (and especially of the *De innumerabilibus, immenso et infigurabilis, seu de universo et mundis*, which has been defined as a compendium of Bruno's original thought) is historically significant. It has already been suggested, at the beginning of this chapter, that the Ninth Earl's role within his circle needs to be recognized for the clarity of the cultural choices operated and financed in the interest of scientific enquiry. In the *Advice* he defines in these terms the 'doctrine of the Metaphysics' which

containeth in it the division of *Ens* in his full scope and amplitude, which *Ens* ought first to be known, to conduct our knowledges to all arts that follow, which as yet is very slenderly delivered and uncertain, itself being a general stem from whence all other subjects of sciences do spring.[11]

Such a definition shows how aware Northumberland was of the intimate and crucial connection between the new philosophy and the new science. When he wrote this passage, Bruno's work was already acting as a powerful stimulus in this regard. In the words of Eugenio Garin:

> Non a caso per circa due secoli sembrano indugiarvisi quasi inseguendosi filosofi e scienziati, in una fervida circolazione di idee: da Copernico a Bruno, da Bruno a Galileo. Come non si intenderebbe tanta parte di Bruno senza Copernico, cosí senza Bruno – e sarà Keplero a rilevarlo – sarebbero difficilmente concepibili certe prospettive generali della scienza del Seicento.[12] (It is not by chance that for nearly two centuries philosophers and scientists seem almost to loiter over this, chasing each other in a fervid circulation of ideas: from Copernicus to Bruno, from Bruno to Galileo. Just as, without Copernicus, it would be impossible to understand much of Bruno, so without Bruno – and it is Kepler who makes the observation – many general prospects of seventeenth-century science would be hardly conceivable.)

It is in this historical prospect that the Northumberland collection of Bruno texts acquires its full significance. Quite apart from the question of the value of the scientific results achieved by the Northumberland circle (still a subject of investigation and debate), their Bruno collection requires us to recognize their participation in a movement of thought which was changing the traditional vision of the reality in which we live.

THE *HEROICI FURORI* AND THE 'ESSAY ON LOVE'

The annotated copy of *De gl'heroici furori* presents a problem of particular interest in the close connection it establishes between Bruno's text and Northumberland's 'Essay on Love'. Frances Yates first published and discussed Northumberland's 'Essay' in her book on *Love's Labour's Lost*, and in her discussion she already suggested that there was a close link between the Northumberland circle and Bruno, and specifically between Northumberland's 'Essay' and the *Heroici furori*.[13] She makes the connection in the context of an interpretation of Shakespeare's comedy as an unequivocal rejection of the new scientific learning, with its suspicions of passion and poetry and its emphasis on cold reason. A crucial event behind this debate between love and learning, passion and reason, is seen by Frances Yates to have been the Gray's Inn revels of 1594, recorded in the *Gesta Grayorum*, and in particular the speeches of the Second and Sixth Councellors of the Prince of Purpoole, the first of whom advises the study of philosophy which through the piercing sight of divine reason 'seeth into the bottom of the Sea', while the Sixth Councellor affirms the values of music, dancing, triumphs, comedies, ladies, and love.[14] Frances Yates sees Northumberland's 'Essay' as a reply to this debate in support of the Second Councellor, and Shakespeare's play as an answer in support of the Sixth. Behind both of them she sees the debate between Bruno and Sidney in the anti-Petrarchan satire of the *Argomento* of the *Furori*, which Bruno had addressed deliberately to Sidney as the arch-Petrarchan of the English scene:

> The Earl of Northumberland's essay gives us the second half of the answer to the stars-eyes, love-learning antithesis in L.L.L. The scientific study theme is stated and rejected in the play, though accepted and enlarged upon in the essay; whilst the writing of arcadian 'platts' to ladies, stated and rejected in the essay, is accepted and enlarged upon in the play. Berowne and his friends, when they have given up mathematics, are deeply intent on expressing their lethargious passions in pleasing order thus exactly reversing the process described by Northumberland. Northumberland's essay, in which Sidney's *Arcadia* is mentioned as a pattern for the 'platts', contains a memory of the previous argument between Bruno and Sidney on the relative merits of Women and knowledge, 'spectrum' and stars, a subject which is echoed in Sidney's sonnets.[15]

Whether Shakespeare's comedy can be interpreted in the light of such a reconstruction is a subject outside the scope of this chapter. I will consider here Northumberland's annotations of the *Furori* in the light of the general historical perspective outlined by Frances Yates to see how far they support her interpretation of the 'Essay on Love'.

The annotations confirm Northumberland's deep interest in Bruno's anti-Petrarchan satire in the *Argomento* and first dialogue of the *Furori*, which is precisely the part of the text in which we find his careful translations of difficult phrases and words. Northumberland's 'Essay', for instance, starts off by describing with contempt his distracted state of mind when his behaviour as a young man was regulated by the canons of the post-Petrarchan lover intent, above all, on the writing of 'platts' to women: 'how disgested, how contrived, yow may remember, the inventions from what conceate they proceeded yow did see and weare sorry, my violent passion yow were content to yeeld vnto out of necessitie, because it was otherwise booteles.'[16]

Turning to the *Furori* we find that Northumberland's annotations begin in earnest on page 5 of the first edition at precisely the following passage:

Ecco vergato in carte, rinchiuso in libri, messo avanti gli occhi ed intronato a gli orecchi un rumore, un strepito, un fracasso d'insegne, d'imprese, de motti, d'epistole, de sonetti, d'epigrammi, di libri, de prolissi scartafazzi, de sudori estremi, de vite consumate, con strida ch'assordiscon gli astri, lamenti che fanno ribombar gli antri infernali, doglie che fanno stupefar l'anime viventi, suspiri da far exinanire e compatir gli dei, per quegli occhi, per quelle guance.[17]

(Here we find traced on paper, closed in books, shown to the eyes and sounded to the ears, a noise or rather a din of emblems, 'imprese', mottoes, letters, sonnets, epigrams, books, abundance of waste-paper, of intense sweats, of consumed lives, with shrieks which deafen the stars, groans which shake the halls of hell, sufferings which amaze the souls of the living, sighs fit to make the gods blanch with pity, and all for those eyes, those cheeks.)

This and other passages annotated by Northumberland in the *Argomento* of the *Furori* lend weight to Frances Yates's thesis that in his 'Essay on Love' he was interpreting his youthful courtly experience in the light of Bruno's anti-Petrarchan satire. But, this being the case, the annotations appear to contradict the further Yatesian hypothesis that the 'Essay' is to be dated immediately after the Gray's Inn revels in 1594 and just before the composition of *Love's Labour's Lost*, which she puts at 1595.[18] For a close study of Northumberland's translations of Italian words and phrases shows an evident use of Florio's dictionary in the revised and amplified version published in 1611.[19] Florio did not modify all his definitions in his *New World of Words*, so that very often it is impossible to tell if Northumberland was referring to this or to the first edition of the dictionary published in 1598.[20] However, in seven separate cases his translations correspond to definitions given in the 1611 edition but not present, or present in a different form, in the earlier dictionary. The most striking of these is the translation of the phrase 'l'entusiasmo per solcar' as 'the fury from which to ploughe or furow'. In his first edition, Florio fails to list the word 'entusiasmo', but it appears (as 'enthusiasmo') in his second edition with the significant definition 'a Poeticall or propheticall fury, a ravishment of senses from above'.[21] On other occasions Northumberland's definition is an exact quotation from Florio's *New World of Words* or too close to be coincidental, for example the translation of 'facelle' as 'littel brand or burning lights' (See Plate 3): 'a little brand or burning light' in the *New World*.[22] The cumulative evidence of seven such cases of clear reference to Florio's new dictionary leaves little doubt that the reading of the *Furori* and the composition of the 'Essay on Love' were undertaken by Northumberland not during his period of Court life under Elizabeth in the 1590s, but in the very different circumstances of his confinement in the Tower after investigations into the Gunpowder Plot.[23]

The new date is consistent with the documented evidence that an intense study of Italian was undertaken by Northumberland during his imprisonment. It is probable that, like most of Elizabeth's Court, he knew some Italian before going to the Tower; but the extreme difficulty of the *Furori* suggests a reading after a concentrated and organized study of the language, which he undertook during his confinement. We know from a book list which has survived[24] that he sent back to Syon House from the Tower in 1614 a consignment of books including 'Florio's New Dictionary'. As well as a large number of books in Italian on various subjects, there were several Italian language books[25] including *Le observationi* by Dolce, an erudite

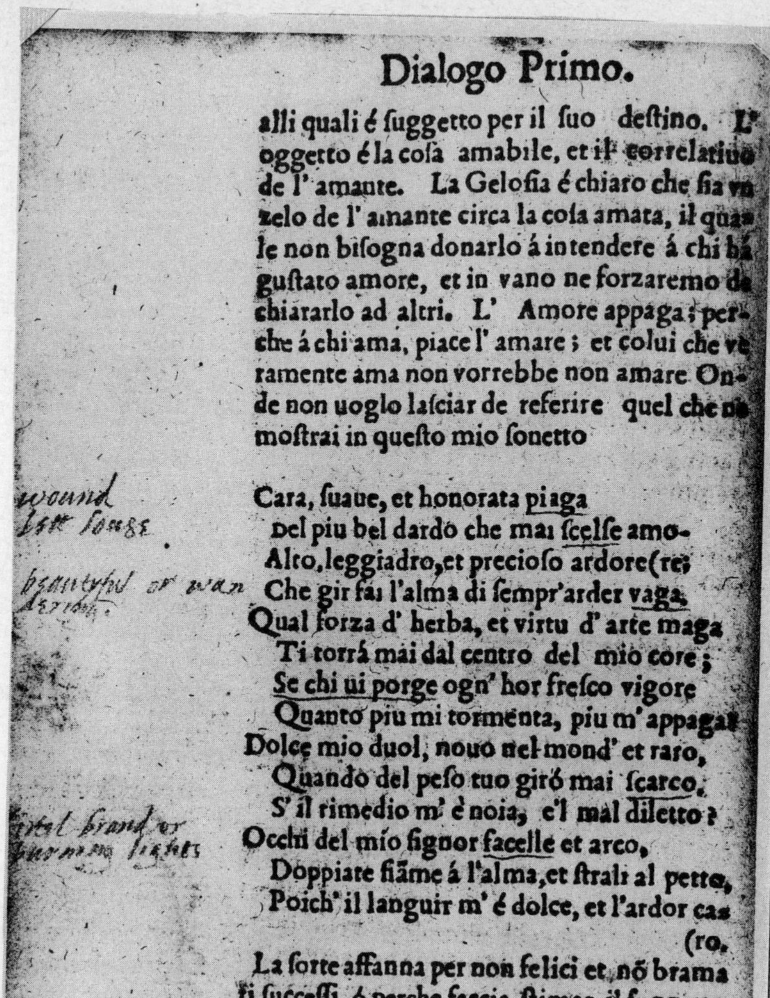

alli quali é fuggetto per il fuo deftino. L'
oggetto é la cofa amabile, et il correlatiuo
de l' amante. La Gelofia é chiaro che fia vn
zelo de l' amante circa la cofa amata, il quale non bifogna donarlo á intendere á chi há
guftato amore, et in vano ne forzaremo de
chiararlo ad altri. L' Amore appaga; perche á chi ama, piace l' amare; et colui che ve-
ramente ama non vorrebbe non amare On-
de non uoglo lafciar de referire quel che ne
moftrai in questo mio fonetto

wound

low foule

Cara, fuaue, et honorata piaga
  Del piu bel dardo che mai fcelfe amo-
Alto, leggiadro, et preciofo ardore (re)

beautyful or wan desious

Che gir fai l'alma di fempr'arder vaga;
  Qual forza d' herba, et virtu d' arte maga
    Ti torrá mai dal centro del mio core;
    Se chi ui porge ogn' hor frefco vigore
    Quanto piu mi tormenta, piu m' appaga;
Dolce mio duol, nouo nel mond' et raro,
  Quando del pefo tuo giró mai fcarco.
    S' il rimedio m' é noia; e'l mal diletto?

firel brand or burning lights

Occhi del mio fignor facelle et arco,
  Doppiate fiáme á l'alma, et ftrali al petto,
    Poich' il languir m' é dolce, et l'ardor ca-
                   (ro.
La forte affanna per non felici et nó brama
fi fucceffi, ó perche faccia ftimar il fuggetto
men degno de la fruition de l' oggetto, et
men proportionanato á la dignitá di quel-
lo; o perche non faccia reciproca correla-
tione, ó per altre caggioni et impedimenti

Plate 3 Translations in the hand of the Ninth Earl of Northumberland
in his copy of Bruno's *Heroici furori*. Petworth House Library. Reproduced by courtesy of Lord Egremont.

exposition and discussion of the structure and various parts of Tuscan Italian. Northumberland's copy of this book survives in the collection at Petworth House, Sussex;[26] it is heavily annotated in pen from the first blank fly-leaf, which contains a list of irregular verbs, to the final fly-leaf which contains a list of pronouns. A complicated set of tables, made up of letters and numbers, appears to have been used as a memory aid for learning the various pronouns. Throughout the volume blank spaces are filled with notes on verbs, vocabulary lists (Italian into Latin as well as Italian into English), and notes on the linguistic problems discussed by Dolce. The volume is an eloquent testimony to the study of Italian undertaken by Northumberland to while away the long years in the Tower.[27] The return of the language books and a large number of Italian texts to Syon House in 1614 suggests that the linguistic study was by that time complete. Given that Florio's new dictionary was also sent away at that date, the reading of the *Furori* may be assigned to the years 1611–14, with the probable composition of the 'Essay on Love' in the same years or shortly afterwards.

Intrinsic characteristics of the 'Essay' also suggest that it was composed during the years in the Tower. In the second part of his *Advice to his Son*, which is dated 1609 and claims to have been written 'fourteen years after the former', Northumberland himself draws attention to the dramatic change in his literary style which had taken place with the sombre turn of events in his life:

> Wonder not at the alteration of the style, which perhaps you may find, for either have I forgot much since that time in looking after other matters of greater weight, or lost much form in phrase, which youth pleaseth itself commonly in . . . I know that things plainest written are the best way for doctrine; fine phrases and laboured styles are but to please.[28]

Frances Yates is of the opinion that the 'Essay' resembles the earlier, more elaborate and laboured style of the first part of the *Advice*, rather than the plainer and more terse style of the second part.[29] The thesis appears at first sight to be supported by some of the passages she quotes, as, for example, these lines in which Northumberland sums up the sense of hopeless agitation and frustration caused by his concentration on his 'lethargious' passions:

> Tumblinge these conceites from corner to corner of my braynes, nothinge resting vndone but how to compownd a mixture fittest to purchase my idle determination, both I and my fancies walked in a Cirkell, the one about the Chamber, the other to the first period of obteininge vntill I grew giddie with thinckinge, and thinckinge gyddelie, made me gyddie in walkinge.[30]

But the *Advice* shows that Northumberland was sensitive to questions of style, and it may be argued that this and other elaborate passages in the first part of the 'Essay' are suitable stylistic expressions of an elaborate, over-complicated and ultimately frustrated state of mind. When, in the second part of his 'Essay', Northumberland describes his rejection of his 'finite' mistress and his discovery of the superior claims of scientific investigation and learning, we find him expressing himself with the new plainness and directness he refers to in the *Advice*:

> Knowledge I fownd spake gravely my Mistris, idelly, it constant, shee fickle, it treated of hidden misteries shee of vulger trifles, it contented ever shee displeased often, it discourst with assurance, shee weakly, it produced out of conclusions p[er]petuall contentment, shee in conclusion p[ro]duced sadnes, for they say *Omne animall post coitum triste*.[31]

Nor could there be anything more plain and direct than the conclusion of the 'Essay', which shows Northumberland writing with terse assurance of the values he has been weighing in the balance and the respective importance he is prepared to allow them:

> But least I showld open my humor to be over enclyning to a *Cynicall* disposition, and that knowledge could not be enterteyned w[i]thout the losse of a Mistris, I must conclude that to enioye a Mistris together with learninge is possible, but to gaine a Mistris with longe sute, mutch passion, and many delaies, and follow knowledge in his hight is impossible.[32]

It is further noticeable that an overtly autobiographical element appears only in the second part of the *Advice,* when the prisoner in the Tower begins to meditate on the experiences he has lived through. The 'Essay on Love' is an intensely autobiographical composition which attempts in a few pages to communicate the sense of a life which has yielded to and then controlled the claims of sensual passion, discovering the superior claims of an intellectual pursuit of knowledge and truth. Although working in a much smaller dimension, Northumberland follows Bruno's *Furori* in attempting a psychological reconstruction of a life-experience which he, like Bruno, divides into three main stages: an initial rejection of natural passion as the key to happiness; an intermediate stage of uncertainty and search, undecided between the claims of passion and intellect; and a final breakthrough of the intellect which declares its service to 'this infinite worthy Mistris' knowledge who brings with her 'myndes quiet, sowles felicitie'. The intelligence works quietly, not in agitation ('l'opra d'intelligenza non è operazion di moto, ma di quiete'), Bruno had written in a passage closely annotated by Northumberland.[33]

The assignment of Northumberland's reading of the *Furori* and the composition of the 'Essay on Love' to the years of confinement severs the connection of the 'Essay' with the composition of *Love's Labour's Lost,* but leaves it still very much a part of the debate between love and learning, passion and reason, the senses and the intellect. For that debate was to continue well into the seventeenth century with its increasing emphasis on scientific enquiry accompanied by the gradual affirmation of sterner moral values. Northumberland's 'Essay' is concerned with one of the central themes of that debate, the necessity of bringing the natural passions under the curb of an enquiring reason. It is of the greatest interest in this context to discover that another carefully annotated passage of the *Furori* is a page containing one of the book's central metaphors: that of the will seen as a helmsman in the stern of the ship of the human soul, intent on the task of controlling with his tiny tiller of reason the waves of natural 'furyes, force or outrages' (Northumberland's translation of Bruno's 'empiti'). In spite of the efforts made by the will to bend the natural forces which surround it to its determined purpose, some refuse to listen to its call and against these the will is forced to proceed, killing some with the anger of the sword and punishing others with the whip of contempt ('vien a mostrarsi come uccidesse quelli e donasse bando a questi, procedendo contra gli altri con la spada de l'ira, ed altri con la sferza del sdegno').[34] Northumberland needed equally extreme language to describe his 'greate strife of humours' in which, struggling between the claims of the senses and the intellect, only too often he 'lost the iewell of tyme, and exchanged light for darkness' until finally, immersing himself in intellectual enquiry, he was carried by an unhampered reason to 'the veary principles most simple of knowledge in generall'.[35]

The annotated copy of the *Furori*, therefore, not only confirms Northumberland's deep interest in Bruno's work but suggests that the influence of Bruno on the 'Essay on Love' (and thus on Northumberland's whole conception of the sense of his intellectual enquiry) went beyond the limits of the anti-Petrarchan polemic in Bruno's opening pages. Indeed Northumberland's treatment in his 'Essay' of the theme of the simplicity of truth brings us back to the other Bruno texts which we know were in his library. At the height of his detailed description of the stratagems he meditated and adopted in his unruly youth to obtain the desired mistress, Northumberland, from the standpoint of his later experience, comments on his blind dedication to his 'pretended happynes, little thinckinge that a *Mathematicall* line beinge lesse then an vntwined thredd could have bene stronger to have stayed me, then eyther fetters or Chaynes'.[36] This comment in its turn links up with a further image of imprisonment in a 'circular maze' of frustrating desire, from which he is freed by his first scientific enquiries which will eventually lead him to those 'veary principles most simple of knowledge in generall'. Truth as a straight line, unique and powerful in its brevity and simplicity; falsehood as a twined thread, a 'circular maze'. The images lead us straight to Bruno's extraordinary opening to his book on measure (the fifth book of the *De triplici minimo*) in which the straight line is presented as 'an archetype of truth' and exalted, in very similar imagery, for its unique power derived from its simplicity and brevity in contrast with the 'falsity' of the innumerable curves which join the same two points meandering through devious figures and forms.[37] The true, the sacred, the good, Bruno writes, everywhere and eternally tend directly towards a single point. A '*Mathematicall* line', writes Northumberland, 'beinge lesse then an vntwined thredd' is stronger than 'eyther fetters or Chaynes'.

A concept of truth as liberation: this seems to be a central idea which Northumberland receives from Bruno's work. His reading was far from being confined to Bruno. Indeed his library, once its full extent is known, will probably have to be considered among the most important collections of the Elizabethan and Jacobean periods; and many other works will have had their effect on Northumberland and his circle. Nevertheless, the wandering Neapolitan, so proud of being unaristocratic, inelegant, and unrefined, of bearing a message not honey-sweet but breathing the honest flavour of chestnuts and cheese, as he writes in the remarkable confession which closes his *De innumerabilibus, immenso, et infigurabili* (and perhaps he already foresees that for such honesty he will have to pay the highest price), appears to have had on the haughty and aristocratic Earl a particularly rich and varied influence. Not only does Bruno help to establish the crucial link between philosophical and scientific investigations, but he offers Northumberland the concepts with which to interpret the intimate sense of his life-experience: his struggle to rise above unrestrained passion and fashionable trifling in order to dedicate himself to an unswerving pursuit of knowledge and truth.

3

THE NORTHUMBERLAND CIRCLE: HARRIOT'S PAPERS

'NOLANUS, DE UNIVERSO ET MUNDIS'

Bruno's strong influence extended beyond the Ninth Earl to the scholars and scientists in his circle. Before defining that influence, however, it is necessary to face the problem of widely differing interpretations of Bruno's thought, and therefore of differing assessments of his impact on the development of contemporary culture, and particularly, in this case, of contemporary science.

One way of interpreting Bruno (the most distinguished example is probably to be found in the work of Alexandre Koyré) is to divide him into two different people: on the one hand the advanced thinker who destroyed the Aristotelian cosmos and with it Aristotelian physics; on the other hand the esoteric magician. 'Not a modern mind by any means', Koyré remarks drily of this second Bruno.[1] Others have considered Bruno essentially as a mystic searching for the divine unity behind the multiplicity of appearances, and have denied him any real importance in the modern scientific revolution.[2] In a more complex approach, which has exercised much influence, Frances Yates stressed the Hermetic and magical aspects of Bruno's thought, while at the same time insisting that Renaissance science was permeated with such influences right up to Newton himself.[3] Bruno, the Renaissance magus, was thus saved as a figure of influence on the science of his time. But the thesis was pushed too far. The Yatesian Bruno remains primarily a mystic, his Copernicanism itself confined to a marginal position except in so far as it can be considered a mystical diagram or Hermetic seal:[4] definitions which place precise limits on Bruno's influence on scientific thought. Some of the most recent work on Bruno shows a marked reaction against such a primary emphasis on his mysticism and magic. His Copernicanism has been re-examined and revalued. His interest in, and knowledge of, the scientific enquiries of his times, such as the study of comets, has been underlined. In general, it is precisely where Bruno breaks away from the Neoplatonic magi to establish a new cosmic vision that he is attracting the attention of many scholars today.[5]

It is in this context of a renewed interest in his more specifically scientific enquiries that Bruno's influence on the Northumberland circle has to be considered. For the Bruno texts in the Northumberland library allow us to place in a new light the circle's knowledge of and interest in Bruno's work. That there was, somewhere, an influence of Bruno is not a new idea. It has been suggested most convincingly in the work of Jean Jacquot, who considers the influence certain in the case of Nicolas Hill, rather less certain in the cases of Harriot and Warner, while he allots little or no space to the Earl himself.[6] But it has not yet been established what precise aspects of Bruno's thought were acting most strongly on the group, with what results in their work and on their reputation. Using the new knowledge of the particular works of Bruno which were being read by the Northumberland circle, it will be possible to gain a more exact idea of what his philosophy meant to them.

The Northumberland library, as we have seen, contains seven of Bruno's texts, considering each part of the Frankfurt Trilogy as a separate work. Six of them are Latin texts written after Bruno had left England, while there is only one of the celebrated Italian dialogues written in England during his visit from 1583 to 1585. It has generally been assumed that English readers of Bruno were referring to these Italian dialogues, which caused heated discussion in English circles during the 1580s. They are, indeed, works of great importance for they represent Bruno's first efforts to clarify the terms of his total cosmic vision. They already contain the essential elements of his philosophy, including his Copernicanism and his atomic theory of matter, but neither of these elements is as yet fully worked out. Bruno is still primarily concerned with the divine unity of the one principle and cause; he retains a sense of the transcendent, and Neoplatonic influences are still strong. Of these works only the last, the *Heroici furori*, is present in the Ninth Earl's library. I have already argued that this text, annotated by the Earl of Northumberland himself, was the model used for his interpretation of his intellectual life as we find it described in his 'Essay on Love'. Besides his annotations, the book carries his book-badge, but it has no sign of his library catalogue numbers. I am inclined to think that he kept it for private reading during his imprisonment in the Tower, where he wrote his 'Essay on Love'. I have so far found no evidence of a direct knowledge of the *Furori* in the members of the group discussed in this chapter, whereas they appear to have been deeply influenced by the three great Latin poems published in Frankfurt in 1591, all of which are present in the Northumberland collection. These are the works in which Bruno, after years of further wandering through Europe and numerous publications on diverse subjects, reworked his total cosmic vision, giving his philosophy its final shape. Although his vision is not new with respect to the Italian dialogues written in London, the emphases are different. The divine unity behind the whole is remembered in occasional, often passionately intense pages, but Bruno's attention here is primarily directed towards the nature and order of the physical universe.[7]

The last of these poems, and the one in which Bruno himself considers that he has revealed precise truths about physical things, is the *De innumerabilibus, immenso, et infigurabili* (usually known as *De Immenso*). This work offers us Bruno's final vision of the immense, the unbounded universe. It also contains, as Bruno's major nineteenth-century commentator, Felice Tocco, pointed out, his most advanced scientific intuitions: the criticism of the theory of the lunar epicycle and the planetary orbs; the geometrical refutation of the spheres of air and fire; the theory of spiral motion; the theory of comets, which Bruno used as a fundamental argument against the immutability of the heavens; and the theory of the movement of the sun round its own axis.[8] In some of these pages Bruno reached, through philosophical argument, intuitions which would later be developed scientifically by Galileo. It is then of the greatest interest to note that this work (and only this) is specifically mentioned by title in the writings of the Northumberland group. In one of Harriot's unpublished papers we find the jotting: 'Nolanus, de universo et

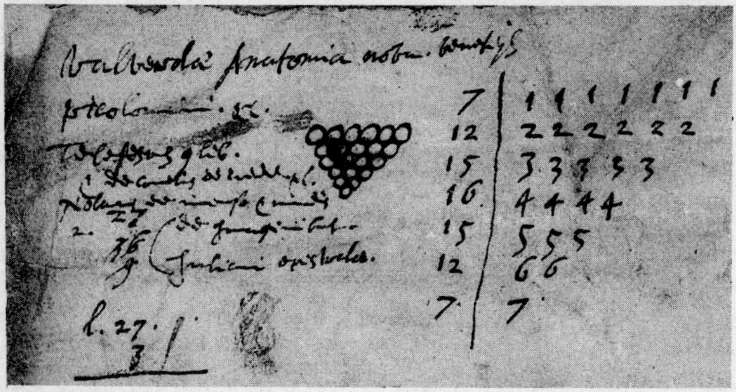

Plate 4 Thomas Harriot's book list containing the annotation 'Nolanus, de universo et mundis' beside mathematical notes on progressing series of numbers. Add.MSS. 6188, fol.67ᵛ. Reproduced by courtesy of the British Library.

mundis' (see Plate 4), which is Bruno's second title for his *De innumerabilibus, immenso, et infigurabili, seu de universo et mundis.*[9]

The context in which this note occurs indicates clearly the terms in which Bruno's works were being consulted by Harriot and therefore (given the close relationship between their activities) by his associates. The note occurs on a working page of Harriot's mathematical manuscripts, in a corner of which, apparently without direct connection with the calculations he was attempting, he wrote out a brief and hurried book list. It may have been for his own reading, or perhaps to be referred to his patron the Earl. It is a significant list, for it shows that Bruno was not consulted by Harriot in a context of Hermetic mysticism, but was included and read in the context of study of the natural philosophers of the period.[10] The list opens with a medical text on anatomy which links up with the known interest of the Northumberland circle in questions of medical science. More significant still is the group of texts which immediately precede the Bruno title. These are a number of works of Telesius, the philosopher from Cosenza; his writings on the nature of the universe and his critique of Aristotelian physics were much admired by Bruno, who refers to him in his Italian dialogue *De la causa* as 'il giudiciosissimo Telesio', and praises him again twice in the Latin trilogy (*De monade*, v, and *De immenso*, II, ix). Moreover, the influence of Telesian ideas on the beginnings of modern scientific enquiry in England has recently been underlined (Bacon is an interesting case in point),[11] and there can be no doubt that Harriot was studying him carefully, linking this study with that of Bruno's *De immenso*. The first work of Telesius's mentioned in Harriot's list is referred to simply as in nine books, and is obviously his best known and major work *De rerum natura iuxta propria principia,* first published in its complete form in 1587. Immediately after this, Harriot also refers to the less well-known pamphlets, *De cometis* and *De iride*, which appeared in the collection of Telesius's shorter works published in 1590, after his death, by Antonio Persio. The references to these titles are particularly interesting in view of the importance of Harriot's own observations of comets and his work in optics; and his debt to Telesian ideas on these subjects could well be looked into. For the purposes of this study, however, it is above all the general context of enquiry into natural phenomena, and the inclusion of Bruno's major work in this context, which indicate the sense of the Northumberland circle's reference to the Nolano.

The influence of the *De immenso* on the Northumberland circle can be clearly traced in a series of passages in other works of the group. In his philosophical book published in Paris in 1601, Nicolas Hill mentions Bruno in a marginal note to his aphorism 434 entitled: Terrae motum sufficienter probant.[12] Shortly afterwards, in aphorism 438, Hill extends the heliocentric theory to the concept of an infinite universe in terms which closely follow Bruno, although his name is not mentioned again. However, Hill's innumerable globes dispersed in an infinite spatial envelope are clearly inspired by Bruno's cosmic vision. Although his name, again, is not mentioned, it is obvious that Bruno similarly inspired Walter Warner's definitions of space in his philosophical papers.[13] These definitions constitute one of Warner's clearest and most succinct pages:

> Space is corporeally or spherically infinite, that is according to all dimensions and all local respects. . . . It is absolutely continuall throughout his whole infiniteness and all his parts . . . it is absolutely immoveable but is the base and fundamentum of all motion for whatsoever is moved is moved in

space. . . . Space may be defined. . . an infinite eternall nothing, but the universall vessell or receptacle of things. (See Plate 5.)

One of Aristotle's arguments against the infinity of the universe was that an infinite body could not be conceived to move; to which Bruno retorts that the more ancient Greek philosophers, whom Aristotle was attacking, had never conceived of infinite space as movable but simply as the envelope or receptacle of things.[14] In the first book of the *De immenso*, Bruno's own concept of infinite space had found its final expression in terms almost identical to those used by Warner: 'Space', Bruno writes, 'is a certain continuous physical quantity, in three dimensions, which contains everything indifferently . . . it stretches beyond everything and includes everything. . . . Space is not movable but gathers within itself the things which move'.[15]

In his *Etudes galiléennes*, Alexandre Koyré has pointed out the enormous implications, for the development of a new physics and a new astronomy, of Bruno's concept of infinite space.[16] The Aristotelian idea of privileged places and movements has been completely destroyed. Space has become indifferent to the motion or rest of the bodies contained within it. Some of the important implications of this new (or if we like antique) concept of space were drawn by Bruno himself. The second chapter of the third book of the *De immenso* is entitled, with a typical Brunian blend of philosophy and poetry: 'By better wings we are led into the skies'.[17] Here Bruno meditates on the absence of a centre in the new infinite universe. Wherever you are everything will appear to rotate round you. Wherever you are everything will have the same aspect as it would if you were in any other place. It is known that the Northumberland circle was familiar with 'that opinion . . . of Nolanus by which he affirmed that the eye beinge placed in anie parte of the Universe the appearance would still be all one as vnto us here'. The words are written by Sir William Lower in his much-quoted letter to Harriot about the recent discoveries of 'my diligent Galileus'.[18] The letter is well known, and has often been used to underline the remarkable speed with which the Northumberland circle received and absorbed the great Galilean discoveries, for the letter, dated 21 June 1610,[19] was in answer to a previous letter of Harriot's sending Lower

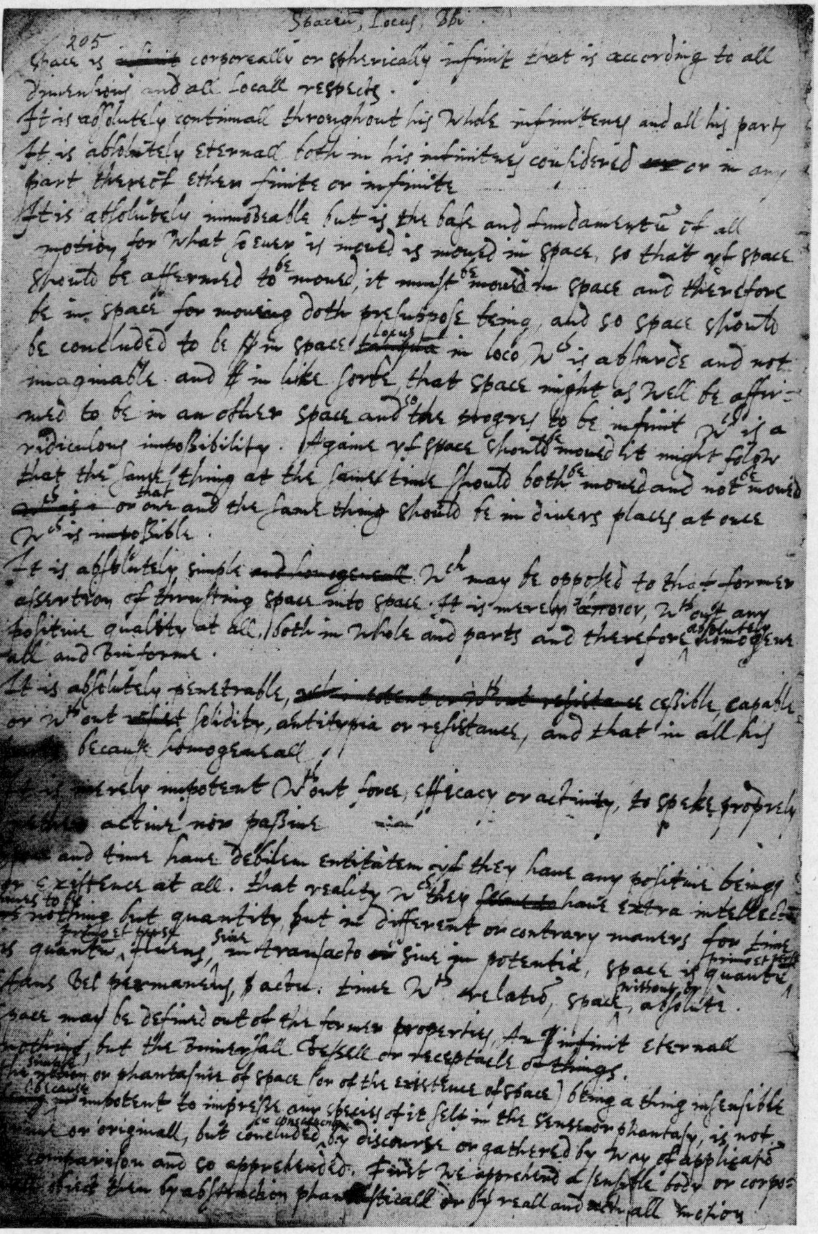

Plate 5 A page of Walter Warner's philosophical manuscripts entitled 'Space, Locus, Ubi'. Add.MSS.4395, fol.204ᵛ. Reproduced by courtesy of the British Library.

news of the *Sidereus nuncius*, which had only been published on 12 March of the same year.

It is worth looking at this letter yet again, for it demonstrates to an extent not yet realized the importance of Bruno's thought for the Northumberland circle's astronomical speculations. Lower quotes Bruno's concept of the relativity of universal space in a discussion of Kepler's doubts about the infinity of the universe expressed in his *De stella serpentari* (1606). In the course of his discussion, which rejects Kepler's objections to an infinite cosmology,[20] Lower refers to a hypothesis which he says he has learnt from Harriot himself:

> for sayd I (havinge heard you say often as much) what if in that huge space betweene the starres and Saturne, ther remaine ever fixed infinite nombers which may supply the appearance to the eye that shalbe placed in ♋ [Cancer], which by reason of ther lesser magnitudes doe flie our sighte, what if aboute ♄. ♃ .♂. [Saturn, Jupiter, Mars] etc. ther move other planets which also appeare not. Just as I was a saying this comes your letter, which when I had redd, loe. qd I, what I spoke probablie experience hath made good.

The opinion which Lower ascribes to Harriot was one of the important conclusions that Bruno had already drawn from his new concept of infinite space. In the fourth book of the *De immenso*, meditating on 'the order of the worlds in the universe and their disposition in the ethereal space', Bruno had pointed out how the observing eye, which has become the relative centre of the new centreless universe, observes only what it can see from its relative position in the immense whole:

> As you have seen these planets move round the sun, do not believe it impossible to discover others, although your sight cannot of itself detect them, nor can those bodies send out light reflected to us for three reasons: they possess no light of their own; they are tiny and far from us.[21]

Harriot's familiarity with Bruno's hypothesis, which he has passed on to Lower, demonstrates how thoroughly he had studied the book whose title he jotted down in his notes.

It must be remembered that Bruno's cosmological speculations were considered, by none other than Kepler himself, a primary stimulus behind Galileo's discoveries, which included the satellites of Jupiter, announced in the *Sidereus nuncius*. Kepler's opinion is contained in a letter written by Martin Hasdale, Librarian to the Imperial Court at Prague, to Galileo himself on 15 April 1610. Hasdale has just made friends with Kepler and reports a conversation with him that morning to Galileo: in it Kepler had lavishly praised the new discoveries announced in the *Sidereus nuncius* (which had been presented to him on 8 April by the Tuscan ambassador) while at the same time suggesting that Galileo

> had given some cause of complaint not only to the German nation but to his own, having failed to mention any of those authors who had proposed and stimulated an investigation into those things which had just been discovered, naming among these Giordano Bruno for Italy, as well as Copernicus and himself.[22]

Kepler, of course, did not accept Bruno's concept of an infinite universe, although recognizing the importance of his cosmological speculation. Lower's letter to Harriot, together with Hill's reference and Warner's definition of space, demonstrate that, on the contrary, the Northumberland circle as a whole accepted the full Brunian thesis of an infinite, homogeneous universe. This means that they were interpreting their astronomical investigations within a philosophical concept which represented the most extreme consequence to be drawn from the Copernican revolution, so extreme that Kepler would never accept it in full while Galileo himself would hesitate to endorse it.[23] It was their study of Bruno's *De immenso* which prepared Harriot and his associates to respond so quickly and enthusiastically to Galileo's discoveries, perhaps even, as has been argued, to anticipate some of them.[24]

THOMAS HARRIOT'S PAPERS *DE INFINITIS*

In a rather different context of enquiry, a study of Harriot's manuscript papers entitled *De infinitis*[25] again leads to Bruno, although to a less well-known aspect of his thought. These papers have recently been the subject of some curiosity and much perplexity. They discuss in quasi-mathematical, quasi-logical terms questions relating to infinite quantities, both the maximum and the minimum infinites. In a paper on Harriot's use of the minus sign, Dr Tanner has pointed out the basis in Aristotelian logic of Harriot's speculation here.[26] The question to be asked is why Harriot thought it necessary to go back to Aristotle's often baffling meditations on infinite quantities, getting himself involved, in those dawning years of modern scientific enquiry, in ancient and scholastic paradoxes such as that of Achilles and the tortoise. The answer is to be found in Bruno's *De triplici minimo*,[27] the first book of the Frankfurt Trilogy, of which the *De immenso* is the last.

The *De triplici minimo* is an important work for in it can be found Bruno's fullest treatment of his atomic theory of matter. And as, in the *De immenso*, Bruno will establish the infinity of the universe through a point-by-point refutation of Aristotle's arguments against infinity in the *De caelo*, so here he establishes the existence of the atomic minima through point-by-point refutation of Aristotle's arguments against the atomic theory, above all in books III and Vl of the *Physics*. Bruno uses the method of Aristotelian logic to reverse the conclusions reached by the Stagirite himself. Aristotle, it can thus be said, stands at the centre of Bruno's speculations on minimum and maximum quantities as the great authority to be dethroned. Bruno recognizes his stature as an antagonist. Purely philosophical argument will not be enough to convince a reading public still thoroughly schooled in Aristotelian doctrine. So Bruno does not hesitate to add invective and insult. Aristotle looms at times in his work as a kind of primal source of mental and physical darkness, the very principle of falsehood: in short, the devil himself.[28] Only by remembering Bruno's use of such extreme metaphors in what was, after all, a philosophical adventure of extreme daring is it possible to understand the sense of the quotation from Revelation jotted down by Harriot as a heading to one of his pages *De infinitis*: 'The devell that was bound for a thousand years and after let loose to deceave the people in the four quarters of the earth'.[29] The start of the first line is missing and the corners of the page torn off, but it may be deduced from the remains of the letters that the word attached to the quotation was Aristotle.

Aristotle's speculations on infinity in the *Physics* had covered the minimum as monad, or the prime number, the minimum as minimum magnitude or atom, and the minimum as point. He drew careful distinctions between these three minima, admitting the monad in the abstract as the prime number or basic principle of arithmetical calculation, denying the existence of a physical minimum or atom on the basis of the infinite divisibility of matter, and conceiving the point as an abstract element in geometrical speculation and not as an indivisible line.[30] Bruno replies by ignoring Aristotle's distinctions between actuality and potentiality, and insisting on a related actual existence of the minimum in its three forms. Firstly it is monad, the first number, the basis of every principle of quantity. Secondly it is atom, the physical minimum, the life-giving centre of energy at the basis of matter and all its vicissitudes. Thirdly it is point, the basis of every principle of measure.[31] Through this threefold definition, Bruno establishes the minimum as the fundamental element of all existence. Without it there is nothing, but at the same time, developing an insight of Nicolas Cusanus, the ultimate minimum, in so far as it represents the first principle of all existence, coincides with the ultimate maximum, the all-embracing one.[32] The thought is not without subtlety, although it may well be considered as paradoxically anachronistic from a mathematical point of view. For in order to save the physical atom from Aristotle's logic, Bruno has gone back to a Pythagorean conception of number as the basis of actual quantitative existence and of the point as indivisible line. Indeed the second work of Bruno's great Latin trilogy, the *De monade*, is an enquiry into the various traditions of visionary meditation on numbers as the basic elements of sensible things. Bruno himself was not entirely satisfied with the *De monade*, and admits that in this work his search for truth gives uncertain results.[33] Nevertheless, throughout the trilogy, he assumes a Pythagorean position, refusing to make a clear distinction between the logic of mental processes, or what he calls 'art', and the natural universe comprehended by that 'art'. Thus he can overturn Aristotle's conclusions by arguing that as the mind, in dealing with decreasing numbers, is ultimately arrested at the monad, the first number and first principle of quantity, so the division of matter cannot proceed infinitely, but must ultimately be arrested at the physical minimum or atom. Conversely, as the mind continues infinitely to add number to number, so matter stretches out infinitely without meeting any bounds.[34]

This still leaves Bruno with the Aristotelian objection to the continuity of atoms; for Aristotle had argued in the *Physics* that since indivisibles have no parts, they must be in contact with one another as whole with whole, and so will not form a continuum.[35] Bruno replies with an important distinction between the concept of atoms as minimum parts and what he calls their *termini*. These are not to be considered as parts of the minimum, which indeed has no parts, but only as limits which touch the limits of other minima separated by an indivisible distance.[36] At times Bruno identifies this indivisible distance with the Democritean vacuum which seals adjoining atoms.[37] Thus continuity of matter is substantially saved, and combinations of atoms are the basis of all physical reality.

There can be no doubt that Harriot had Bruno's *De triplici minimo* in mind when he meditated on the infinites, for his meditations follow strikingly the directions of Bruno's thought. Propositions concerning the continuum formed by *minima* at an undivided distance are clearly related to Bruno's concept of *termini*;[38] meditations on the relative characteristics of infinite quantities (whether, for example, it is possible to apply the notions of equality and inequality to infinites) appear clearly related to Bruno's similar meditations derived from the speculations of Cusanus.[39] We have a whole series of geometrical meditations which relate the speculations on minimum and infinite quantities to Euclidean geometry as Bruno attempts to do in the second part of his book. And in an important page there is a passage which we may consider as Harriot's clearest expression of adherence to Bruno's cosmic vision. The passage, as can be seen from the quotations below, is largely made up of propositions which precisely echo passages in the *De triplici minimo*:

> Porro nobis statuendum est, materiam finitam quantamcumque obiectam partibus constare non infinitis, cui apponendo magnitudinem, sicut et numero finito multitudinem, infinitum percurrere licet. E contra vero a finita magnitudine partes adimenti et subdividenti minimum, sicut a finito numero numerum subtrahenti monadem, tandem occurrere necesse est. (Bruno)[40]

(And yet we must affirm that finite matter, however extended, is not composed of infinite parts, but if we continue adding to it, like adding innumerable numbers to a finite number, then it really is possible to proceed to infinity. On the contrary, by subtracting and dividing the parts of a finite magnitude, we necessarily arrive sooner or later at the minimum quantity, just as by subtracting a number from a finite number we must arrive at the monad.)

And yet for a last in decreasing progressions we must needes understand a quantity absolutely indivisible; but multiplicably infinitely infinite till a quantity absolutely inmultiplicable be produced which I may call universally infinite. And in encreasing progressions we must needes understand that for a last there must be a quantity inmultiplicable absolute, but divisible infinitely infinite till that quantity be issued that is absolutely indivisible. That such quantity which I call universally infinite: hath not only act rationall, by supposition: but also act reall, or existence . . . with many reall consequences or properties consequent. (Harriot)[41]

Here we have Harriot, in what I find a moving passage, standing up beside Bruno to declare the physical and actual reality of both the minimum atom and the infinite universe; and this moment of solidarity with Bruno's daring must surely be allowed its full importance. But this does not mean that Harriot's *De infinitis* papers as a whole should be interpreted as a mere underlining of Bruno's thought. They appear far more complex and subtle than that. I believe Harriot found himself in a paradoxical position; for in his attack on Aristotle, Bruno was prepared, as we have seen, to go back to antiquated mathematical reasoning in order to save his infinite universe. Indeed Bruno's insistence on relating his mathematics to his metaphysics led him inevitably to his much-criticized refusal of some of the most advanced mathematical thinking of his time, for example the developments in trigonometry. 'The doctrines of irrationality and asymmetry are the mothers of the ignorance which surrounds the minimum', is Bruno's title of the sixth chapter of book III of the *De triplici minimo*, where his criticism of the modern mathematicians reaches its height. The doctrine of the minimum lay at the basis of his new cosmology and was not to be renounced. Every figure must resolve itself into its own minimum (the triangle into a minimum triangle, the sphere into a minimum sphere, etc.), and every residual quantity, however minute, must be taken into calculation, or the concept of the minimum would be nullified. So Bruno wishes to sweep away all the 'useless' trigonometrical tables devised, in his opinion, 'by an ignorant century'. Harriot's relationship to such thinking could not be a simple one, for his own mathematical enquiries had led him into many of the fields which Bruno so ferociously attacks.[42]

The question which is raised here is the complex and much discussed one of the contradiction between Bruno's anachronistic mathematics and his advanced cosmology.[43] It is probably true, as one modern commentator has pointed out, 'that Bruno was so intensely aware of the relationship of geometry to metaphysics, that he found it impossible to make purely geometrical deductions'.[44] And it was inevitable that a nineteenth-century commentator like Felice Tocco, in his detailed commentary on the *De triplici minimo*, should dismiss Bruno's arguments against the new mathematicians as unsound and unjust.[45] But it must be remembered that behind the whole phenomenon of the emergence of a new mathematics there lay a crisis of an antique mystical concept of quantity and number which had played a prominent part in sixteenth-century philosophical speculation. The note of doubt in Bruno's own judgement of his *De monade* is an interesting sign of growing unease among philosophers of the late sixteenth century with respect to the mystical, Pythagorean concept of number as the basis of sensible things, which still carried the authority of the most prominent thinkers of the Florentine Neoplatonic school. Another nearly contemporary expression of similar tensions is John Dee's *Mathematicall Praeface* to Billingsley's translation of Euclid's *Elements*. Although Dee on the one hand aligns himself with 'the noble Earle of Mirandula' who, in his eleventh Conclusion disputed at Rome had claimed that 'by numbers, a way is had, to the searching out, and understandyng of every thyng', he nevertheless points out that 'the peculiar maner of handlying and workyng with numbers' developed by the new mathematicians and astronomers 'may seeme an other forme of

Arithmetike'.[46] In the late sixteenth and early seventeenth centuries, two different concepts of number and quantity could exist side by side, with some of the most advanced cosmological speculation, as in the case of Bruno, still referring to Neoplatonic concepts. Giovanni Aquilecchia, in his presentation of two previously unknown texts of Bruno's, closely related to the Euclidean sections of the *De triplici minimo*,[47] has underlined the fact that Bruno's mathematical thinking, linked as it is to the logic of Raymund Lull and Nicolas Cusanus, fits into a vast current of Renaissance speculation in which mathematical and metaphysical considerations were inextricably enmeshed. Aquilecchia points to documented evidence of the widespread interest of Bruno's contemporaries for his mathematical speculations, particularly after the publication of the Frankfurt Trilogy. Such interest seems to have been especially lively in Venice and among the German scholars who probably attended Bruno's lectures of 1592 at Padua, where Aquilecchia thinks he may have aspired, unsuccessfully, to the vacant Chair of mathematics shortly to be awarded to Galileo. It is thus evident that Harriot was far from being alone in paying serious attention to the mathematical-logical aspects of Bruno's thought even if, as the *De infinitis* papers suggest, he had reservations about his method of enquiry.

These reservations would appear to be most clearly expressed in those pages of his notes in which Harriot considers, with apparent impartiality, Aristotelian proposals on infinite quantities which are the direct opposite of Bruno's own. At times he will accept a Brunian proposition, such as that of a line composed of atoms instead of abstract points, in order, as he puts it, to 'propound some difficulties'.[48] There is even a page of his manuscripts, certainly related to his papers *De infinitis*, in which he suggests that the whole exercise of considering infinities in the light of Aristotelian logic may lead to questionable results.[49] The page presents a series of contradictory propositions concerning minimum and maximum infinites, such as 'whether at the maximum be finite and at the minimum too', or, alternatively, 'whether at the minimum be infinite and at the maximum too' ('An sit maximum et minimum finitum', 'An sit minimum et maximum infinitum'). Such impartial speculation on the very question which Bruno had argued against Aristotle with such ferocity sounds like an ironic critique of his vigorous logical methods. For against Aristotle's finite maximum, which gave him his closed universe, and his infinite minimum which allowed him to refute the atomic theory by propounding the infinite divisibility of matter, Bruno proposed as a certainty his triple finite minimum (monad, atom, and point) leading by ever-increasing progression to an infinite maximum: the theoretical or logical premise on which his vision of the infinite universe was based. Harriot, as we have seen earlier on, was quite prepared to align himself at one point of the *De infinitis* papers with Bruno's central cosmological proposition, accepting both the atomic minimum and the infinite maximum in their 'act reall, or existence . . . with many reall consequences or properties consequent'. It would appear, then, that what Harriot's more scientific mind was perceiving on this further page was the impossibility of proving, in scientific terms, either the Aristotelian or the Brunian position. We might say that, with a particularly modern perception, he was recognizing the essentially hypothetical nature of both cosmological propositions. For, as Bruno himself admits in the *De triplici minimo*, the finite minimum is an 'occult' quantity which he is unable to demonstrate in any but logical terms, while the infinite maximum can be argued, as he does most persuasively, but hardly demonstrated or proved. Thus we see Harriot, who at one point appears to accept Bruno's cosmology without reserves, put forward on this other page his central proposition on the resolution of a finite quantity into indivisibles as a speculative one not susceptible of proof: 'whether a finite may be resolved into indivisibles' and 'whether a finite be composed of indivisibles' ('An resolvatur finitum in indivisibilia' , 'An componatur finitum ex indivisibilibus'). On the same page he proposes in similar, impartial terms questions of the passage from finite to infinite which had long been the subject of traditional scholastic debate and which Bruno tends to ignore: 'Whether the infinite be generated of finites', 'whether the infinite be composed of finites' ('An ex finitis generetur infinitum', 'An ex finitis componatur infinitum'). Or again 'whether from finite to infinite transit be made through a finite maximum' ('An ab finito ad infinitum fiat transitus per maximum finitum'). Harriot has given no indication of how to resolve such problems, but he has pasted in, in English, at the bottom of his page, these three enigmatic lines: 'Much ado about nothing. Great warres and no blowes. Who is the foole now?'. Harriot's sardonic vein of humour, and the subtlety of his logical reasoning still have to receive their full due.

'THE CONCEITS OF OUR MINDS'

Though Harriot may have had reservations about Bruno's mathematical thinking or his logical premises, it remains clear that the philosophical background to the scientific enquiries of the Northumberland circle was closely dependent on their study of Bruno's works, and particularly of the *De triplici minimo* and the *De immenso*. The first book of the great Frankfurt Trilogy offered them the basis on which to develop their atomic conception of matter and their speculations into minimum and maximum quantities. The *De immenso* offered them the concept of an infinite, homogeneous universe in which to carry out and interpret their physical and astronomical enquiries. Many more particular links could be suggested between the group's philosophical papers and these two works. It would be interesting, for example, to relate Warner's concept of *vis*, which he associates with power and the composition and decomposition of atoms, to Bruno's pages on the power of the atom as a centre of life;[50] or Hill's concept of the soul and its relation to matter to Bruno's ideas on the soul, which had caused so much concern to his inquisitors.[51] But it is perhaps more interesting to conclude with a brief mention of another work of Bruno's found in the Northumberland library, which leads into somewhat different fields of speculation: the *De imaginum, signorum et idearum compositione.*[52]

This is the last of Bruno's works published with his consent and participation. It appeared in Frankfurt at the end of 1591 just after the publication of the trilogy, and was considered by Bruno as closely associated with it. It is the last of his voluminous works on memory and shares with the others an assumption which has already been underlined as central in his thought: the inextricable connection between the ordering of mental process and the order which regulates the natural universe. Thus, for Bruno, the man who achieves the heroic task of uniting in a coherent system the images which pass through his memory can be said to have reconstructed within himself the principle of cosmic order. The complex intricacies of Renaissance works on memory and their vast historical background have been studied in Italy by Paolo Rossi in his book *Clavis universalis*[53] and in England by Frances Yates in her *Art of Memory*.[54] It is Frances Yates's book which examines Bruno's memory works most closely, and among her conclusions on them generally and the *De imaginum* in particular, the following comment is of particular interest:

> If Memory was the Mother of the Muses she was also to be the Mother of Method. Ramism, Lullism, the art of memory – all those confused constructions compounded of all the memory methods which crowd the later sixteenth and early seventeenth century – are symptoms of a search for method.[55]

The Renaissance works on memory were, through their insistence on the question of method, closely connected with speculations on the ordering, expression, and communication of the new scientific knowledge. Bruno fully understood the problem when he characterized the basic method of the new enquiries as a method of doubt. All received knowledge, he insists in the first book of the *De triplici minimo*, is to be debated, weighed in the balance, and accepted only if it corresponds to the light of reason. And immediately after this he meditates on words, themselves often causes of ignorance and iniquity, the tainted vessels in which we receive our knowledge from others. The answer, Bruno claims, must be found in simplicity of expression: a simple sign may be enough to express a divine truth.[56] Bruno himself can hardly be said to have followed his own advice. Rather he seems to find words too few and limited to express his complex and intense intuitions, which so often escape from their logical articulation into poetic imagery and mystical vision. But in the complex systems of 'imagines' established in his memory works, in his frequent use of emblems, his interest in hieroglyphs and seals, his evident delight (not always illuminating) in figures and diagrams, there is, as the studies of the Renaissance memory tradition have often pointed out, much more than a visual Renaissance imagination. It is the aspect of Bruno's thought which is most closely and frequently related to the Neoplatonic tradition, and particularly to the influence of Ficino.[57] The signs ('simulacro, imagine, figura') are the vehicles which link the human mind to the pattern of connecting principles which animate nature, the only means the mind possesses of penetrating those principles. The correct ordering of the 'imagines' is thus an issue of vital importance, for through such a process the guiding principles of the universe are known by the intellect. Hence the urgency of Bruno's desire to communicate essential knowledge through simple signs.[58]

The Northumberland circle was deeply concerned with the problem of expression. Warner's philosophical papers, often repetitive and diffuse, are most interesting where he can be seen groping towards new concepts and finding difficulty in expressing them. For example, many pages demonstrate an intense preoccupation with the nature of time. What is time? In what sense, if any, can it be said to 'exist'? Is it not a condition of existence rather than something which itself exists? Precisely where we see him searching for a new concept of time, Warner breaks out into an attack on the conventional language of philosophy: 'many terms are inapplicable incomparable irrationall incorrespondent', he writes, 'and between which there is no reference which being applied or compared never so much will bring forth no conclusion of use or verity for the progress and augmentation of science'.[59] The Earl of Northumberland himself, in his *Advice to his Son*, underlines his search for 'the plainest characters I could devise, since I know that things plainest written are the best way for doctrine'.[60] In his interesting pages of cultural advice to his son, Northumberland explains to him the importance of what he calls 'universal grammar', meaning by this 'not those rules vulgarly taught for the attaining of any received language ... but such a doctrine general, as discovereth amongst the whole variety of means sensible the best ways to signify the conceits of our minds'.[61] Interestingly, the passage on universal grammar immediately precedes a passage on metaphysics in which Northumberland points out to his son that 'the division of *Ens* in his full scope and amplitude is ... as yet very slenderly delivered and uncertain'.[62] The enquiry into the nature of being is thus closely linked to the question of a universal grammar, or adequate means of expression of the 'division of *Ens*'.

Northumberland's speculations on memory, method, the logical ordering of the 'conceits' of our minds, may be connected on the one hand to Harriot's achievements in reducing his mathematical enquiries to symbolical signs, and on the other hand to Bruno's meditations on memory and expression. Harriot's numerous manuscript pages, entirely composed of formulae and calculations, are recognized by historians of mathematics as far in advance of his time,[63] while Bruno, in the *De imaginum*, writes: 'Conferunt imagines, sigilla et characteres ad agendum, percipiendum et significandum tum physice, tum mathematice, tum logice'[64] (Images, seals, and characters contribute to action, perception, and meaning in a physical sense as well as a mathematical and a logical sense). It is true, as has often been pointed out, that Bruno's mathematics is linked to his magical or Pythagorean concept of number as the basic structure of sensible things, while, as we have already seen, he scorned the modern mathematicians for their ever more subtle calculations of abstract quantities. But it would be unwise to push such a distinction too far, confining Bruno to a Neoplatonic and Hermetic position with Harriot on the other side of the divide moving towards a 'modern' mathematical and scientific vision. For Bruno's enquiry was directed towards a search 'inwards' to penetrate the logical structure of the universe as the ultimate object of knowledge rather than towards a Neoplatonic or Hermetic gnosis or religious ascent. Although in many pages of his papers *De infinitis* Harriot develops purely mathematical speculations into infinite quantities outside the range of Bruno's thought, he was deeply concerned to associate himself at the same time with a cosmic vision which closely echoes Bruno's. Perhaps the point of contact is to be found in their mutual search for a new logic 'at the meeting point between reasoning about living things and calculatory reasoning, in the light of a new unified cosmology'.[65] For both Bruno and Harriot, although with different emphases, the instruments of the new logic were symbols and signs.

THAT WHICH WILL PRESS MEN TO DEATH

In these diverse ways Bruno deeply coloured what Warner calls the Northumberland circle's 'high and abstract speculation of natural verity'.[66] It remains to be asked what effects their adherence to Bruno's cosmic vision had on their lives and position in the society of their time. For it must be remembered that if Bruno offered them an advanced and stimulating philosophical context in which to interpret their scientific investigations, he also projected them well beyond what the religious and cultural orthodoxy of their time was prepared to accept.

Bruno himself was convinced that his new cosmic vision was the means of reconciling the intellectual and religious strife which had bedevilled history, and which made the present the abode of error and conflict. Hierarchical knowledge – the official priest or sage – would collapse together with the vision of a hierarchical universe. Every man would be free to dedicate himself to a study of nature which would raise him towards God, for God acts on the reason through nature. 'Unhappy the man who seeks protection beneath the plume of his helmet',[67] Bruno writes in one of his last works. In the now infinite universe, without centre or degree, it is the depth and range of his intellectual enquiry, and no longer the prestige of his birth or position, which establish a man's true value. But such optimism found little counterpart in the reactions of his readers, and led him, on the contrary, to an eight-year-long trial and a horrible death: the price paid by Bruno for his temerity in sweeping away the Aristotelian-Ptolemaic cosmos, which constituted one of the most deep-rooted common assumptions of Catholic and Reformed Christianity.[68] In fact, Bruno's clear stand for the principle of free thought and enquiry remains throughout his work closely linked to his breakaway from the traditional cosmology. This central strand of his thought, which already runs powerfully through the Italian dialogues (is, in fact, largely expressed in his use of the dialogue form as a means of representing dramatic clashes of opinion between authority and the new philosophy), finds its culmination in a striking page, near the end of the *De immenso*, in which we can clearly hear the echoes of one of Bruno's chief literary and philosophical models, the *De rerum natura* of Lucretius. In a series of powerful images which denounce the 'fantastic' Aristotelian construction of a closed system of revolving spheres, Bruno denounces in the same breath a dogmatic culture which honours only those who bow to the accepted creeds, separating nation from nation, son from parents, on the basis of differing dogmatic orthodoxies.

The true believer appears as the voice of pure folly in an Erasmian reversal of values which expresses the paradoxes of a distorted civilization, related directly by Bruno to a distorted cosmology. And so he raises his voice to exhort his readers to fear no more, to break out of the shadowy prison – the closed universe – of accepted ideas and orthodox thought in a spirit of free and fearless enquiry into the true nature of things:

> Nam quid concludunt sycophantum dogmata passim?
> Non male pro factis Iustus, Divum oppetit iram,
> Non bene pro factis capitur deus optimus unus,
> Sed si animo tantum dominetur opinio qua se
> Subtrahat a populo populus, natusque parentes
> Deserat atque aliter credentem nemo salutet,
> Defendatque deos sint quamvis cunctipotentes
> Quivis mortalis, sine vi, phanaticus, excors.
>   Ergo age solve metus, solve, inquam, e carcere caeco
> Egrediare, animum super effer imagine tecti
> Arcentis totum, torquentis, conque prementis,
> Desine terreri, compactasque ordine nullo
> Aeque distantis convexi concavitate
> Credere desistas magnas, parvas, minimasque
> Stellas, cum sensus visum vult fallere pictor.
> Nempe aliter quia sunt immensi corpora mundi
> Distincta in spacio.[69]

(And so, what conclusions do the dogmas of flatterers lead to? Not for evil actions is the just man punished by the anger of the gods. Good actions do not serve to raise him in the favour of god the most high. Rather, to obtain such favour, his soul must be filled with a false belief which plucks one people from another, the son from his parents, and permits no one to hail a believer in another faith: such a believer as, in his mortality and weakness, praises the gods in a paroxysm of folly.

So now, forget your fears, I say, and resolve to escape from your shadowy prison. Raise your soul beyond the image of the limiting roof which closes and constrains all within it. Escape from your terrors. Cease to believe that the stars, great or small, are in any way fixed to the concave surface of that equidistant convex sphere as if a painter had tried to deceive the sense of sight. For it is in a quite different order that the bodies of the immense universe are spread out in space.)

It would be historically unjustifiable to equate the situation in Italy with that in England at the beginning of the seventeenth century, in the years following Bruno's execution. Nevertheless, the advent of the Stuart dynasty undoubtedly represented a decided turn in the direction of authoritarianism in every field. The expulsion from Court of a figure like John Dee,[70] or the anxiety of Nathaniel Torporley to dissociate himself from the philosophical views which had given his close friend Harriot his reputation for impiety[71] are sufficient indications of a situation in which liberty of philosophical and scientific enquiry was being systematically suffocated. Indeed James I's judges' obstinate determination in imprisoning the Earl of Northumberland, and for a time even Harriot himself, for presumed complicity in the Gunpowder Plot, on what is now generally considered insufficient evidence, was almost certainly helped by suspicions, already surrounding them, of dangerous and unorthodox opinions and enquiries.[72] It is surely necessary to bear in mind their relationship to Bruno's philosophy when we discuss not only the Northumberland circle's reputation for wizardry and impiety, but their retreat underground, their decision to confide only to private papers and close associates scientific enquiries which were often breaking original ground.

The unorthodoxy of the Northumberland circle's cosmology and their tendency to assume a cautious silence on crucial points of philosophical and scientific speculation are well illustrated by Harriot's brief correspondence with Kepler on the nature of light. This important episode in Harriot's scientific career has already been fully discussed by various commentators, but is worth referring to here for it shows how closely the unorthodox views of the circle were linked to their advanced cosmological speculation, which was to a large extent dependent on their knowledge of the works of Bruno. In this case it is the atomic theory of matter which Harriot proposes to Kepler to resolve his perplexities about the behaviour of light, and particularly the phenomenon of refraction. The first part of Harriot's letter is of a purely scientific nature, supplying angles of refraction in air and certain transparent bodies for a given angle of incidence. But when he comes to explain the atomic theory of matter on which his concept of the behaviour of light is based, Harriot's words reflect the intense attitude of 'ammiratio' which is so characteristic of Bruno's ecstatic vision of the new cosmic order:

I have led you to the doors of nature's mansion, where her secrets are hidden. If you cannot enter on account of their
narrowness, abstract yourself mathematically, and contract
yourself into an atom, and you will enter easily. And after you
have come out, you will tell me what wonders you have seen.

Kepler, whose objections to Bruno's cosmology are well known,
was not a sympathetic recipient of theories which threatened his
more orthodox views of the universe and its creation; and in his
reply he refuses to follow Harriot's 'allegories in the manner of
the alchemists'. In the final letter of the exchange, which seems
to have tailed off due to the incompatibility of their theological
and philosophical positions, Harriot refuses significantly to
develop his ideas more fully. He cannot philosophize freely, he
writes to Kepler, for here 'we still stick in the mud'.[73]

The Northumberland circle's awareness of the dangers inherent in the issues at stake and of Bruno's own story appears
clearly in a remarkable page of Harriot's papers *De infinitis*.[74] It
is a crowded page in which we find some of his most complex
considerations of mathematical infinites and infinitesimals (see
Plate 6). The starting-point of his considerations is clearly
indicated by a title word: 'Unitas'. This leads to the concepts
developed from the unit: number, the finite, the infinite.
Further down the page the basic philosophical concept behind
the mathematical reasoning is developed more fully: 'All the
mistery of infinites lieth in *formali ratione unitatis* which is only
respective, and from whence the knowledge and judgement of
formalis ratio of quantity doeth spring'. Here we have Bruno's
monad, the basis of multiplicity which leads us by increasing
progression to the universal infinite, the whole mystery of the
immense. But Bruno's 'one' and his 'infinite' were no mere
mathematical or physical concepts. They had destroyed a world
picture, brought down a centuries-old cosmos. Harriot knew
just how far such speculations had taken him. On the same page
he writes 'Minimum', and beside it: 'that will kill men by percing
and running through'. Underneath he writes 'Maximum – that
which will presse men to death'.

Plate 6 A page of Thomas Harriot's manuscripts *De infinitis* with notes on minimum and maximum, finite and infinite quantities. Add. MSS.6782, fol.374[r]. Reproduced by courtesy of the British Library.

4

BRUNO AND MARLOWE:
DR FAUSTUS

The Faust legend lives predominantly in the European mind through Goethe's great re-creation of it. Written at a time when European culture was reacting dramatically against a rationalistic, scientific era, the Goethian Faust's eager dialogues with ideal, transcendental forces were one of the great literary expressions of a period which was reconquering areas of experience suffocated or ignored by illuministic empiricism.[1] But the Faust legend in its original form had emerged over two centuries before, at the beginning, not the end, of the first modern scientific era. Almost at once it found its first dramatic expression in a tragedy which is an intimate part of specifically sixteenth-century, late-Renaissance enquiries and crises. Christopher Marlowe's Dr Faustus, in a time of violent religious and civil conflict, turns deliberately to magic in its traditional, forbidden medieval form, but through that magic he searches for a new kind of knowledge of the universe, making his bid, in the face of the devil and the armies of hell, for the advancement of human learning about natural things.

The exact date of composition of *Dr Faustus* is unknown, but most modern commentators are agreed that it was Marlowe's final work, probably written only shortly before his premature death in a tavern brawl in May 1593.[2] It is thus an expression of the final years of the century, which were not only rich in new scientific investigations, but characterized on many sides by a breakaway from conventional humanistic enquiry within a fundamentally Christian framework, a period which sees the emergence of numerous figures who challenge the conflicting cultural and religious orthodoxies of the times in their claim to create a new cosmology and a new physics: a new image of the universe.

In a European dimension, the figure who assumes this role with most power and daring is Giordano Bruno, whose image of the heroic searcher for new knowledge of the structure of the universe directly inspired Marlowe's dramatic and poetic articulation of the Faust myth. This does not mean that Bruno was, in any simple way, the model for Marlowe's Faust figure. Other candidates who have already been put forward such as the Elizabethan mathematician-magician John Dee, who had begun his conjuring of spirits in the 1580s, have just as good a claim to that role.[3] What Bruno offered Marlowe was far more important: the philosophical framework in which to create a new image of man, unsuccoured by theological dogma, committed to enlarging the sphere of human knowledge and to acquiring an ever-increasing dominion over nature. Like so many Renaissance problems, the Bruno–Marlowe link is a delicate relationship to investigate, for it disregards our modern boundaries between scientific, philosophical, and artistic experiences. But then Bruno's whole career was articulated in just such complex terms. Not only did he begin his writing experience as a dramatist, but in the *Heroici furori* (written and published in London in 1585, when Marlowe was an already unorthodox student at Cambridge) and in the Frankfurt Latin Trilogy (published in the autumn of 1591, possibly within months of the conception of *Dr Faustus*) he had broken down the barriers between philosophical and poetical discourse by presenting the sixteenth-century dilemma of the opening up of new vistas of knowledge, unauthorized by the theologians, as at once a philosophical and a dramatically human and poetical motive.

The imperfections in the text of Marlowe's last and most challenging work are worth underlining, for they suggest that Marlowe's argument, and above all his way of developing it, met at once with objections, giving rise at times, it would seem (I shall be referring to one such place in this chapter), to deliberate cuts and manipulations.[4] This is not surprising in view of the biographical facts which accompany his final months, and about which we now possess considerable documentary evidence: the warrant for his arrest, on the charge of unsafe opinions, issued by the Privy Council on 18 May 1593; the investigation by the informer Baines, issuing in his startling list of outrageous heresies; the written testimony of 'atheism' by Marlowe's former friend, the dramatist Thomas Kyd, extorted while under torture for suspicions of heresy; and then the final act, the death by stabbing in the tavern at Deptford (see Plate 7). The official documents surrounding Marlowe's death, which have come to light this century, all agree in presenting his stabbing as a result of a sordid brawl over the paying of a bill. But the free pardon, on the basis of self-defence, granted so rapidly to the killer, has seemed to more than one of Marlowe's most qualified biographers to suggest that the official reports may have been hiding a deliberate attempt to eliminate him from the scene.[5] For certain, we do not know. But what such evidence tells us with certainty is that Marlowe, in his final months, which probably saw the composition of *Dr Faustus*, had become a dangerous figure whom the authorities were anxious to control. It is a

Plate 7 Engraving of a stabbing in a tavern by A. Van Ostade (1610–85). Reproduced by courtesy of the Instituto Nazionale per la Grafica, Rome, cat. no. F.C. 121323.

situation which corresponds surprisingly to Bruno's own, and it is perhaps not just a coincidence that Marlowe's death in London (1 June 1593) and Bruno's arrest in Venice (26 May 1592) are so near in time. Even in the comparatively open-minded and tolerant atmospheres of a mildly Protestant Elizabethan London and a mildly Catholic independent Venice, it was dangerous in those years to pose the problem of gaining new knowledge of the universe as a primarily human endeavour, beyond or outside a specifically Christian framework of thought.

HISTORICAL FACTS AND DOCUMENTS

Historical evidence of Marlowe's knowledge of Bruno, outside the evidence of his literary texts themselves, is indirect. We know little with certainty of Marlowe's early formation or cultural relationships. There is no mention of Bruno, even less an account of a meeting during Bruno's London years when Marlowe was studying at Cambridge but probably visiting the capital. Nevertheless, there are a number of historical facts and documents which strongly suggest a connection.

The principal factor which connects Marlowe to Bruno in historical terms remains the so-called 'School of Night', or group of thinkers, writers, and scientists centred first of all on Sir Walter Ralegh and later, after his disgrace, on the Ninth Earl of Northumberland. Marlowe's connection with this circle has long been established, and there is no need to examine once again the documentary evidence linking him not only to Ralegh, but more particularly to figures such as Thomas Harriot and Walter Warner considered in the previous chapters.[6] What needs to be underlined once again here is that Harriot and Warner, whom Kyd mentions in his letter as the men closest to Marlowe and with whom 'he conversd withall', are now known to have associated themselves, in their later philosophical papers, with Bruno's advanced, infinite cosmology; and although they may not have fully elaborated their philosophical views until the following century, after Marlowe's death, it is certain that already in Elizabeth's reign they were being attacked for unorthodox views on the creation of the world and the nature of the soul which clearly suggest an early influence of

Bruno. Warner, though less prominent than Harriot both as a scientist and an unorthodox thinker, was a trusted member of Northumberland's household from as early as 1591. As for Harriot, we know that the poets of the group (not only Marlowe, but also his close friend and collaborator George Chapman) selected him at an early date as a figure-head and symbol of a new kind of learning in terms which remind us clearly of Bruno's heroic searcher: an enquirer into the nature of the universe who reached, in their eyes, almost miraculous new powers in the understanding and dominion of natural forces. 'My admired and soule-loved friend Mayster of all essential and true knowledge M. Harriots', Chapman calls him; and in a poem celebrating him he savagely attacks (with what are surely Brunian echoes) 'the formes of fooles or Parasites' who were impeding the new enquiries, praising Harriot as a

> rich mine of Knowledge, ò that my strange muse
> Without his bodies nourishment could use
> Her zealous faculties, onely t'aspire,
> Instructive light from your whole Sphere of fire.

Marlowe himself makes no explicit reference to Harriot in his work, but we know the almost Faustian terms in which he thought of him from the much-quoted report of the informant Baines: 'He affirmeth that Moses was but a Jugler & that one Heriots being Sir W. Raleigh's man can do more than he'.[7]

The Baines report on Marlowe's heresies is, in fact, the historical document which links him most closely to Bruno, for many of the accusations are strikingly similar to those which the Inquisitors, first in Venice and later in Rome, were bringing against him from the summer of 1592.[8] Both men were accused of denying the orthodox account of a creation in time and, in particular, of promoting the pre-Adamite heresy. The Baines note begins with this accusation: 'That the Indians and many Authors of antiquity have assuredly writen of above 16 thousand yeares agone wheras Adam is proved to have lived within 6 thousand years'. Marlowe's use of the recent discoveries of the cultures and beliefs of the New World to deny orthodox accounts of the creation of man links him once more to Harriot, who had made Ralegh's Virginia expedition of 1585–7 famous throughout Europe with his *Briefe and True Report of the New Found Land of Virginia*, first published in London in 1588 and reproduced in Frankfurt in 1590 with Theodore de Bry's etchings based on the splendid drawings made on the spot by John White. Harriot's own deduction of the pre-Adamite theory from his Virginian experience has received much attention, and has already been associated with the provocative page of Bruno's *Spaccio* in which Momus ironically suggests sending Aquarius to the earth to teach men stories of the creation and the flood which the discoveries of the New World cultures, with their memorials of 10,000 years ago or more, had already proved to be erroneous.[9] It has also been pointed out that Bruno's reference to the Virginia expeditions in the *De immenso*, though critical of the greed and self-interest which were nourishing the English colonial adventures only somewhat less than those of Spain, suggests he had had direct contacts with the Ralegh circle during his London years.[10] Certainly Bruno, in the *Spaccio*, goes straight to the heart of the problem from a religious point of view, for he sees at once that the increasing knowledge of primitive religions will facilitate a relative vision of the truth of every established divinity.[11] In view of Bruno's highly polemical treatment of the pre-Adamite argument, it is surprising to find no reference to this heresy in the official documents of his trial. The known documents, however, are incomplete, and we learn from the letter of Gaspare Scioppio of 17 February 1600 that Bruno's adherence to the pre-Adamite heresy was considered in Rome as among the principal reasons for his execution. Scioppio had personally attended both the public condemnation of 8 February and Bruno's death on the 16th, so his testimony is considered by Bruno scholars valid documentary evidence.[12]

Many of the other imputations which are common in the cases of Marlowe and Bruno were normal coin in any trial for heresy of the time. Both men were accused, generically, of holding opinions contrary to the Christian religion, while on a level of vulgar blasphemy both were said to have imputed impure acts to Christ, the Virgin, and the saints. Bruno repudiated these last accusations indignantly, judging them futile and insisting on being tried for the serious substance of his philosophical doctrines. Marlowe did not live to make a reply. More substantial are the precise accusations in both cases of denial of the fundamental miraculous events surrounding the Christian incarnation: the immaculate conception and the Virgin birth. Here we are approaching Bruno's concept of a universe united throughout by rigorous, intelligent laws: a denial, in practice, of the miraculous event. This concept was to have a number of important repercussions in the cosmological field, such as his consideration of comets as natural phenomena rather than the miraculous portents they were still widely believed to be even by prominent scientific investigators.

The whole question of the status of miracles and the consequent definition of magic lies behind the other accusation which strikingly links Marlowe's case to Bruno's: the affirmation that Moses was a juggler. Bruno had already stated his conviction publicly in another polemical page of the *Spaccio*,[13] which Marlowe may well have derived it from. It is the second accusation brought against Marlowe in the Baines note and it finds its exact counterpart in Bruno's trial. Probably in the same months of 1593 which saw Baines writing to the Privy Council about Marlowe, a certain Fra Celestino presented to the Inquisitor in Venice a series of written accusations against Bruno which included the affirmation that he had spoken scathingly of Moses 'mago astutissimo'. In Mocenigo's earlier accusations, Bruno was accused of having called Christ himself a juggler whose miracles were only apparent. Kyd in his letter to Walsingham affirms that Marlowe said the same things of St Paul. Behind all these accusations emerges a new concept of knowledge, which becomes the right and possession of anyone capable of pursuing and achieving it. Bruno was prepared to follow this concept to an openly heretical conclusion, reducing the prophets, saints, and Christ himself to the same level as other exceptionally learned men. In the *Sigillus sigillorum* he had already given a list of those who were for him the true 'prophets' of history: Pythagoras, Moses, Jesus, Raymund Lull, Paracelsus.[14] He puts all of these figures on the same level, according them special status only in so far as they are truly exceptional men who have achieved (not been 'given') special knowledge and powers. According to the logic of this point of view, as Bruno tried to explain to his Inquisitors, it is no offence to Moses to consider him a magus, for magic is 'a knowledge of the secrets of nature with the faculty of imitating nature in her works and doing things considered marvellous by the vulgar crowd'.[15]

THE ICARUS IMAGE

When Marlowe turned for inspiration to the anonymous English translation of the German *Faust-book*, published in 1592 with the title *The Historie of the Damnable life, and deserved death of Dr. Iohn Faustus*, he found in his source a pregnant poetic image applied to the figure of Faustus himself: 'and taking to him the wings of an Eagle, he thought to flie over the whole world, and to know the secrets of heaven and earth'.[16]

The *Faust-book* creates, almost unawares, a strongly ambivalent and at times ambiguous image of the Faust figure, although these ambiguities and tensions are constantly held in check by the homiletic approach it basically develops. In the first chapter Faust is described simply as 'being of a naughty mind', and the writer hardly seems to realize how strongly he creates a contradictory pole of meaning by his use, in the second chapter, of the eagle image to evoke the daring of Faust's intellectual enquiries. For the eagle image had assumed a significant role in Renaissance thought, becoming ever more strongly associated with a new concept of man as a bold and brilliant searcher into the truths of nature and the universe.

A glance through the emblem books which were so popular a phenomenon of the period, shows the eagle, as a visual image, present above all in its classical role as a part of the Prometheus myth: the torturer sent by Jove to consume the liver of the hero who had been so presumptuous as to contest his divine power in the name of man. But gradually the Renaissance writers had assumed the eagle itself into the role of the Promethean hero, developing it as an image of the human mind in its fearless contemplation of the truths of nature. In these terms, at the end of the fifteenth century, Pico della Mirandola had adopted the eagle image in a text which resounded through Renaissance Europe: the *Oratio de hominis dignitate*. In a powerful passage of his *Oratio*, Pico urges his reader to accept no limits to his search for knowledge, but to accustom his eyes to endure in the contemplation of nature the still feeble light of truth as it were the first rays of the rising sun, so that at last . . . we may like heavenly eagles boldly endure the most brilliant splendour of the meridian sun.[17]

Nearly a century later, in almost identical terms, Bruno himself uses the eagle image in the closing lines of his dedication to Rudolf II of the *Articuli centum et sexaginta*, his major defence of philosophical liberty, where he writes:

So we raise our heads towards the splendour of the dazzling light, and we listen to nature who speaks to us in a loud voice, and we pursue knowledge with simplicity and purity of heart preferring her before all else: and she not only refrains from abandoning us, or waits while we draw nearer, but she comes swiftly towards us, cleans our eyes, and as if we were the off-spring of eagles she trains us to gaze on the sun, enabling us to contemplate ever more firmly.[18]

It is with such a use of the eagle image in the background that the *Faust-book* applies it to the figure of Faust himself straining 'to know the secrets of heaven and earth'. But Marlowe changes the image, without losing the soaring, birdlike dimension of meaning, by replacing it with the myth of Icarus. It is in terms of the Icarus image that, in the introductory speech of the Chorus, the figure of Marlowe's Dr Faustus is presented to the audience. After brief news of his humble birth and arrival at Wittemberg, the Chorus comments on his intellectual history by identifying him with Icarus:

> So much he profits in Divinitie,
> The fruitful plot of Scholerisme grac'd,
> That shortly he was grac'd with Doctors name,
> Excelling all, whose sweete delight's dispute
> In th' heavenly matters of Theologie;
> Till swolne with cunning of a selfe conceit,
> His waxen wings did mount above his reach,
> And melting, heavens conspir'd his over-throw:
> For falling to a divellish exercise,
> And glutted now with learnings golden gifts,
> He surfets upon cursed Necromancie.[19]

Marlowe gives the Icarus image here powerful poetical expression. The striking physical immediacy of a Faustus 'swolne with cunning' evokes his intellectual presumption as a palpable reality; while the insistence on words like 'glutted' and 'surfets', which find their source in the myth of the fall of man (Genesis 3) and are normally associated with carnal excesses, at once places the concept of learning in the context of a shameful, deadly sin. The image is being used by the Chorus in entirely conventional terms. It echoes classical sources, such as Book VIII of Ovid's *Metamorphoses*, in presenting Faustus-Icarus as an example of impudent presumption in disobedience to Dedalus's wise advice to fly neither too high nor too low. The Christian tradition had adopted the Icarus image with ease, for it was a simple step to see the presumption the figure represents as a sin against the rule and commands of divine wisdom. These are the terms of the Chorus's use of the Icarus image, and what we are left with at the end of this introductory speech is an already 'fallen' and damned hero, who has strayed out of the 'fruitful plot of Scholerisme' preferring a 'divellish exercise' of the mind to 'his chiefest bliss', or traditional studies of divinity.

The fact that Marlowe's Chorus introduces Faustus in these terms does not mean that the drama develops as an exemplary Christian tragedy of presumption and punishment. For Marlowe at once creates on the stage a dramatic dialectic, shifting the audience's gaze abruptly from the point of view of the Chorus to Faustus himself 'discovered in his study'. And Faustus at once expresses himself in a monologue which is a provocative denial of all the traditionally pious sentiments of the Chorus. At the end of this speech, Faustus recalls the Icarus image, but in his mouth it assumes a new and positive value; for he exults in his determination not only to fly into the skies but to 'raise the wind' and 'rend the clouds': that is, to know and dominate the most distant and mysterious forces of nature herself.

Critical debate of *Dr Faustus* has always centred on the interpretative problem raised by Marlowe's dialectical treatment of the Faustus theme. Is Marlowe to be identified with the Faustus figure itself, as many commentators have argued, linking the dramatic facts of Marlowe's personal history to the tragedy of his hero? Or can the critic, as most recent comment has been doing, stretch to its limits the claim that literary criticism should be a reading of a text without reference to historical and biographical facts, making of the play a rigorously Christian comment on an impious and imprudent hero? Between these two poles, some of the best criticism has stressed the historical impasse from which Marlowe's tragedy arose, seeing it as essentially a dramatic expression of a moment of tragic conflict between new concepts of man and the requirements of a traditional and deeply embedded religious faith.[20] Yet it remains important to define the precise moment of the historical impasse which Marlowe dramatizes: a moment which, in the final years of the sixteenth century, was assuming the tragic character of a direct clash between exasperatedly dogmatic religious approaches to the problem of gaining new knowledge, and an approach which was attempting to wrench the problem of knowledge from its religious centre, developing it in primarily human and at times provocatively heretical terms. It is here that Marlowe links up once more with Bruno who, in two of his Italian dialogues, the *Heroici furori* and the *Cabala del cavallo pegaseo* ('Cabala of the Pegasean horse'), had re-elaborated the central western myths concerning the problem of knowledge, the eating of the fruit in the garden of Eden, the Prometheus myth, and the Icarus myth itself. It may have been with Bruno's interpretation of the Icarus myth in mind that Marlowe modified the already powerful image of the eagle suggested to him by the *Faust-book*.

In its classical form the Icarus myth could have a general meaning applicable to any form of over-eager and imprudent presumption. It was the humanists who associated the myth primarily with the question of knowledge, and once again it is Pico who provides a passage which will sanction this interpretation for the following century or more. In his *Disputationes adversus astrologiam divinatricem,* he associates himself with those who were proposing allegorical interpretations of Homer, indicating in the myth of Icarus the evil fate of the astrologers who 'raising themselves to the sky on the wings of their daring art, collapse into the pool of lies when they have to predict the future on the basis of their celestial principles'.[21] It was probably under the influence of Pico that Icarus appeared linked specifically to the unfortunate errors of the astrologers in one of the

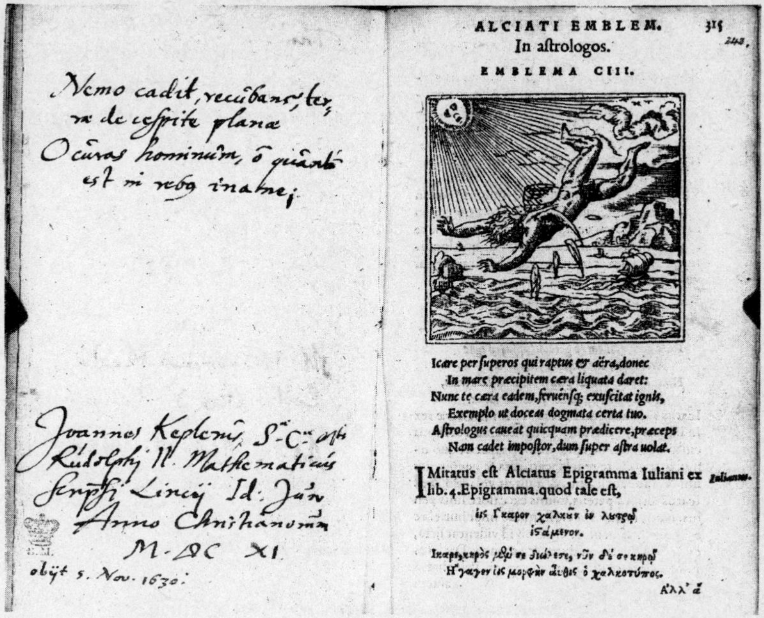
ALCIATI EMBLEM. 315

In aſtrologos.

EMBLEMA CIII.

Icare per ſuperos qui raptus & aëra, donec
In mare præcipitem cera liquata daret:
Nunc te cera eadem, feruénsq; exuſcitat ignis,
Exemplo ut doceas dogmata certa tuo.
Aſtrologus caueat quicquam prædicere, præceps
Nam cadet impoſtor, dum ſuper aſtra uolat.

IMitatus eſt Alciatus Epigramma Iuliani ex lib. 4. Epigramma. quod tale eſt,

Plate 8 Emblem of Icarus in Andrea Alciati's *Emblemata* printed at Lyons in 1573 with a commentary by Francisco Sanchez of Salamanca and an autograph comment by Johannes Kepler. Egerton 1234, fols.242^{v}–243. Reproduced by courtesy of the British Library.

most popular emblem books of the century, Andrea Alciati's *Emblemata*, which combines a delightful visual image of the falling Icarus (see Plate 8) with a brief poem ending: 'Astrologus caveat quicquam praedicere, praeceps/Nam cadet imposter, dum super astra volat' (The astrologer should beware of foretelling events, for the impostor falls headlong when he flies beyond the stars).[22]

Bruno found the myth already part of his subject when, in the *Heroici furori*, he began tracing the intellectual history of the new heroic enquirer into the nature of the true structure of the universe. But rather than to the still cautious and traditional interpretation of Pico, Bruno turned to Tansillo, the Neapolitan poet he admired so deeply that he incorporated many of his sonnets into the *Furori*, introducing the poet in person as the main speaker in the dialogue for all the first part of his text.

Tansillo's sonnet commented on by Bruno gives an entirely new dimension to the myth, presenting Icarus not in the tragedy of his fall but as the positive hero ready to risk failure and death for a glimpse of new and higher truths than man has so far attained:

> Poi che spiegat'ho l'ali al bel desio,
> Quanto piú sott'il piè l'aria mi scorgo,
> Piú le veloci penne al vento porgo,
> E spreggio il mondo, e vers'il ciel m'invio.
>
> Né del figliuol di Dedalo il fin rio
> Fa che giú pieghi, anzi via piú risorgo.
> Ch' i' cadrò morto a terra, ben m'accorgo;
> Ma qual vita pareggia al morir mio?
>
> La voce del mio cor per l'aria sento:
> – Ove mi porti, temerario? China,
> Che raro è senza duol tropp'ardimento. –
>
> Non temer, respond'io, l'alta ruina.
> Fendi sicur le nubi, e muor contento,
> S'il ciel sí illustre morte ne destina.[23]

(Now I have spread my wings towards a fine desire, I spurn the air beneath my feet and open my swift feathers to the wind. Skywards I fly, leaving the world behind me in disdain.

Nor does the sad fate of Dedalus's son induce me to turn back, but spurs me higher. Well I know that I shall plunge towards the earth and die: but what life is worth my death?

I hear my heart's voice crying through the air: 'Where are you carrying me so boldly? Turn back, for too much courage is rarely without pain'.

Fear not such high disaster, I reply. Rend the clouds securely, and die content, if heaven such a glorious death decrees.)

Tansillo glories in 'rending the clouds' (the exact expression used by Faustus at the end of his first monologue), uncaring of the fall which may await him. In Bruno's comment on the poem this concept is rendered even clearer:

it is enough that all should run the race; that all should stretch their powers to the uttermost; because the heroic spirit is satisfied rather with falling or losing with honour an arduous undertaking where the dignity of his spirit is revealed, than in succeeding perfectly in lower and less noble tasks.

In the context of the dialogue in which they occur, these meditations on the Icarus myth could seem no more than an apology for intellectual daring and vigour, against the plea for caution and constraint which the myth had traditionally expressed. In the context of the whole development of the *Furori*, however, they assume a more explicitly subversive character with respect to a culture which, on both sides of the religious divide, was urging an intellectual enquiry contained within a Christian faith and framework. For Bruno's idea of the 'sommo bene' on earth, or the new truth about the universe and its relation with the One Divine Principle and Cause, which his philosophy is proposing to uncover, is articulated throughout the text quite independently of Christian concepts of creation or salvation.[24] He is thus free to develop in his own terms the traditional western myths about knowledge which the Christian tradition had taken over from classical or Hebraic sources. To find him doing this in ways which appear especially relevant to the Faustus story, we must turn to the *Cabala*.

This is the most brilliantly satirical and provocatively heretical of Bruno's Italian dialogues. In it we find him extending the concepts which surround his treatment of the Icarus myth in the *Furori* to the other myths concerned with the problem of knowledge, above all the story of the garden of Eden, which, like the Icarus myth in Tansillo's sonnet, appears rewritten as a positive heroic adventure rather than a tragic failure. Bruno is working here in the particular satirical tradition of 'asinine' literature, and he introduces this page by branding as 'asses' those who are prepared to limit their intellectual enquiry, 'listening only and believing'. Extending the ass metaphor, Bruno likens these to beasts who have closed up their hands, catching all five fingers under a single nail,

so that they remain unable to stretch out their hands like Adam to pluck the forbidden fruit from the tree of knowledge, and in consequence they remain without the fruits of the tree of life, or to hold out their hands like Prometheus (which is a metaphor of the same kind) to take the fire of Jove to light the lamp of rational ability.[25]

Bruno's daring treatment of the figures of Icarus, Adam, and Prometheus seems clearly related to Marlowe's introduction of Faustus to his audience in terms first of a traditional 'fallen Icarus' and then in Faustus's opening monologue as a positive heroic searcher for new forms of truth and knowledge. Seen in the light of Bruno's concepts, the ambiguities, contradictions, at times the evident fragility of Faustus's search for new kinds of truth and power, which have so worried many of Marlowe's recent critics, become justifiable, even heroic, failings: 'it is enough for all to run the race'. And the race in question is concerned with new forms of knowledge: the slow and arduous emergence of new sciences and enquiries. The implications of the Icarus myth in the context of this development were complex and far-reaching, and appear to have profoundly involved the figures concerned; thus by the beginning of the seventeenth century we find some of the major new scientists referring directly to the myth in terms of their own intellectual experiences. Bacon, whose relationship to Bruno has to be further investigated, may well have had in mind his provocative treatment both of Icarus and the story of the garden of Eden when, in his mythological studies, he compared the sins of excess to those of defect claiming:

> Icarus chose the better of the two; for all defects are justly esteemed more depraved than excesses. There is some mag-nanimity in excess, that, like a bird, claims kindred with the heavens: but defect is a reptile, that basely crawls upon the earth.[26]

For Bruno, it had become a sin not to stretch out the hand for the forbidden fruit of the tree of knowledge. For Bacon, the serpent has become the base enquirer who refuses to take the risks of 'excess' intellectual daring. Yet the warnings of Marlowe's Chorus reached deep down into the moral and religious consciousness of the period. There were those among the new scientists who preferred to refuse the Faustian excesses. Johannes Kepler, for example, who wrote in a copy of Alciati's *Emblemata* beside the illustration of Icarus: 'No one falls down if he is already lying on the ground' (see Plate 8, p. 85).[27] Marlowe's dialectical opening of his tragedy of *Dr Faustus* in terms of differing elaborations of the Icarus myth expressed the intellectual dilemma of a new scientific epoch.

'*DIVINITIE*, ADEIW'

Faustus's opening monologue, as he sits alone in his room in Wittemberg trying to 'settle' his studies, is a brilliantly synthetic, radical review of the orthodox culture of the late sixteenth century: a Christian culture whose intellectual structure was still predominantly Aristotelian and which presents itself to Marlowe with its Protestant face. The first crux of the monologue is Marlowe's choice of the order in which to develop his review of this cultural situation. He begins not with the question of faith, nor with a primarily theological argument, but with the question of logic. Faustus thus approaches his problem in philosophical terms, choosing to reject initially the authority of Aristotelian analytics.

Aristotle, the master of 'sweet Analytikes', is presented at first in an impetus of unreserved acceptance, almost a poetic embrace ('tis thou hast ravisht me'). The verse is immediately qualified with a Latin definition of the aims of logic: '*Bene disserere est finis logices*' (To dispute well is the end of logic). This complicates the question under review, for although his name is not explicitly linked to Aristotle's, the verse, as Marlowe critics have long recognized, is the opening sentence of the *First Book of Dialectic* of Peter Ramus. The influence of Ramist logic throughout the Protestant countries of Europe was rapidly growing in this period, and was strong in both the English universities, but particularly Cambridge where Marlowe himself had studied. Faustus's rejection of the traditional logic is thus a double act of deliberate cultural provocation: not only Aristotle is swept aside but with him the modern logician acclaimed by the Protestant cultures as the great reformer of the intricacies of Peripatetic discourse, the inventor of a new and simplified method of reasoning in the search for truth.

Yet the terms in which this rejection is developed suggest an extremely complex, even ambiguous, relationship between Faustus and Ramist logic. For his rejection of Ramus's definition has no psychological build-up or descriptive preparation, but is itself stated as a logical proposition. As such, it is a logical proposition of a peculiarly Ramist flavour, reflecting two special tenets of Ramist thinking: the necessity for brief, clear-cut discourse, and the particular emphasis placed upon the 'figure of difference' or the 'definition of dissimilitude', which was to make Ramist discourse a sharp instrument in controversial argument. In Chapter XI of his *Logike*, Ramus insists on the importance of developing with particular clarity differing arguments of dissent from a stated proposition: 'The agreable argumente being expounded, now followethe the disagreable, which dissentethe from the matter. The arguments disagreable are equallie knowen amonge themselves, and disproueth equallie one another: yet by their dissention, they do more clearlie appeare'. The movement of Marlowe's poetry in Faustus's opening lines suggests that he was using Ramist logical concepts (generally interpreted today as differing in emphasis rather than kind from the basic tenets of Aristotelian analytics) in a radical rejection of traditional logic itself as the highway towards the new knowledge he dreams of:[28]

> live and die in *Aristotles* workes.
> Sweet *Analytikes*, tis thou hast ravisht me,
> *Bene disserere est finis logices.*
> Is to dispute well Logikes chiefest end?
> Affords this Art no greater miracle?
> Then read no more, thou hast attain'd that end;
> A greater subject fitteth *Faustus* wit.[29]

It is in terms of this same logical movement from 'agreable argument' to 'disagreable', or clear-cut dissent, that Faustus's monologue develops in its second section: a rapid invocation and rejection of the disciplines at the basis of the academic life of the period. First of all medicine is reviewed and then law, in the figures of Galen and Justinian: names closely linked to Aristotelian methods and doctrines. Marlowe offers no explicitly named alternative authorities, but his rejection of Galen clearly invokes Paracelsian concepts of magical healing, thus linking Faustus to an already developed, if semi-underground, English school of 'alternative' medicine and alchemical enquiry.[30] It is in this part of the monologue that a closely related Hermetic image of man as magus begins to emerge in terms of a provocatively stated concept of a human intellect capable of achieving, through its enquiry into natural truths, almost divine vision and powers. Marlowe at once states this concept as an act of intellectual liberation, exposing the dreary drudge of routine academic enquiry, the fastidious professor who Faustus himself had been until only a few minutes back, in all his obsequious respect of the cultural status quo: 'This study fits a Mercenarie drudge/Who aimes at nothing but externall trash/Too servile and illiberal for mee.'[31]

It is only when this sense of man as free to achieve for himself, through his own intellectual impetus, an almost divine status has already been hinted at that Faustus reaches, in the central verses of his monologue, the hard kernel of his problem: his studies of divinity. In eleven terse and concise verses he offers to his audience his answer to the problem at the centre of his culture. And he does it, as his culture was doing in academic places throughout Europe, by linking the problems of divinity to the methods of traditional logic. Here, in fact, Faustus reaches back beyond Ramus and picks up the traditional, accepted method of Aristotelian reasoning. For he ironically and provocatively rejects the Christian godhead by developing from biblical sources a regular and, in logical terms, perfectly acceptable syllogism: 'The reward of sin is death? that's hard. . . . If we say that we have no sinne we deceive our selves. . . . Why then belike we must sinne, and so consequently die'. It has often been pointed out by Marlowe's commentators that the syllogism is a traditional one, to which Christianity offered its answer by the Christian act of salvation itself: faith in Christ's mercy breaks up the apparently acceptable logic of the syllogism. In fact Faustus fails to quote his biblical sources in full, giving only the opening part of Romans 6:23 and failing to add the following and opposing proposition, 'but the gift of God is eternal life through Jesus Christ our Lord'.[32] The fact that Faustus does not qualify the syllogism with this central tenet of the Christian doctrine has seemed to some an act of intellectual irresponsibility, or even of almost infantile, wilful forgetfulness.[33] But Marlowe makes it quite clear that it is to be seen as a deliberate intellectual choice, and he leaves his audience in no doubt as to the considerations which lead Faustus to that choice. The

Christian solution to the drastic conclusion to the syllogism is rejected on two grounds: first of all because its concept of death in terms of rewards and punishments leaves open the possibility of everlasting torment; and second because it develops a doctrine which leaves man dependent for his salvation on an act of mercy on the part of God: 'What doctrine call you this? *Che sera sera*:/What will be, shall be; *Divinitie*, adeiw'.[34]

Once again the deliberate and daring provocation offered by Faustus's reasoning (it must be remembered that Marlowe connects him constantly with Wittemberg, the intellectual centre of Protestant Christianity) can only be fully understood in terms of the historical situation which Marlowe was expressing. He was writing at the end of a century in which opposing Christian factions had been making ever more drastic use of visions of hell and eternal punishment to ensure the obedience of their adherents. Writers such as Thomas Beard on the Protestant side or the notorious English Jesuit Robert Parsons were equally unscrupulous in conjuring up visions of the tortures awaiting those who died with the wrong beliefs; and men like the playwright Robert Greene, who cursed Marlowe's influence on him with the last strokes of his pen, were dying filled with horror at the fate which might await them. It is against this vision of death as, for some at least, an 'everlasting punishment', that Faustus reacts already at the opening of his drama; and it is in a much expanded, anguished meditation on the same subject that Marlowe will depict his death. In part, Marlowe's play can be seen as an early text making a plea for a 'decline of hell': certainly Faustus refuses an idea of death which involves the possibility of such a fate.[35] But his refusal appears to be also a protest against some of the special tenets of Protestant Christianity, and particularly against Luther's vision of a humanity saved from eternal punishment entirely by an act of faith in God's mercy, and not at all by its own works.[36]

Marlowe is expressing here, in the dialectic between his Chorus and Faustus, one of the fundamental issues of his times: man's new faith in his own intellectual resources against a deeply rooted Christian concept of the vanity of human endeavour alone. The issue was acutely felt by the newly emerging magus of the sixteenth century, as well as by his more scientific counterpart in the century to come. Cornelius Agrippa, whose

De occulta philosophia (1533) had become established as one of the central texts on magic of the century, and whom Faustus will acknowledge explicitly as his master, hoping to become 'as cunning as Agrippa was,/Whose shadows made all Europe honour him', had also written his widely read attack on the vanity and uncertainty of arts and sciences, *De vanitate scientiarum* (1530). Here the natural magic of the philosophers is depicted, in terms which the Chorus would certainly have approved, as 'oftentimes . . . entangled in the craftes and errours of the deuills of hell'.[37] Agrippa seems to have oscillated rather ambiguously between two opposing positions, but later more scientific enquirers would feel the need to resolve the dilemma. On the Protestant side, efforts to do so would be especially concerned with the question of vindicating an active concept of enquiring man against the dominating theories of predestination. Bacon will elaborate with care, at the beginning of the seventeenth century, his theory of first and second causes, limiting the activity of the modern scientist to the latter but claiming for him, in his proper sphere, unreserved freedom of enquiry. We now know that Harriot, shortly before his death, was studying the works of the Dutchman Arminius, who had abandoned the doctrines of predestination developed by Calvin and Beza, proposing a doctrine which considered 'elect' only those who were capable of responding to the divine call.[38] Once again Marlowe expresses in Faustus's opening monologue a particular moment of exasperation and a particularly dramatic solution to the dilemma. Opposing himself without compromise to the warning and admonitions of the Chorus, Faustus not only omits to qualify his syllogism with the central statement of Christian belief, but cuts short all niceties of theological debate by bidding '*Divinitie*, adeiw'.

At this point in his monologue, Faustus also abandons the rigorous logical structure which has so far informed the pattern of his reasoning, and Marlowe's poetry opens out into freer and more impetuous rhythms invoking an alternative 'metaphysic', which is at the same time a different concept of man and a different way of reaching the heavens. The conventional magical symbols which Faustus invokes – 'Lines, Circles, Signes, Letters and Characters' – appear here in the impetus of Marlowe's poetry as the means of satisfying Faustus's desire to achieve new forms of knowledge unknown so far to man. Although he appeals to the traditional 'Negromantick bookes', Faustus's image of the knowledge he yearns for is represented in terms of new, unlimited spaces for the human mind to move in, and looks forward to new forms of power and dominion over the forces of nature which will make of the 'Studious Artizan' a triumphant demi-god.

The points at which this monologue connects with and echoes the thought as well as the poetry of Bruno are so many that it is difficult to select precise passages for comparison. All the arguments Faustus touches on find their counterpart in similar terms in Bruno's works: the initial love, followed by the violent repudiation of Aristotle; the dismissal of Galenic medicine in favour of Paracelsus; the particularly strong attack on the Protestant refusal of works and on concepts of predestination; the refusal of the central assertion of the Christian incarnation in favour of a metaphysic which sees the whole universe as the sign or seal of the divine intelligence (the unknowable 'Deus optimus unus'); the reference to traditional magic as a means of achieving new knowledge of and powers over the natural world; and finally the inebriating vision of a human mind capable of reaching unbounded vistas of knowledge and truth, becoming assimilated, in its moment of understanding and power, into the divine whole. The very concept of an intellectual-poetical biography of the mind in its action of repudiating accepted cultural methods and doctrines to reach out into vastly expanded spaces of new learning and understanding of the universe recalls the *Heroici furori*, a text which, as we have seen, would later be used by Northumberland as his primary source for his own intellectual biography. But the Bruno text which offers the closest parallels to Faustus's opening soliloquy is the *De la causa*, the second of his Italian dialogues written in London. This work opens with a strong attack against the academic culture of the period, particularly in its pedantic dependence on Aristotelian doctrine. Bruno is still burning with indignation after his Oxford débâcle, coupled with the outcry caused by the publication of the *Cena*; and the first dialogue of the *De la causa* develops in rather more calm and meditated terms than the *Cena* his criticism of an English academic tradition which he sees as exhausting itself in ever more subtle disputes while ignoring the true substance of metaphysical enquiry. The statutes of the university, we are reminded, which the student is obliged to obey on his oath, include the principle: 'Nullus ad Philosophiae et Theologiae magisterium et doctoratum promoveatur, nisi epotaverit e fonte Aristotelis' (That none be promoted to the rank of doctor or allowed to teach Philosophy and Theology if he has not drunk from the fountain of Aristotle).[39]

It is in the third dialogue of the *De la causa* that Bruno also launches his heaviest attack on Peter Ramus: 'francese arcipedante'. Ramus's attack on Aristotelian logic, which one might have expected Bruno to appreciate, is heavily criticized as misdirected, and insufficient to save the French logician himself from the accusation of being still, in the end, a pedantic grammarian. This page of the *De la causa* has recently been much discussed in the light of Bruno's earliest memory work, the *De umbris idearum*, also published in London, which opposes to the Ramist theories of a logically articulated art of memory a system based on the zodiacal images. Much more than a logical technique, Bruno's memory system was an attempt to create a symbolic pattern of 'shadows' or 'signs' through which the mind recreates and learns to penetrate the intimate structure of the universe. Bruno's work was much admired and imitated by the Scot, Alexander Dicson, whose own *De umbra rationis* triggered off a lively polemic with the Cambridge Ramist William Perkins. The whole story of the dispute has been told by Frances Yates in her *Art of Memory*, where it is judged as 'one of the most basic of all Elizabethan controversies';[40] and one which surely Marlowe is recalling in Faustus's repudiation of Ramist logic which leads him, in the final lines of his monologue, to an alternative metaphysic of 'things': 'All things that move betweene the quiet poles'. Even the ambiguity of Faustus's attitude to Ramus finds its counterpart in the Brunian anti-Ramist polemic, for, as Giovanni Aquilecchia has pointed out in his introduction to the *De la causa*, Dicson in his reply to Perkins's attack accuses him of being an abstract Ramist disputer, while at the same time he praises Ramus as a defender of the liberty of philosophical enquiry. Certainly Ramist doctrines were not only well known but also highly influential in the circle that both Bruno and Dicson moved in, for both men were close to Sir Philip Sidney whose protection of the English Ramists is well known.[41] None the less, both Yates and Aquilecchia argue that Dicson's ironically presented Socrates, identified with subtle and arid forms of Greek sophism, is intended to be a representation of Ramus himself, contrasted with the positive figure of Thamus who 'with a swelling religious passion . . . inveighs against the disputatious Socrates, who reduces wise men to the level of boys, who does not study the way of the sky, does not seek God in his vestiges and "umbrae" '.[42] In the context of the anti-Ramist dispute caused in Elizabethan England by Bruno's *De umbris*, Faustus's monologue can be seen as a rejection of his academic-Ramist self to assume the part of Thamus, a 'sound Magitian' intent on penetrating the secrets of the universe:

> Emperors and Kings,
> Are but obey'd in their severall Provinces:
> Nor can they raise the winde, or rend the cloudes:
> But his dominion that exceeds in this,
> Stretcheth as farre as doth the mind of man:
> A sound Magitian is a Demi-god,
> Here tire my braines to get a Deity.[43]

MEPHOSTOPHILIS: WORDS AS DECEIT

No sooner has Faustus decided to dedicate himself to the 'metaphysicks of Magitians' than he is visited by a Good and a Bad Angel:

GOOD ANGEL. O *Faustus*, lay that damned booke aside,
And gaze not on it least it tempt thy soule,
And heape Gods heavy wrath upon thy head.
Reade, reade the Scriptures: that is blasphemy.

BAD ANGEL. Go forward *Faustus* in that famous Art
Wherein all natures treasury is contain'd:
Be thou on earth as *Jove* is in the skye,
Lord and Commander of these elements.

The two angels are traditional figures taken straight out of the medieval drama, and the theme of the two books which they introduce is also traditional and of medieval origin. The damned book is obviously a necromantic book such as the *Picatrix*, one of the most popular of the medieval magical works, originally written in Arabic, probably in the twelfth century, but widely available to the Renaissance reader in Latin translation. Or, as Marlowe introduces the name of Agrippa more than once and underlines his point by calling one of Faustus's magician friends Cornelius, perhaps it is the notorious and spurious fourth book of Agrippa's *De occulta philosophia.*[44] It is certainly a necromantic book of spells in which Faustus finds his instructions for his first attempts at conjuring. But the terms in which the Bad Angel refers to the 'damned booke' indicate that Marlowe is deliberately treating these traditional themes in the light of new emphases and experiences which had been slowly developing in his century. For the Bad Angel sees 'Negromantick Art' as one 'wherein all natures treasury is contain'd'. He is thus placing the book of God or the Scriptures against the symbol of a 'book of nature', creating a contraposition through which, as Cassirer argued in some of his most celebrated pages, the consciousness of a new more scientific enquiry into the truths of nature would gradually develop.[45] The development would be neither simple nor linear, for the whole concept of the 'book of nature' would be subject to conflicting interpretations and pressures. On one side occult and Hermetic currents of thought would develop the idea of the 'book of nature' as a pattern of signs, symbols, and hieroglyphs veiling the impenetrable secrets of a mystically conceived divine unity; on the other, the newly emerging scientific enquirers such as Leonardo or Galileo would dedicate themselves to discovering the rigorously mathematical relationships which define the pattern of nature herself, considering them as the interpretative key to a rational understanding of natural truth.[46] Such conflicting attitudes to the symbol of the 'book of nature' coexisted in a rich and at times ambiguous amalgam for a long period before 'the book' freed itself from spiritualistic and demonic contents to lay itself open to rationalistic enquiry. Marlowe's Faustus expresses the typical ambiguities of his period. He is unhesitant in accepting the Bad Angel's invitation to study the art 'Wherein all natures treasury is contain'd', but the ends he is pursuing through that art are uncertainly defined. At times he expresses his desired end in terms of the penetrating of Orphic or Pythagorean mystical secrets beyond the veil of an obscure, phenomenal natural world. Faustus will thus instruct his spirits to 'read me strange Philosophy', while he approves the promise of Cornelius: 'Then doubt not *Faustus* but to be renown'd,/ And more frequented for this mysterie,/ Than heeretofore the *Delphian* Oracle'. Yet such occult and mystical definitions of his purpose are rare. Rather than a purifying ascent beyond an obscure, phenomenal natural world, Faustus's dominating passion appears the bending and controlling of that world to his will and desire. In Faustus the *libido sciendi* is also a *libido dominandi*; and Marlowe's poetry accepts and accentuates the identification by expressing Faustus's aims as magician in terms of an almost physical appetite for new forms of control and power over the natural world:

> How am I glutted with conceipt of this?
> Shall I make spirits fetch me what I please?
> Resolve me of all ambiguities?
> Performe what desperate enterprise I will?[47]

When Marlowe introduces Mephostophilis, Faustus's deceiving demon, he presents him in strictly traditional terms as the servant of Lucifer and the powers of hell, developing his theme with subtle differences of emphasis which will make of Faustus's tragedy a primarily human rather than supernatural or demonic experience. Most particularly is this evident where Mephostophilis, like the Good and Bad Angels, becomes associated with the theme of books, which are language or words. For Mephostophilis, it soon becomes clear, is not only the guardian but also the censor of the books on which Faustus depends for his speculative adventure in search of new forms of truth.[48] In a central moment of Faustus's eager dialogue with his newly conjured demon, Mephostophilis presents him with a book of powerful spells, presumably more powerful than those in the book which Faustus has already used to conjure Mephostophilis himself. Inexplicably, Faustus not only at once accepts the new necromantic book, but repeats his request to Mephostophilis, who yet again offers him the book he asks for. The really important aspect of this scene, however, is the fact that Faustus is not satisfied with these multiple necromantic books:

FAUSTUS.   Now would I have a booke where I might see al characters of planets of the heavens, that I might knowe their motions and dispositions.

MEPHOS.	Heere they are too.	*Turne to them*
FAUSTUS.	Nay let me have one booke more, and then I have done, wherein I might see al plants, hearbes and trees that grow upon the earth.	
MEPHOS.	Here they be.	
FAUSTUS.	O thou art deceived.	
MEPHOS.	Tut I warrant thee.	*Turne to them*[49]

The inexplicable repetition concerning the gift of the necromantic books, and the abrupt ending of this scene after Faustus's
crucial 'O thou art deceived', clearly suggest that the text is
imperfect and has been interfered with and cut. We are at once
reminded of another (historically true) scene similarly interfered with and cut: Bruno's Oxford débâcle. Here too the drama
centred on a book, and just such a one as Faustus demands of
Mephostophilis: 'where I might see al characters of planets of
the heavens, that I might knowe their motions and dispositions'.
The book in question was Copernicus's *De revolutionibus orbium
caelestium*, and Bruno's reference to it as the book which
revealed a new message of natural truth had caused the Oxford
dons to accuse him of madness and interrupt his lectures. In the
words of an indignant contemporary witness of this seminal
Elizabethan scene:

> when he had more boldly then wisely, got vp into the highest
> place of our best & most renowned schoole, stripping vp his
> sleeves like some Iugler, and telling vs much of *chentrum* &
> *chiriculus* & *circumferenchia* (after the pronunciation of his
> Country language) he vndertooke among very many other
> matters to set on foote the opinion of Copernicus, that the
> earth did goe round, and the heavens did stand still; whereas
> in truth it was his own head which rather did run round, & his
> braines did not stand stil.

Less than a year later Bruno published his *Cena*, where he not
only returned the Oxford dons' insults with as good as he got,
but continued with undiminished vigour to propose the book of
Copernicus as the new message of truth about the cosmos. But
he knew by then how strong the resistance to the new message
was, and in his text he represents it in the figures of the
supercilious Torquato and the pedantic Nundinio, who express

here the 'discourteous incivility and the imprudent ignorance' of the doctors, refusing to listen to the new message but hurrying away still convinced of the fitness and unchangeable justness of the traditional Aristotelian cosmology. The dramatic clash within the text was punctually reflected in the outside London world by a reaction so harsh and scandalized to the publication of Bruno's book that he was forced to stay closed indoors and seek protection against bodily harm.[50]

There could be no question, only a few years later, and with Bruno himself by then in prison and on trial, of the public theatres of London accepting an open debate into the Copernican question. The fact that in *Dr Faustus* Marlowe makes no mention of Copernicanism does not necessarily mean that he was unaware of this revolutionary theory. It is true that in none of his writings – as they have reached us – does Marlowe ever mention a heliocentric universe, while his poetic imagery often contemplates a 'centric' earth and the revolving spheres; none the less, many of his critics have found it surprising and even contradictory that he did not include Copernicanism among his unorthodox and unlicensed opinions.[51] His documented intimacy with Harriot and Warner, who were confirmed Copernicans, suggests it as a probability; and his evident relationship to Bruno in other contexts makes it unlikely that he could have ignored this central element of Bruno's cosmic vision. Such considerations give a precise meaning to the crucial point in the drama when Faustus looks through the book offered him by Mephostophilis presenting the truth about the universe, and cries in disappointment: 'O thou art deceived'. It is a cry which echoes through the immediately succeeding scene, the famous astronomical debate (or 'dispute' of 'divine Astrology' as Faustus calls it) which Faustus and Mephostophilis undertake in his study. The scene is a key one, for in it the demonic role of Mephostophilis becomes comprehensible in a new light.[52] No longer a traditional devil or fearful fiend, he suddenly appears in recognizably human and historical terms as an Aristotelian academician. Nor is he any less fearful for that. Seen in Brunian terms, he is the most deadly of enemies: the doctor who interrupted his Oxford lectures, the Torquato of the *Cena*, perhaps even the Inquisitor already officiating at Bruno's trial in

Venice: the voice of a rigorously exposed, centuries-old cosmology integrated into a traditional, theological vision of the universe.

When Francis R. Johnson brought his wide knowledge of the history of astronomy, particularly in England, to bear on this scene, he illustrated with fine technical expertise the niceties of the debate between Faustus and Mephostophilis.[53] Correcting the numerous blunders of Marlowe's literary critics and editors, he convincingly showed how the scene in Marlowe's tragedy delineates two differing developments of the post-Ptolemaic astronomical debate, and how Mephostophilis offers to Faustus as the undisputable truth the theories of an eight-sphere universe presented by Agostino Ricci of Casale and supported by his friend Cornelius Agrippa. In doing so, Johnson concludes, Marlowe demonstrates his preference for a more empirical astronomy against the more widely accepted ten- (or in some cases eleven- or twelve-) sphere universe; but nowhere does he indicate a knowledge of or interest in Copernicanism, nor does the debate (in spite of Faustus's keen desire for so far unrevealed new truths) ever move outside the dimensions of a dispute taking place in most of the academies of Europe.

There can be no doubt of the importance of Johnson's studies of this scene. No reader of Marlowe can afford to ignore them for they have indicated with clarity and exactitude the background of technical astronomical discussion on which Marlowe depends. Yet it can be argued that Johnson's conclusions represent a total misreading of the drama as a whole. Not only does he consider the scene out of context, without reference even to the preceding scene of the books, but he quite arbitrarily assumes that Mephostophilis expresses the opinions of Marlowe himself, forgetting that his role within the drama is that of an avowed servant of the devil, the master of lies.[54] He even omits to mention the reactions of Faustus to the accomplished academic lecture he is receiving: 'Hath *Mephostophilis* no greater skill?/ Who knowes not the double motion of the Planets?' . . . 'Tush, these are fresh mens suppositions'. If Johnson had related the debate Marlowe presents on the stage to Bruno's *Cena* he would have seen how closely Marlowe is echoing here the scene in the Fourth Dialogue which sees the Nolan himself debating with the Aristotelian Torquato on questions of astronomy. It is important to notice that Torquato, although he represents here the traditional, hidebound thinker, presents exactly the same eight-sphere Ptolemaic system as Mephostophilis embraces, with reactions from the Nolan which closely echo Faustus's taunts. The scene is described by Teofilo, who is narrating the dramatic events of the Ash Wednesday supper in his role of a disciple of Bruno:

> Once this argument had been exhausted, they began to speak among themselves in English, and after they had chattered sufficiently, paper and an ink-stand appeared on the table. Doctor Torquato smoothed out a sheet of paper to its full length and width, took a pen in his hand; drew a straight line through the middle of the sheet from one side to the other; in the centre forms a circle of which the above mentioned line is the diameter, and within a semi-circle of this writes *Earth*, and in another *Sun*. Beside the earth he forms eight semi-circles, where he carefully drew the symbols of the seven planets and around the last sphere writes: *Octava Sphaera Mobilis*; and in the margin: *Ptolemaeus*. At which the Nolan asked him what he meant by this, which even children knew how to do? Torquato replied: – '*Vide, tace et disce: ego docebo te Ptolemaeum. . .*'[55]

In Bruno's text, Torquato goes on to illustrate on the other half of his sheet the Copernican theory, but only to deride it. At this point Bruno intervenes and disputes with Torquato in heated terms, defending the Copernican cosmology. Torquato leaves the supper indignantly after Bruno has 'revealed his ignorance'. Faustus, on the other hand, is obliged by Mephostophilis to remain within the Ptolemaic universe; but then the 'book' revealing the new cosmic truth he had asked for has been denied him. Marlowe makes it clear enough that Faustus is as dissatisfied with Mephostophilis's reasoning as Bruno was with Torquato's. For when his final question, 'Why are not Conjunctions, Oppositions, Aspects, Eclipses, all at one time, but in some years we have more, in some less?' has received the smooth, expected answer: '*Per inequalem motum respectu totius*' (because of the spheres' unequal motion with regard to the whole), Faustus replies with a drily ironic: 'Well, I am answer'd: now tell me who made the world?'.

If the scene of the astronomical debate is considered in the context of Faustus's overall interrogation of Mephostophilis in the first part of the drama, it can be seen how the tension on the stage is derived precisely from Mephostophilis's expertise in frustrating Faustus's eager desire to break new boundaries of knowledge. Nowhere does Mephostophilis allow him so much as to crack the compact shell of conventional dogma and explanation: to Faustus's questioning of the nature of demons and hell, he replies with the accepted biblical explanation of the war in heaven and the defeat of the over-proud Lucifer; to the questions on the nature of the cosmos he replies with an already accepted if debated version of the Ptolemaic-Aristotelian hypothesis; to Faustus's ultimate question about the creator and the creation, he returns a scandalized refusal to offer to man knowledge beyond his station. Systematically and inexorably Faustus is drawn back into the traditional dichotomy between good and evil, salvation and sin; and it is a 'distressed' Faustus, as he describes himself, who finishes his first attempt to 'raise the windes' and 'rend the cloudes' by watching that most dreary of tired spectacles conjured up for him by Lucifer himself: the procession of the seven deadly sins.[56]

Words, Bruno had written in the *De triplici minimo*, must be the servants of meanings, not meanings the servants of words as the grammarians make them.

> We will have made a real beginning when we have uprooted from the depths of the shadows the most famous assertions of antiquity together with the ancient words: we shall be inventors, if necessary, of new words, whatever their origin might be, in harmony with the novelty of the doctrine.[57]

It is here that Faustus, to use another Brunian expression, loses the race, unable to pit against the smooth expertise of Mephostophilis's oratory new doctrines and new words. He can only ask question upon question, and cry disappointedly at the familiar, expected answers: 'O thou art deceived'. It is surely with dramatic irony that when Marlowe's Faustus finally travels through the heavens, as the *Faust-book* required, to investigate the true nature of the cosmos, the dramatist does not allow the journey to be described by Faustus himself (who might have told a very different story), but presents it through the entirely orthodox words of the Chorus:[58]

> Learned *Faustus*
> To find the secrets of Astronomy,
> Graven in the booke of *Joves* high firmament,
> Did mount him up to scale *Olimpus* top.
> Where sitting in a Chariot burning bright,
> Drawne by the strength of yoked Dragons neckes;
> He viewes the cloudes, the Planets, and the Starres,
> The Tropicks, Zones, and quarters of the skye,
> From the bright circle of the horned Moone,
> Even to the height of *Primum Mobile*:
> And whirling round with this circumference,
> Within the concave compasse of the Pole,
> From East to West his Dragons swiftly glide,
> And in eight daies did bring him home againe.[59]

FAUSTUS'S DEATH: 'I'LE BURNE MY BOOKES'

'Let him kiss me with the kisses of his mouth . . . Stay me with flagons, comfort me with apples: for I am sick of love.' Quoting these verses from the Song of Solomon, Bruno in Dialogue Four of the First Part of the *Furori* expresses his sense of the search for knowledge in its culminating moment when the mind dissolves itself in the object. The language he is using, as Bruno himself underlines, is that of the mystical death of the soul, called by the cabbalists the kiss of death. In the Psalms, the kiss becomes a sleep: 'I will not give sleep to mine eyes, or slumber to mine eyelids, until I find out a place for the Lord'.[60] Mystical and Neoplatonic imagery appears to dominate the concept of knowledge Bruno is expressing here, although the passage culminates in an image which gives the traditional theme new and different emphases. The heroic searcher seems, it is true, to be tending towards a pure reality of forms or ideas, beyond the phenomenal, natural world, but in the end Bruno's philosophy in this passage, as in previous dialogues, denies the Platonic dichotomy, and the final image of the object desired by the intellect modulates from the Platonic 'fountain' of ideas into an

Epicurean 'ocean' of truth and goodness, identifiable with the natural universe itself.[61]

The object of knowledge in Bruno's philosophy is thus not a perfect sphere of being beyond the natural world, but the newly defined infinite universe which the finite mind ardently desires to penetrate in its total truth:

TANSILLO. It is right and natural that the infinite, in so far as it is infinite, is infinitely pursued, in that mode of pursuit which is not to be considered a physical but a metaphysical motion; and which is not from imperfect to perfect, but which moves around through grades of perfection until it reaches that infinite centre, which is neither formed nor form.

CICADA. I would like to know how moving in a circle it is possible to arrive at the centre.

TANSILLO. I cannot know that.

CICADA. Why do you say so?

TANSILLO. Because I can say so and leave you to consider it.

CICADA. If you do not mean that pursuing the infinite is like moving round the circumference in search of the centre, I do not know what you mean.

TANSILLO. Something else.[62]

Tansillo's gnomic replies here, as well as indicating the point which lies beyond human knowledge, cover the radically heretical aspects of the discourse from an orthodox, Christian point of view. For the natural universe has expanded into an infinity which if not identical with the idea of divinity itself is the necessary reflection or imprint of the divine intellect. Traditional concepts of a transcendent divinity, of a creation in time and of an individual soul, subject to rewards and punishments after death, are bypassed; for although Bruno's universe is formed of two principles, soul or form and matter, he sees them as complementary and inseparable. The individuality of the soul becomes at most expressible in the image, which Bruno will obstinately hold on to throughout his long trial, of a helmsman in a ship, both to dissolve at death and be reabsorbed into the infinite universe.

It was these ideas which allowed Bruno to dismiss visions of death, both Platonic and Christian, which contemplated in an afterlife the judgement of the individual soul. To such a vision Bruno opposes a Lucretian joy at the idea of a dissolving of individual formations into the infinite whole. Lucretius in the third book of the *De rerum natura* had given poetic expression to the concept of death expressed by Epicurus in the *Letter to Menoeceus* in terms which Bruno was quick to apply to his more fully animated universe. Lucretius had written:

> the nature of the mind and the soul must now be displayed in my verses, and the old fear of Acheron driven headlong away, which utterly confounds the life of men from the very root, clouding all things with the blackness of death, and suffering no pleasure to be pure and unalloyed.

Having defined mind and soul (both of which for Lucretius have a material nature) as composed of tiny round particles, the poem goes on to visualize the moment of death itself as the breaking of a vessel and the flowing away of the water it contained:

> now, therefore, since, when vessels are shattered, you behold the water flowing away on every side, and the liquid parting this way and that ... you must believe that the soul too is scattered and passes away far more swiftly, and is dissolved more quickly into its first bodies, when once it is withdrawn from a man's limbs, and has departed.[63]

It is a vision which denies death as anything but a re-embracing by an infinite whole, in its perpetual transformations and vicissitudes, of the primary particles of substance. So Bruno too denied death:

> But when we consider more profoundly the being and substance of that in which we are immutable, we will find there is no death, not for us, nor for any substance; for nothing substantially diminishes, but everything, moving through infinite space, changes its aspect.[64]

We know that prominent figures such as Ralegh and members of the Northumberland circle shared similar views on the soul and on death which were frowned on by the authorities. Nashe's attack against the so-called 'atheists' in *Pierce Penilesse his supplication to the devill*, which corresponds so exactly to the probable date of composition of *Dr Faustus* in 1592, was primarily directed against Harriot, who, as we have seen, was

closely connected with Marlowe: 'I hear say there be Mathematicians abroad, that will proove men before Adam, and they are
harbored in high places, who will maintain it to the death, that
there are no divels'.[65] One of the 'high places' frequented by
both Harriot and Marlowe was the household of Ralegh, whom
the Jesuit Parsons had accused of forming a 'Schoole of
Atheism' and whose religious views would be the subject of an
official investigation shortly after Marlowe's death.[66] It is in this
enquiry that we hear news of the famous dinner party where
Ralegh's brother had scoffed at the views on the soul proposed
by an Anglican clergyman, Ralph Ironside, who recorded:

> Towards the end of supper some loose speeches of Master
> Carewe Rawleighes beinge gentlye reproved by Sir Raulfe
> Horsey in these wordes *Colloquia prava corrumpunt bonos
> mores*. Master Rawleigh demandes of me, what daunger he
> might incurr by such speeches? whervnto I aunswered, the
> wages of sinn is death. and he makinge leight of death as
> beinge common to all sinner & reightuous; I inferred further,
> that as that liffe which is the gifte of god through Jesus Christ,
> is liffe eternall: soe that death which is properlye the wages of
> sinne, is death eternall, both of the bodye, and of the soule
> alsoe. Soule quoth Master Carew Rawleigh, what is that?
> better it were (sayed I) that we would be carefull howe the
> Soules might be saved, then to be curiouse in findinge out ther
> essence.[67]

Similarly conflicting concepts of the soul and death lie behind
the whole dramatic development of the final scene of Faustus's
tragedy. And the lucidity with which Marlowe poses the
problem as essentially a metaphysical rather than a religious one
clearly links him to Bruno's philosophy. It is a point which
Marlowe's critics have not sufficiently clarified, for they have
always approached Faustus's death scene in moral terms, pointing out how even in the extreme moment of his history Faustus
fails to repent and save himself from eternal torment. But
Faustus himself clearly defines his situation as an intellectual
rather than a moral dilemma, and he does this by underlining his
link with Wittemberg. For it is here in the country of Paracelsus
and Agrippa, and the historical Faustus (and indeed where
Bruno himself had taught), that books 'wherein all natures
treasury is contain'd' had convinced Marlowe's Faustus to make

an irrevocable intellectual choice: to embrace an alternative metaphysic which implied alternative concepts of knowledge but also of the soul and of death. But it was here too that Luther had powerfully reinforced a vision of the universe balanced between heaven and hell, the joy of eternal salvation and the despair of eternal punishment, with the individual soul as the prize to be won in this cosmic struggle. Faustus carries both visions within him, together with the lucid knowledge that having embraced an alternative metaphysic he can no longer be saved in Christian terms, while nevertheless living as he does in the very centre of Protestant Christianity he has no means of escape from a death he must experience in the terms of his world:

> the serpent that tempted *Eve* may be saved, but not Faustus. Ah gentlemen, heare me with patience, and tremble not at my speeches. Though my heart pant and quiver to remember that I have beene a student here these thirty yeares, O would I had never seene *Wittemberg*, never read book: and what wonders I have done, all *Germany* can witnesse, yea all the world: for which *Faustus* hath lost both *Germany* and the world, yea heaven it selfe: heaven the seate of God, the Throne of the Blessed, the Kingdome of Joy, and must remaine in hell for ever. Sweet friends, what shall become of *Faustus* being in hell for ever?[68]

It is in the poetic development of the tensions between two conflicting images of the universe, and two concepts of knowledge and of death in that universe, that Marlowe writes his greatest and final dramatic monologue. A universe in which time brings man inexorably to death, and in which death means God or the devil, eternal joy or eternal despair.

> Stand still you ever moving Spheares of heaven,
> That time may cease, and midnight never come.
> The Stars move still, Time runs, the Clocke will strike.[69]

Throughout the first part of his speech Faustus experiences his death in a Christian universe, in despair at the impossibility of being able to save himself in terms which he has chosen to re-nounce, and in fear of the consequences which necessarily follow:

> The devill will come, and *Faustus* must be damn'd.
> O I'le leape up to my God: who puls me downe?
> See see where Christs bloud streames in the firmament,
> One drop would save my soule, halfe a drop, ah my Christ.

Yet for Faustus it is only a momentary vision ('Where is it now? 'tis gone') which is quickly replaced by that of another God, more wrathful and less merciful, of the Old rather than the New Testament. In front of this vision Faustus, developing a complex set of biblical references, can only wish to hide himself in the earth, or to have his soul separated from his body by the force of the storm clouds 'So that my soule may but ascend to heaven'. Then this vision too fades away to leave only the certainty of damnation. And it is here that Faustus's mind turns at last to the ideas of death implied in the metaphysics he himself has embraced:

> Why wert thou not a creature wanting soule?
> Or why is this immortall that thou hast?
> Ah *Pythagoras Metemsycosis*; were that true,
> This soule should flie from me, and I be chang'd
> Unto some brutish beast.
> All beasts are happy, for when they die,
> Their soules are soone dissolv'd in elements,
> But mine must live still to be plagu'd in hell.[70]

The search therefore is no longer for forms of salvation of his soul within a Christian or Hebraic universe, impossible for Fausttus for whom such images are visions briefly conjured up but soon gone again. Here instead we have a metaphysical hypothesis which, if true, as Faustus lucidly realizes, would allow him to die, even if he has failed in his heroic attempts, in quite different terms. Above all to die without fear, as Bruno had claimed in *De la causa*:

> Every production, of whatever sort it is, is an alteration, in which the substance remains the same; for it is only one, there is only one divine and immortal being. This is what Pythagoras meant, who does not fear death but expects a process of change.[71]

It is in such a vision of death that Faustus's mind longs to come to rest in the last poignant verses of his monologue, which bring him finally to a concept both Epicurean and Brunian of the soul as a drop of water (an image clearly related both to Epicurean and Brunian atomism) which resolves at the death-moment into the universal ocean:

> O Soule be chang'd into little water drops,
> And fall into the Ocean, ne're be found.
> *Thunder, and enter the devils.*[72]

The attempt to escape from the metaphysic which dominates his culture has failed, and the last, tragic moments of Dr Faustus on earth are an expression of his despairing recognition of that failure: he has no choice but to die in terms of the inevitable scenario.

> My God, my God, looke not so fierce on me;
> Adders and serpents, let me breathe a while:
> Ugly hell gape not; come not *Lucifer*,
> I'le burne my bookes; ah *Mephostophilis.*
> *Exeunt with him.*

Marlowe creates in these final verses of Faustus's monologue a subtle contrast between two forms of purification on death. On one side we have the painless purification of water imagery in the vision of the ocean silently absorbing, as one of its cosmic rights, its component 'little water drops'; on the other the roaring, hissing, punishing purification by thunder, serpents, damnation, and hell-fire. Faustus's mind clearly tends with ardent desire towards the first of these visions, although he realizes by now that he can only express such a vision in hypothetical grammatical forms ('Why wert thou not', 'Or why is this', O soule be chang'd'). The alternative form of purification, which is warded off for as long as possible by Faustus's ever weaker negative verbs ('Ugly hell gape not; come not *Lucifer*') is only irrevocably accepted in the final line, and in a spirit of despairing, exhausted recognition of a fact and its consequences.[73] Rather than repenting, Faustus recognizes in his final words the force of a reigning metaphysic too strong and entrenched to resist. As in his opening monologue, although with a far deeper anguish which Marlowe's poetry evokes powerfully in the broken irregularity of his pentameters, Faustus's mind is working according to a logical pattern of thought centred on the theme of a choice of alternative books. With his alternative metaphysic, or art 'wherein all natures treasury is contain'd', relegated to the status of a dangerous heresy by the realities of the situation in that particular Wittemberg (which can stand as well, in this context, for Bruno's Oxford or Venice or Rome) Faustus brings his speech and his life to a close with lucid if exhausted logical precision on the inevitable consequences of his intellectual adventure: 'I'le burne my bookes; ah *Mephostophilis*'.

The pessimism of Marlowe's final tragic vision is only partially qualified by the brief comments of the two scholars who discover Faustus's dead body. For them Faustus's story is not to be concluded on a purely negative note. Although they recognize that in religious terms his experience must be accepted as a negative lesson, they express an understanding of the intellectual dilemma which the Faustian story represents:

> tho *Faustus* end be such
> As every Christian heart laments to thinke on:
> Yet for he was a Scholler, once admired
> For wondrous knowledge in our Germane schooles,
> We'll give his mangled limbs due buryall:
> And all the Students clothed in mourning blacke,
> Shall wait upon his heavy funerall.[74]

Such ambivalence is at once suffocated by the Chorus, who close the tragedy, as it had begun, on a note of unequivocal orthodoxy, bringing the intellectual experience represented by Faustus under a moral and theological sign of rigorous negativity. As in the opening of the tragedy, the Chorus uses a pagan symbol to express the Faustian intelligence, recognized as having made an attempt to re-establish the values of '*Apollo*'s Lawrell bought'. But the bough has been duly burnt, and the lesson must be learned by the audience who are recalled by the Chorus to the values (which are also linguistic and dramatic forms and formulas) of the medieval morality play:

> regard his hellish fall,
> Whose fiendfull fortune may exhort the wise
> Onely to wonder at unlawfull things,
> Whose deepnesse doth intice such forward wits,
> To practise more than heavenly power permits.[75]

The question here is not whether Marlowe's schematically conceived, theologically dominated Middle Ages fully represent the complex characteristics of that period. He is writing in a recognizable Renaissance convention which underlined its own achievements as a reawakening of lost forms of thought and knowledge, and marked out the centuries intervening between the illuminated cultures of classical antiquity and the modern rebirth as a period of shadows and darkness. The new cultural impulses, arriving from Italy through France, had permeated the northern cultures for over a century by the time Marlowe wrote; and a full historical consideration of their influence would have to take account of the part they had played in generating the Reformation itself. But Marlowe was writing in the agitated, blood-filled final years of the sixteenth century, in a Europe torn by the struggle between Reformation and Counter-Reformation, with even the comparatively peaceful Elizabethan England overshadowed by increasing religious tensions and oppressive legislation, aggravated by growing political uncertainty due to the ageing of the Virgin Queen. In such a situation, Marlowe brings his final tragedy to a close on a note of fierce intellectual pessimism which consciously projects his audience backward into a past age. The intellectual impulses forward seem to be irrevocably blocked by the Chorus's assumption of its own intellectual authority and dominion. It has taken possession in its own terms of the two classical images which define the Faustian attempts to break new intellectual territory. Icarus, connected as we have seen with concepts of new forms of scientific investigation, has fallen as the Chorus predicted, and Apollo's laurel bough has burnt. Both a new science and a new poetry or drama appear irrevocably compromised; and Marlowe's final moment of tragic vision seems to lead with both a logical and biographical inevitability towards his shadowy and premature death.

I have suggested that Bruno's thought, and above all his search for new forms of knowledge, informs Marlowe's conception of the Faustian figure. Had Marlowe lived to the end of the century, he would have seen Bruno die in terms which he himself already foresaw as inevitable. But had he followed Bruno's final days in all their dramatic complexity, he would also have heard him making his celebrated and extreme claim that he did not want or have to retract, that he had nothing which needed retraction and that he did not know of anything he should retract: a stand which a few days later Bruno qualified by his penetrating statement to his judges that perhaps they pronounced against him with more fear than he received his sentence.[76] It is tempting to speculate whether a more mature Marlowe, if he had followed the Brunian experience through to the end, might not have found there that movement forward against all odds towards new forms of knowledge and understanding which his tragedy, in its last moments, seems to deny.

BRUNO AND SHAKESPEARE:
HAMLET

The first question we should ask ourselves is – What did Shakespeare mean when he drew the character of Hamlet? He never wrote anything without design, and what was his design when he sat down to produce this tragedy? My belief is, that he always regarded his story, before he began to write, much in the same light as a painter regards his canvas, before he begins to paint – as a mere vehicle for his thoughts – as the ground upon which he was to work. What then was the point to which Shakespeare directed himself in Hamlet?[1]

Some years after he had asked these questions in his 'Lectures on Shakespeare and Milton' of 1811–12, Samuel Taylor Coleridge remembered that 'Hamlet himself was the character in the intuition and exposition of which I first made my turn for philosophical criticism'.[2] But the philosophy Coleridge associated with the figure of Hamlet was very much that of his own age, for he saw Hamlet as the type and symbol of a modern intellectual who tends towards action but whose impetuous thought processes, with their subtle distinctions and ceaseless self-analysis, prevent action from being accomplished.

Shakespeare's design, I shall be arguing, was wider and deeper. For Hamlet's thoughts are not simply intense and all-pervading, but they add up to the rejection of a traditional concept of the universe – cultural, political, cosmological – tending towards a redefinition of the universal order and of man's position and autonomy within that order. If Hamlet has difficulty in passing from thought to action, it is not simply because he thinks too much, but because his ideas involve a process of total 'renovatio' which no single action or 'revenge' can bring about.

The exact date of the composition of *Hamlet* is unknown, but it is now generally thought that the play was written or at least completed in 1601,[3] a date which gives it a particular significance, for not only does it evoke the beginning of the new century, with its closing in on the new enquiries and debates, but it follows at only a year's distance the moment of Bruno's death. Whether Shakespeare wrote his play in the knowledge of that death is not a question of primary importance. What the coincidence of dates tells us is that at the opening of the new century two of the greatest European minds, working, as we shall see, in surprisingly similar terms through an awareness of historical crisis towards an idea of a totally renewed universal order, conclude that thought process in clearly tragical terms.

'BE SILENT, THEN'

As we saw in the previous chapter, we do not know if Marlowe ever met Bruno. The closest way of linking their biographies is through the documents of their investigations and trials, that is to say through the mechanisms by which their respective cultures drove them to silence and, in Bruno's case at least, to death. We have even less knowledge of a direct link between Bruno and Shakespeare, who had probably not arrived in London when Bruno left in 1585. Shakespeare's most recent and convincing biographer, Samuel Schoenbaum, derives much of his conviction by narrating the few known facts of what he calls a 'simple life-story' in less than the first page of his book.[4] All the rest is (and can only be, given the lack of documents and recorded facts) indirect comment, social history, and oblique illuminations. Even the handwriting of this greatest of writers is unknown to us except in the form of two or three signatures to official documents, with the possible addition of some lines of manuscript of the drama *Sir Thomas More*. We do not know how or why it was that one of the world's greatest artists faded out of history on a personal level, leaving an opus in which reality appears through so many shifting planes of human and linguistic experience as to baffle us with respect to the identity of its author, who, inexplicably, left to others the task of preparing his collected works for the attention of posterity. It is difficult not to conclude that behind such an opus its author carried out a deliberate erasure of his personality and personal faiths, and with good reason. For had his dramas been fully understood by his public, it is unlikely that he would have been able to pass those years of prosperous retirement at Stratford where he would be enshrined, shortly after his death, in a statue which shows him as a wealthy, self-satisfied bourgeois citizen.[5]

Around Bruno's name the silences are of a different order, for he was not one to draw back from public notice. Yet silences there are, which have baffled his biographers almost as much as Shakespeare's, although it is probable that they were created around him rather than, like the more reserved Shakespeare, by himself. Keeping within an English context, it is striking, for example, that it has taken nearly 400 years for a text to be discovered which confirms Bruno's claim to have spoken, and more than once though with disastrous results, at the University of Oxford, which appears to have been at pains to eliminate his name from all official records, to the great frustration of generations of researchers.[6] As for government records, after an ominous announcement of his arrival from France in a message sent by the English Ambassador in Paris, Sir Henry Cobham, warning Walsingham of the danger of his religious ideas,[7] we find no further mention of Bruno in the government papers of the times in spite of the fact that his own account of his stormy stay in London suggests some kind of official measures having been taken against him. Equally strange is the total lack of the least mention of his name in either the public or private papers of the eminent figures with whom he claims to have had both a personal and a cultural relationship, foremost among them Sir Philip Sidney and Fulke-Greville.[8] Given the prominence which his work achieved throughout Europe in the last years of the sixteenth century in contesting the foundations of a culture whose principal occupation was rapidly becoming the making of wars between differing concepts of Christianity, it is curious that the overt memories of Bruno's three-year visit were confined in England to figures of secondary importance and even then most usually to his few easily acceptable ideas and pronouncements. His name is most consistently linked to the English works on the art of memory which relate to his early ideas in that field;[9] but although the discussion on this subject involved some figures of a certain eminence, they are totally out of proportion with Bruno's own cultural stature, and his main ideas never seem to have reached the foremost cultural practitioners of the time except in indirectly 'silent' forms, as in the case of Marlowe's *Dr Faustus.* Occasionally his name appeared, though as briefly as possible, in discussions of Copernicanism and the new cosmology. On the whole, however, his most-quoted statement is an appreciation of the quantity and quality of Elizabethan translations of foreign texts.[10] But his remark is always quoted out of context and becomes simply a pleasing compliment to the Elizabethan culture. It is doubtful if it is the remark he would have chosen to be remembered by; and all in all, a list of contemporary English references to Bruno adds up to a meagre booty for such a primary thinker of his time. It would appear that Elizabethan culture took some pains to forget such an uncomfortable visitor, and effectively to eliminate him from collective memory.

Silence thus becomes a fact: a form of historical refuge in the case of Shakespeare or, as in the case of Bruno's impact on English culture, a form of historical deceit. The importance of prudent silences in this period is well illustrated by Vincenzo Cartari's widely read mythological study *Le imagini de i dei de gli antichi*, where silence is associated with wisdom in the figure of Minerva whose helmet

> signifies that the prudent man will not always reveal what he knows or offer his advice to anyone he meets; nor does he speak in a way which can be understood by all, but only by those similar to himself, according as events require it, so that to others his words seem like the intricate pronouncements of the Sphinx.

And Cartari's Minerva following, as he informs his reader, an ancient Athenian precedent, is shown with a small symbolic sphinx surmounting her helmet (see Plate 1, p.9).[11] The relevance of such silences, either chosen or imposed, can only be appreciated by a consideration of the corresponding danger of words: 'Be silent, then, for danger is in words'.[12] Dr Faustus, talking to the Wittemberg scholars as he prepares himself for his final act of magic, the conjuring up of the shadow of Helen of Troy, is concerned above all to warn them of the dangers

involved for those who choose the new 'metaphysics of magitians'. But Faustus himself will be the first to disregard his own
warning. For as soon as he sees the shape of Helen before him,
he bursts out with the famous eulogy of her overpowering
beauty: 'Was this the face that launched a thousand ships,/ And
burnt the topless towers of Ilium?/ O Helen, make me immortal
with a kiss'. And Faustus had undoubtedly been right to sense
the danger inherent in words, for no sooner does he express his
sense of a divinity and immortality to be found within the human
form, and to be possessed through an ardent act of love, than he
is admonished by the Old Man, the guardian of Christian
orthodoxy and order, that thus he has lost his soul, and
condemned himself for ever to the torments of hell.[13]

Hamlet, speaking to his Wittemberg student-friend Horatio
and his companions, is equally insistent on the necessity for a
close silence: 'Swear by my sword/Never to speak of this that you
have heard'.[14] For he has just been communing with the Ghost
of his dead father on the castle ramparts, and already he knows
that the message that Ghost has brought to him will threaten
him and his friends with death. And so once again Hamlet urges
his companions to silence before leaving the haunted castle
battlements: 'And still your fingers on your lips, I pray'.[15]

Given the presence of the Ghost, we may consider the silence
referred to here as in part a Hermetic silence (the jealous
reservation among a few selected adepts of occult or mystical
secrets); but it is also, and much more, a 'politic' silence, dictated
by the sense common to both Faustus and Hamlet of living in a
distorted and deceptive world where a search for human beauty
and truth becomes inevitably a suspect and dangerous activity.
Such a realization is reached by the eloquent and at times
garrulous Faustus only towards the end of his tragic story, but it
dominates Hamlet's sense of his world from the opening scenes
of the play. And precisely because he starts from such a
realization, Shakespeare operates a radical change of emphasis
in his fable, at the same time as he establishes close links between
his hero and Marlowe's Faustus. For although Hamlet's intellectual powers are clearly projected towards enquiries into new and
unexplored areas of truth which are reminiscent of Faustus
('There are more things in heaven and earth, Horatio,/ Than
are dreamt of in your philosophy'), such enquiries appear at

once, in Hamlet's world, to clash with a prevailing power structure based, as Hamlet himself immediately suspects, on corruption and deceit. Not for nothing does Claudius, the wily uncle-Prince, unhesitatingly forbid his return to Wittemberg. As Hamlet is quick to realize, for truth to reappear in clear and unsullied terms, the order and organization of society have to be radically restructured and reformed. The principle of corruption which dominates the 'unweeded garden' of a bloodstained Court must first be extirpated; for only when this has been accomplished will it be possible freely to pursue the new intellectual enquiries. For Shakespeare's hero, although reluctantly, it is precisely this process of extirpation of evil which becomes his heroic if tragic mission: 'The time is out of joint, O cursed spite,/ That ever I was born to set it right',[16]

Such a change of emphasis corresponds not only to the increasing sense of historical crisis which marks the last years of the century, but also to the central theme of one of the most important of Bruno's Italian dialogues written and published in London between 1583 and 1585, the first of his works of moral philosophy in which he had already dealt with the problem posed by Shakespeare as the moral dilemma of Hamlet: the visualization of a hoped-for renewal of a hopelessly compromised historical reality. For Bruno, too, in the *Spaccio*, the extirpation of evil and the accompanying visualization of a radical 'renovatio', culminating in the arrival of a new and uncorrupted Prince, become the necessary and essential premises for the heroic pursuit of new enquiries into cosmic or natural truths.

In formal terms the *Spaccio* may seem at first sight to develop its visionary reform at a considerable remove from historical reality, for the renewal of a corrupted and distorted situation is presented by Bruno in terms of a cosmic revolution: a 'purge' operated by an ageing and repentant Jupiter of the 'forty-eight famous images of the sky', or the astrological planetary gods as they were visualized according to the classically inspired vision of the heavens which was to take such a strong hold on men's minds throughout the Middle Ages and the Renaissance. Yet through this complex mythical machinery, Bruno presents a powerful critique of the distortions and corruptions of the times:

here you will see introduced a repentant Jupiter, who had filled the sky with so many beasts, with so many vices, according to the forms of the forty-eight famous images; but now calls a consultation to eliminate them from the sky, from the glorious and exalted regions, sending them down to certain places on earth and in those heavenly regions reinstating the long-exiled and scattered virtues.[17]

There can be no doubt of Bruno's own sense of the relevance of the *Spaccio* not just to the European, but specifically to the English, cultural and historical situation of the time. For not only does he write and publish this work in London, but it is the first of his works to be dedicated to an Englishman, Sir Philip Sidney, 'that very illustrious and excellent knight', as Bruno defines him. Sidney is certainly present here not just as the protector who, according to Bruno's own statement at the beginning of the Explicatory Epistle, supported him after the scandal caused by his earlier metaphysical dialogues with their ardent pro-Copernican and anti-Aristotelian bias, but also as the figure most likely to appreciate this first dialogue of moral philosophy with its search for a new world founded on more solid ethical principles. Bruno has little hope of finding more than the rare spirit, like Sidney himself, who will be his wise and just reader, for he is about to reveal to the world the corrupted and distorted bases of its government, its public and private immorality, its linguistic and philosophical assumptions and deceptions. All he can hope for from his studies and his writings, states Bruno wryly, is 'material for disappointment': any prudential reckoning will consider silence more advisable than speech. What spurs Bruno to write at all is what he calls 'the eye of eternal truth'. It is in relation to this higher and divine dimension of justice that his message must be unfolded, the terms of a total reform worked out. The Explicatory Epistle then goes on to indicate briefly the vices associated with the various constellations and to visualize their defeat followed by the reinstatement of the corresponding virtues. What Bruno's work involves is thus the visualization of a new era, the arduous working out of a plan of total reform. Only when this task has been completed can the heroic intellect allow itself to rest: 'There is the end of the stormy travail, there the bed, there tranquil rest, there a safe silence.'[18]

Hamlet, at the beginning of his play, confronted like Bruno by a world become 'rank and gross', weighs the dangers and uses of words in very similar terms: 'It is not, nor it cannot come to good./ But break, my heart, for I must hold my tongue'.[19] Then the Ghost, who announces himself as Hamlet's 'eye of eternal truth', spurs him to speak. Only when Hamlet, like Bruno, has penetrated and denounced the vices which dominate his world does he reach the end of his stormy drama with the advent of a new Prince. There he too finds 'the bed', the moment of ultimate quietness and safety: 'the rest is silence'.[20]

THE SILENUS IMAGE

Throughout the opening scenes of *Hamlet*, the play between appearance and reality lies behind the development of setting, action, and words: the almost transcendental spaces of the castle platform, open to the night sky and the stars, contrasted with the closed, oppressive interior which sees the political action of Claudius in his take-over of power in the state; his able, slippery rhetoric of power, in the act of marrying his brother's wife and thus sealing his claim to the throne, contrasted with Hamlet's insistence on establishing both linguistically and conceptually the rightness and reality of his particular pain for his father's death:

> Seems, madam? Nay, it is. I know not 'seems'.
> 'Tis not alone my inky cloak, good mother,
> Nor customary suits of solemn black,
> Nor windy suspiration of forc'd breath,
> No, nor the fruitful river in the eye,
> Nor the dejected haviour of the visage,
> Together with all forms, moods, shapes of grief,
> That can denote me truly. These indeed seem,
> For they are actions that a man might play;
> But I have that within which passes show,
> These but the trappings and the suits of woe.[21]

The same inner/outer contrast lies behind Hamlet's pained questioning of sentiments and events in his first monologue as well as the puzzled comments by Horatio and the guards on the platform after the appearance of the ghost. 'Something is rotten in the state of Denmark' is an assertion which not only expresses one humble guard's sense of how things stand but suggests what lies in the inner, hidden core of the state under the gay and celebratory noises which reach the anxious group waiting for the message of a king's ghost on the castle battlements. The contrast is built up in intensity and complexity throughout the whole scene of Hamlet's meeting with the Ghost, and clearly projects on to the figure of the Ghost itself, whose words and identity are thrown in doubt first by the scepticism of Horatio and then by Hamlet's own uncertainties as to whether he is dealing with 'a spirit of health or goblin damned'. Inner realities which can be reached, known, and expressed by the language of 'is' are nowhere easily available in Hamlet's Denmark, and the whole first half of the play will see him trying to understand whether the deception, which clearly exists, finds its essential principle in the Uncle who claims a right to his father's throne or the Ghost who claims to be his father's spirit.

The final resolution of the problem in favour of a villainous Claudius and honest Ghost is carried out in two distinct moments: Hamlet's initial burst of confidence in the Ghost's message after it has revealed the story of its murder, and then later on in the performance of the 'play within the play' which clinches the question by inducing Claudius to betray his guilt. Shakespeare's treatment of both these moments suggests that he had in mind an image which he never explicitly mentions, but which had a long and significant history in both classical and Renaissance culture, originating in Plato's *Symposium* to pass through the work of free-thinking humanists as different as Pico, Erasmus, and Rabelais until it was picked up by Bruno and developed in emblematic terms in the opening pages of the *Spaccio*. To trace the history of this image as it passes from Plato to Bruno can illuminate the terms in which Shakespeare deals with those crucial moments of Hamlet's drama in which the intellect and the word succeed, at least momentarily, in penetrating the inner truth of things: the 'is' rather than the 'seems'.

The Sileni of Alcibiades first make their appearance as a central emblematic image of the Socratean character and quest at the end of Plato's *Symposium*, when Alcibiades erupts noisily into the gathering to develop his image of Socrates himself as a Silenus and the whole sense of the Socratic quest is given immediate visual reality. The Sileni, sons of the satyr Silenus, the companion and master of Bacchus, were considered genii of fecund waters, images of what is rough and unkempt outside but rich and fertile in its essential nature. Alcibiades, in the elaboration of his image, refers to the statues of Sileni which were then common in the sculptors' workshops: kinds of boxes decorated with uncouth players of pipes which, when opened, revealed inside images of divinity.[22] He likens Socrates personally to a Silenus-box, referring to his carelessly unkempt and unprepossessing person which contrasts so dramatically with the divine philosopher within. But in a final and revealing development of the image, which once again distinctly recalls Hamlet in his apparent madness, he applies his contrast to the Socratic discourse rather than to his person. For his language, Alcibiades points out, seems ridiculous in its repetition and commonplace terms, almost the skin of a petulant satyr. But if you try and open his discourse, and look inside, you find profound, even divine sense, rich in every virtue and tending always towards the sublime, or rather towards those things which make a man sound and true.

Although it seems more than probable that Shakespeare had a direct knowledge of Plato's *Symposium*, available throughout the Renaissance in Ficino's Latin translation,[23] there was no need for him to know it as far as the Silenus image was concerned. For the theme of the Sileni of Alcibiades had been taken up and reworked in one of the central sections of the most popular work of that most popular and revered of northern humanists, Erasmus of Rotterdam.[24] The image of the Silenus-box of Alcibiades, Erasmus points out in his extended treatment of the theme in his *Adagia*, quickly acquired proverbial value in Greek culture, affording a happy way of indicating those who hide jealously, under a rough exterior, the truest and most authentic values. For the Christian-humanist Erasmus the clearest examples of Sileni figures in this original sense are Socrates and Christ. But the interest and originality of Erasmus's treatment of the Silenus image derive from his perception that history itself and above all the society of his own day afford few examples of Sileni in this sense. Rather the world is full of what Erasmus calls Sileni-turned-upside-down, or negative Sileni images: theologians with long professorial titles, swollen with Aristotelian doctrine and erudite definitions but who 'if you crack the nut' have no real religion; noblemen decorated with antique coats-of-arms and illustrious names but without any genuine nobility: the Erasmian list of negative Sileni is long and detailed, amounting to a profound critique of the society of his time. It culminates in a portrait of the modern Prince which could well serve to introduce the figure of Claudius seen through the eyes of Hamlet:

> Your eye sees the royal emblems, the sceptre, the body-guard; your ear catches the titles of most high, most gentle, most illustrious. Then – is it not true? – you bow to the prince and it seems to you that you are faced by a god on earth, a super-human being. But try to open a little that negative Silenus: inside you will find a tyrant, an enemy even to the public good and to civil peace, a sower of discord, an oppressor of the innocent, a flayer of the law, a destroyer of cities, a robber of the church, a brigand, a blasphemer, a practiser of incest, a gambler, in short, to use a Greek proverb, an Iliad of ills.[25]

The negative-Silenus image, as it is here developed by Erasmus, also recalls a specific linguistic question which is that of the proverb or adage; for it is precisely as such that we find Erasmus's discussion of the Silenus image in his *Adagia*. It is therefore linked to the whole Erasmian conception of the proverb as a linguistic jewel, tiny but cutting in its brevity, its reference to common experience in unexpected terms, also, at times, its function of allegorizing with a great degree of boldness and pushing the allegory to enigmatic lengths. Erasmus finds the simple proverbs embedded in refined discourse, above all that of the classics, rich sources of truths worth spending years of passionate research on.[26] The complexity of Erasmus's comment on his *Adagia* is partly due to his habit of weaving into his own discourse many of the jewels of proverbial wisdom he has found in his search. In particular, as in the passage on the negative-Silenus Prince above, he tends to clinch a passage of criticism effectively by amplifying and clarifying his meaning with a final, brief sentence of a proverbial nature. This rich reference to proverbial wisdom serves at the same time to disguise and universalize his dangerous critique of the society of his times, and frequently Erasmus intervenes with his own voice to claim that he is not concerned with making particular attacks on particular targets: 'I remind you once more', he writes at the apex of his discussion of the negative-Sileni, 'that no-one need be offended by what I say: we name no names. If you are not one of these, then all of this touches you not'.

In *Hamlet* the treatment of Claudius as a negative-Silenus image in the Erasmian sense reaches its climax at the staging of the 'play within the play' which forces Claudius to reveal his hidden nature. At the dramatic crux of this scene, when the actors are presenting the play and Lucianus is about to enter and proceed to the stage-murder of the lawful king, Claudius nervously asks Hamlet the name of the play. Hamlet's reply appears consciously to echo the Erasmian passage just quoted:

> '*The Mousetrap*' – marry, how tropically! This play is the image of a murder done in Vienna – Gonzago is the Duke's name, his wife Baptista – you shall see anon. 'Tis a knavish piece of work, but what o' that? Your Majesty, and we have free souls, it touches us not. Let the galled jade wince, our withers are unwrung.[27]

Bruno's use of the Silenus image in the *Spaccio* is also clearly developed in a direct reference to Erasmus's text. He is explaining to Sidney why he has been spurred at all to write a book of moral philosophy which will attack the evils of the times and attempt to visualize their replacement by the corresponding virtues. Given that stupidity and perversity are the dominating notes of humanity, Bruno observes, it might well be considered wiser for the moral philosopher to stay silent rather than attempt to find words of truth. But when he considers 'the eye of eternal truth', then Bruno realizes that he is called to speak, whatever the consequences. It is here that Bruno introduces the Sileni, to characterize a reading public who will inevitably prefer to 'laugh, joke, play and enjoy themselves on the mimic, comic, and histrionic surface of things' rather than search for goodness and truth under the surface. But at once Bruno proceeds to a consideration of the Erasmian negative-Sileni figures pointing out that besides this frivolous mass of readers, and far more dangerous than them, are the corrupt men of power: those who 'under the severe brow, the reserved expression, the long beard and the grave, flowing gown of the master, studiously and dangerously hide an ignorance which is vile and arrogant and far more pernicious than a celebration of ribaldry'.[28]

The terms in which Bruno in the *Spaccio* goes on to elaborate his theme appear to recall the Socratic quest and are of vital importance for an understanding of his whole work, for he at once makes it clear that the principal elements of his attempt to bring about a radical reform will be words rather than deeds. It is in their vision and understanding of themselves and the universe they live in that men have gone so wildly wrong. Thoughts, words, and gestures are what must be radically changed to bring men back to the virtues of sincerity, simplicity, and truth. The expulsion of the triumphant beast and the reinstatement of the virtues in their proper places are therefore, for Bruno, primarily questions of correct distinctions and judgements, which imply redefinitions in the sphere of language. The new era will have begun when the forms of human conduct are given their proper names, when

> it is no longer considered the highest wisdom to believe without discretion; where human impostures are distinguished from divine decrees; where it is not judged an act of superhuman piety and religion to pervert the natural law; where studious contemplation is not considered madness; where honour no longer consists in greedy possession; splendour in avarice; reputation in having many servants of whatever character; dignity in dressing richly; greatness in having most; truth in marvels; prudence in malice; cunning in treachery; cleverness in deception; wise living in pretending; strength in fury; the law in brute force; justice in tyranny; judgement in violence.[29]

It is in the passage following this one that Bruno, in a famous page, justifies his use of Italian rather than Latin in his London dialogues, for

> here Giordano . . . names things freely, gives its proper name to that to which nature has given its proper being . . . considers philosophers as philosophers, pedants as pedants . . . mountebanks, charlatans . . . parrots . . . for what they say, show themselves to be, and are.[30]

In Bruno's elaboration of what by this time (the *Spaccio* was written and published in London in 1584) had become a key Renaissance image, we can find the essential, underlying theme and shape of Shakespeare's first great tragedy. For Hamlet too will dedicate himself to penetrating through the myriad surfaces of deceptive appearances until he is able to present to the world, in the final sequences of his play, the pedants, mountebanks, and parrots of his Court not for what they seemed to be ('nay, madam, I know not "seems"') but for what they 'show themselves to be, and are'. It is, in fact, in what are surely Brunian terms, the moment of the free and proper 'naming' of things, and above all of people, which constitutes the culmination of *Hamlet*: the moment in which the chief courtier Polonius, after Hamlet has unwittingly killed him, can finally be named and known as a 'wretched, rash, intruding fool';[31] or when the parrot of Hamlet's Court, the effeminate and obsequious Osric, after his exit, can be recognized, through a complex metaphorical statement, for the 'waterfly' that Hamlet had immediately suspected him to be:

> Thus has he – and many more of the same bevy that I know the drossy age dotes on – only got the tune of the time and, out of an habit of encounter, a kind of yeasty collection, which carries them through and through the most fanned and winnowed opinions; and do but blow them to their trial, the bubbles are out.[32]

The final phase of this process is inevitably reserved for the last moments of the duel, when Hamlet can at last publicly name his dying uncle not as the triumphant, virtuous king he 'seemed' in the first scenes of the play, but for what he has shown himself to be and is: incestuous, murderous, and damned. And yet even here, at the apex of the dramatic effect in this sense, it is made clear to the public that the dramatist's freedom to name things 'as they are' is hedged in by clear limits. For Claudius is finally denounced by Shakespeare as 'thou incestuous, murd'rous, damned Dane',[33] although by this time it must have been clear to a contemporary audience, as it immediately is to a modern one, that the Denmark of the play is no less symbolic than its Wittemberg. Just as Bruno, in the *Spaccio*, declares his intention of describing things and persons 'as they are', only to continue explaining himself through a complicated structure of metaphor and myth, so too Shakespeare has to accept the necessary use of oblique forms of expression even at the apex of his

dramatic revelation. The total opening-up of the negative
Silenus-box of history, which is already seen as necessary for the
'renovatio' to take place, is put off until a still undefined future
in which a shadowy Fortinbras may, or may not, reveal himself
as the ideal new Prince.

A BATTLE OF WORDS

The development of the Silenus image through the sixteenth
century implied a corresponding division of language into false
and contorted linguistic models capable only of perpetrating
deceit, and, conversely, the possibility of elaborating language
to penetrate the essence of what things are. Bruno's Explicatory
Epistle to the *Spaccio* shows that he accepts this distinction, but
also that he has no illusions about the ease with which clear and
just definitions can be reached. On the contrary, he underlines
the complexities of human discourse, and the facility with which
mankind habitually bends and uses words according to his own
interests and points of view. Although it is Bruno's intention to
name things 'as they are', he warns us that the truth can only be
reached through the arduous working out of a new vision of
things. Thus he does not wish anything that he says to be taken
'assertively' or categorically. For 'these are dialogues, with
characters who speak together and whose speeches are given
with those of many others, each of them with their own sense
and each one arguing with that fervour and zeal which is proper
to him'.[34]

Significantly, Bruno sees this first work of moral philosophy in
terms of a work of art whose meaning is not given as an assertion
but appears through the creation of the work itself. So he likens
his dialogues to the prelude of a musician, the preparatory
sketch of a painter, the initial setting of his threads by the
weaver, or the foundation work of an architect. Every situation,
he tells us, is depicted without a definite conclusion: 'everything
is posed as a problem, placed before us, pushed into the theatre
to be examined, discussed, compared'.[35] We are reminded of
Bruno's own early experience as a dramatist, a form which, he
tells us in the dedication to his drama *Il candelaio*, satisfied his
sense of the human condition as essentially one of mutability, of
incessant vicissitude. The awareness of such a state is the basis of

human happiness, an awareness which magnifies the human intellect while, at the same time, accentuating the relativity of the truths which it can reach.[36]

The human predicament can thus be expressed as a linguistic predicament: the necessity felt by the heroic intellect to elaborate simple but entirely adequate words, signs, or gestures which satisfy 'the eye of eternal truth'. These, perhaps (and *Hamlet's* Ghost exemplifies this point), may only be available after death, which thus becomes desirable as a positive melting away of individual limitations. Yet the heroic intellect has no choice but to continue, within its mortal coil, its work of progressive clarification and discovery. Bruno insists on the relativity of individual discourse to such an extent that he pictures Jupiter himself as implicated in the incessant vicissitudes of universal nature. His reform is arduously worked out, step by step, with the help of Momus, who stands for the light of the intellect; but no guarantee can be given that, once achieved, it will prove a perfect or final solution. On one point, however, Bruno never wavers. The reform is in some very essential way a reform of language, a movement towards a new and more direct way of using words. It is therefore inevitable that it should finish in an order in which words have reacquired their proper and therefore divine meaning. 'Words, words, words' (an essential passage in the Bruno-Shakespeare relationship which we will come back to later on) have, once again, become the Word. Bruno would have had the essential biblical passage in mind, but he elaborates this theme in his own non-Christian terms. In his vision, it is the demi-god and constellation, the Centaurus, who figures at the linguistic apex of the reform, for in this symbol the gods, man, and brute nature are united in an indissoluble whole. With such unity, there is a recovery of 'divine Parable, sacred Mystery, moral Fable', or the word as once more able to name divine truths. At the same time, senile and bestial Fable is banished once and for all, and with it 'vain Analogy, weak Anagoge, foolish Trope, and blind figurative forms of speech'.[37] Only then is silence to be contemplated, with the return of true virtue and justice which depend on true words, for false words are at the root of all evil.

Bruno's Explicatory Epistle to the *Spaccio* reminds us that Hamlet too battles against his triumphant beast by questioning words, from the very moment of his entrance into the play; not 'cousin' or 'son' as the new King falsely calls him, but 'A little more than kin, and less than kind'. In the very next scene of the first act, we hear Polonius declaiming pompously to his children in his own house in what he himself defines coquettishly as 'poor phrases' or 'foolish figures', clearly reminiscent of Bruno's 'foolish Trope' or 'senile and bestial Fable'. So Polonius comments on Ophelia's moving admission that the Prince Hamlet had 'of late made many tenders of his affection to me':

POLONIUS.   Think yourself a baby
        That you have ta'en these tenders for true pay
        Which are not sterling. Tender yourself more
        dearly
        Or – not to crack the wind of the poor phrase,
        Running it thus – you'll tender me a fool.

Later on in Act III, when Claudius, for a moment, shows his first sign of guilt and remorse, it is the relation of his evil deed to his false word which most strikes him as a heavy load to bear:

        The harlot's cheek, beautied with plast'ring art,
        Is not more ugly to the thing that helps it
        Than is my deed to my most painted word.
        O heavy burden!

Hamlet's chosen form of revenge can thus be seen in Brunian terms as a questioning of false words, a pitting of truer words against the able but treacherous words of his Uncle, the pedantic linguistic formulas of Polonius, the transparent falsity of Rosencrantz and Guildenstern, the parroting of Osric; for the distortions of their world were seen by both Bruno and Shakespeare as intimately related to distortions in the field of language.[38]

Coming at the end of a humanistic cultural revival, both men appear to have related these linguistic distortions to certain characteristics of the humanistic conscience itself; for humanist culture had elaborated a clear-cut distinction between ignorant, barbarous forms of language, and cultured, civilized ones. These last found their great historical models in the Greek, Latin, and, to some extent, the Hebrew. A knowledge of these multiple forms of civilized language was considered a necessary requirement of the serious humanist, who had done so much to enrich modern European culture with his recovery of ancient texts and his learned and intense discussion of the new forms of knowledge which could be derived from them. But by the end of the sixteenth century the new learning had degraded to a crystallization into forms of cultural and linguistic pedantry which had already been mocked by Italian writers of comedy and satire. Bruno inherited this current of thought and was merciless from the beginning in his fierce mockery of what he called the 'grammarians'. In the opening of the third dialogue of the *De la causa*, he illustrates this mockery through the figure of Gervasio, a type of the valid thinker and one of his English followers, shown in a lively discussion with Polinnio, the Aristotelian pedant.

GERVASIO.   Very learned master Polinnio, what I wish to say is that if you knew all the languages which exist, which (as our preachers say) are seventy two . . .
POLINNIO.   – *cum dimidia*
GERVASIO.   – for this reason, not only would it not necessarily follow that you are able to judge the philosophers, but beyond this it would not prevent you from being the clumsiest animal alive: nor would it prevent another with hardly one language to his name, and that in bastard form, from being among the wisest in the world.[39]

Already in the nineteenth century a close connection was noted between Bruno's ironical opposition to the cultural pedants of his time and Hamlet's sharp-witted skirmishes with Polonius. The thesis assumes a particular interest in so far as we find an almost exact identity in names.[40] Seen in the light of Bruno's Polinnio, Shakespeare's Polonius appears as rather more than the garrulous, elderly, foolish courtier he is often considered both in criticism and on the stage. If he were only this, it would be difficult to explain why Hamlet, after his meeting with the Ghost, indulges at such length in skirmishing with Polonius before coming to grips with the King himself. The space in the play and on the stage given to Polonius becomes explicable when it is realized that, with all his apparent absurdity, he is the cultural prop of the new King's Court, and as

such certain kinds of particularly dangerous distortions orig-
inate with him. Like Bruno, in the skirmish between Gervasio
and Polinnio just quoted, Shakespeare presents these distortions
as related to a mistaken concept and use of language: an
'external' sense of words, as Gervasio had put it, as lacking any
real and essential connection with the nature and sentiment of
things. Words which can be many and learned, but which fail to
penetrate the intimate core of nature, and therefore lead
inevitably to distorted misinterpretations both of nature and of
words themselves.

In *Candelaio*, Bruno had shown us the pedant Manfurio
'interpreting' an extremely silly poem he himself had written.
His ecstatic interpretation of his own work is entirely based on
the numbers of his poetic verse: 'Did you ever see such ten-line
stanzas? Some write four-line verses, others six-line, and others
eight; mine is the perfect number'. It is surely not incidental that
the long second scene of the second act of *Hamlet*, which sees the
apex of the hero's skirmishing with Polonius, begins with
Polonius reading to the Queen and King Hamlet's love-letter to
Ophelia and offering a complete misinterpretation of it. He,
too, starts off by commenting on a purely external point: *'To the
celestial and my soul's idol, the most beautified Ophelia* – That's an ill
phrase, a vile phrase, "beautified" is a vile phrase'. Polonius is
perfectly right in his awareness that Hamlet's letter presents a
problem. It is strikingly ungrammatical (*'I love thee best, O most
best'*) and the poetic verses are, at a formal level, absurdly
childish:

> Doubt thou the stars are fire,
> Doubt that the sun doth move,
> Doubt truth to be a liar,
> But never doubt I love.

The modern critic has often joined hands with Polonius in
underlining its lack of eloquence, even suggesting that it was an
early letter written in a more awkward youth. The hypothesis
can hardly be supported, given that Shakespeare himself makes
no suggestion of this kind. What the letter as the text presents it
seems to want to prove is rather the point made by Bruno's
Gervasio: that simple, bastard forms of language can carry
pregnant truths. Hamlet himself underlines the formal inad-

equacy of his letter, connecting it to its 'truth': '*I am ill at these numbers. I have not art to reckon my groans. But that I love thee best*'.[41]

It is, of course, not simply a love-letter but also a repudiation of precisely those aspects of the Aristotelian-Ptolemaic cosmology (the spheres, with the concept of the stars as fire and therefore purer than earth, which lies immobile at the centre) which Bruno was attacking in his proposal of a new infinite vision of an infinitely rich and varied universe. Hamlet's love-letter thus contains in four brief and simple verses a new and revolutionary cosmic vision intimately linked to a declaration of true love. And that it was true, in spite of his cruel behaviour to Ophelia, Hamlet himself will confirm later on when he jumps into her grave declaring:

> I lov'd Ophelia. Forty thousand brothers
> Could not with all their quantity of love
> Make up my sum.[42]

For it is the quality of Hamlet's love which distinguishes him; and an intimate part of that quality lies in his deeply felt link between true love and true philosophy, which involves the question of true words. It was a peculiarly Brunian thesis, developed at length in the *Furori* where the new cosmic vision is seen in terms of an act of love, or even as an act of love itself. This is the true 'heroic fury', which Bruno associates with the poetic muse and 'a certain melancholy impulse' or with a 'divine abstraction' for which in fact 'certain men rise above the ordinary crowd'.[43] Polonius gets it all wrong. He sneers at the vile phrasing and ill grammar which are not necessarily considered by Bruno (and obviously by Shakespeare too) as ignoble vessels for divine truths; while in so far as he recognizes a certain 'fury' behind the verses, he sees it in terms of that 'blindness, stupidity, and irrational impetus which tends towards senselessness', as Bruno had defined the negative form of fury, or madness, which he recognized as dangerously close to, yet clearly distinct from, true forms of heroic fury.

The question at stake here is the reaction, already mentioned, against the dominion of ordered, refined, 'classical' forms of linguistic expression in Renaissance culture. Recent work on Bruno's literary style has placed his theories of language against the background of a wide reaction against Renaissance linguistic niceness which was to lead towards the literary baroque. Writers such as Berni, Aretino, and Folengo, from whom Bruno often borrowed, had already experimented, in contrast to the linguistic refinements of the early humanists, with vulgar forms of language, vividly realistic and often obscene metaphors, the deformation of syntax, and innovations in vocabulary.[44] It would be possible to use the same terms to describe Hamlet's linguistic onslaught on his world, for it is his metaphorical energy and violence which characterize his cruel play with Ophelia and later with his mother, destroying for both of them an illusory vision of a refined and harmonious act of love, become impossible in a deeply distorted world. But it is above all with Polonius, the cultural pedant, that the linguistic battle is waged, in terms which will break down any possibility of communication between them. For Hamlet is searching for new linguistic forms, less elegant but more varied and plastic and alive, in which to express his sense of a reality which, under its apparently ordered and serene surface, he has glimpsed in its falsity and corruption but also in its infinite vicissitudes and variety.[45] As for Polonius, he is at least acute enough to see that it is in his ferocious linguistic play, even more than in his love-sickness, that Hamlet is (as Polonius sees it) 'mad':

POLONIUS. Do you know me, my lord?
HAMLET. Excellent well. You are a fishmonger.
POLONIUS. Not I, my lord.
HAMLET. Then I would you were so honest a man.
POLONIUS. Honest, my lord?
HAMLET. Ay sir. To be honest, as this world goes, is to be one man picked out of ten thousand.
POLONIUS. That's very true, my lord.
HAMLET. For if the sun breed maggots in a dead dog, being a good kissing carrion – Have you a daughter?
POLONIUS. I have, my lord.
HAMLET. Let her not walk i' th' sun. Conception is a blessing but as your daughter may conceive – friend, look to't.
POLONIUS [aside]. How say you by that? Still harping on my daughter. Yet he knew me not at first; a said I was a fishmonger. A is far gone.[46]

Hamlet's apparent foolery is pitted here against Polonius's real but insidious foolishness in a linguistic play which through oblique metaphor, unexpected juxtapositions, violent and at times obscene images breaks down the smooth, familiar and trite truths of Polonius's world. He is in a quite literal sense 'playing the fool', and his close links with Shakespearian comic fools such as Feste and Touchstone, but more particularly with the later Fool of *King Lear*, have often been underlined. Another illuminating link is that between Hamlet (and for that matter other Shakespearian fools) and Bruno's Momus in the *Spaccio*. The emergence of this figure in Bruno's work is of great interest. It appears to complement the disappearance of the foolish pedant, whom Bruno will no longer represent after *De la causa* as a single dramatic figure, although multiple forms of cultural pedantry will continue to be present, and violently attacked, in his work up to the end.[47] Already in the *Spaccio* there is no one figure to represent the pedantry and intellectual foolishness, which are seen here as diffused in various and varying guises throughout a deeply distorted universe. On the other hand we have the emergence in a central role of Momus, the classical god of buffoonery evicted from Olympus for his satirical wit (see Plate 9, p. 136). Momus, in his role of satirical rogue, plays a central part in Bruno's celestial reform, for it is he who reveals the absurdities of the universe about to be purged. Also, and perhaps more tellingly still, he reveals those of the gods themselves in their sometimes presumptuous, sometimes over-solemn, and sometimes mistaken efforts to put everything to rights. His caustic wit knows no bounds, and plays freely over the absurdities of the universe in spite of his formal submission to the power of Jupiter, the monarch of the skies. Interestingly Bruno links Momus's role in Jupiter's celestial Court to that of a fool in a Court of his time: a voice which

> often presents more of factual truth to the ear of the prince than all the rest of the Court together, and for which generally, not daring to speak, they speak in the form of a game and in that way they bring their proposals to effect.[48]

If we consider Hamlet's linguistic fencing with Claudius, the tyrant, which assumes such primary importance in the play with respect to the actual duel which solves the plot, we can notice a

Plate 9   Image of Momus, the God of satire, in Vincenzo Cartari's *Le Imagini de i Dei de gli Antichi*, 1571. Reproduced by courtesy of the Biblioteca Nazionale Centrale Vittorio Emanuele II, Rome.

good example of a similar linguistic subverting of pompous, absolute power in Momus's play with Jupiter just before he ascends his celestial throne to inaugurate the divine council:

> Here, after the rest of them, a silence having fallen, with an aspect not less sad and grave than with high presence and masterly pre-eminence, Jupiter directs his steps, while before he rises to the rostrum and appears before the tribunal, Momus whips in front of him and with his usual liberty of speech, with a voice so low that all could hear it, said: 'This council must be put off till another day and another occasion, oh Father, for this idea of coming into conclave now, immediately after lunch, seems to have been occasioned by

the generosity of your tender cup-bearer; because nectar, which is heavy on the stomach, neither consoles nor refreshes, but alters and saddens nature and disturbs the fancy making some gay without cause, others disorderly and merry, others superstitiously pious, others vainly heroic, others choleric, others builders of castles in the air, until, with the vanishing of such vagaries in their passage through differently fashioned brains, everything topples and goes up in smoke'.[49]

It is, of course, the oblique wit and playing with words of Momus, and not the nectar, which 'topples' Jupiter's carefully prepared appearance before the gods, just as Hamlet 'topples' Claudius's equally well-prepared first appearance before his Court in the role of the new king. Even more dramatic and conscious is his mockery of the final carefully designed plot of Claudius and Laertes in the scene which will witness the final and conclusive duel:

KING.   Come, Hamlet, and take this hand from me.
                  [*Puts Laertes's hand into Hamlet's*]
HAMLET.   Give me your pardon, sir. I have done you wrong;
                  But pardon 't as you are a gentleman.
                  This presence knows, and you must needs have heard,
                  How I am punish'd with a sore distraction.
                  What I have done
                  That might your nature, honour, and exception
                  Roughly awake, I here proclaim was madness.
                  Was 't Hamlet wrong'd Laertes? Never Hamlet.
                  If Hamlet from himself be ta'en away,
                  And when he 's not himself does wrong Laertes,
                  Then Hamlet does it not, Hamlet denies it.
                  Who does it then? His madness. If 't be so,
                  Hamlet is of the faction that is wrong'd;
                  His madness is poor Hamlet's enemy.[50]

Through his 'madness', which appears here more than ever to correspond to Bruno's description of Momus or the Court fools who work through 'language in the form of a game', Hamlet 'topples' all the carefully constructed premises of the scene organized by the King ('this presence'). Instead of Hamlet asking the pardon of Laertes, he becomes himself 'of the faction that is wrong'd', and the whole sense of the duel is disintegrated in mockery before it begins. Laertes is well aware that he is being fiercely taunted, together with the tyrannical King to whom he has rashly allied himself. For though Laertes is the more expert swordsman, this is a duel in which the foils are words, and he has no defences against the conscious and subtle verbal attacks in which Hamlet has by now perfected his technique, and which allow him to give his hand to Laertes only when, through his penetrating 'madness' or 'ignorance', he has established the dangerous falsities which pervade every speech and action of a perverted Court:

> HAMLET.   I'll be your foil, Laertes. In mine ignorance
>   Your skill shall like a star i' th' darkest night
>   Stick fiery off indeed.
> LAERTES. You mock me, sir.
> HAMLET.   No, by this hand.[51]

But Laertes is being mocked in precisely the same way as the other characters were: that is, by revealing the conventionality, emptiness, and falsity of the words by which they construct the sense of their own reality and that of the world they live in. The elaborate cosmic image through which Hamlet underlines Laertes's celebrated skill as a swordsman recalls the Aristotelian-Ptolemaic sphere of the so-called 'fixed stars' which the new cosmology, with Bruno among the foremost, was sweeping away in a new concept of an infinite space in which all the celestial bodies have their proper, ordered, even if imperceptible movements. Laertes's sense of his own superiority as a cultured, courtly dueller, prepared and perfected in Paris, is thus ridiculed as pompous and antiquated and perhaps also (as of course it is) based on deception. At the same time the image suggests far deeper and more daring enquiries into cosmic phenomena which obviously interest Hamlet but appear impossible until the ethical bases of society have been refounded and renewed. Once the duel is over, bringing with the poisoned foils the apocalyptic destruction of Claudius and his Court, it will above all appear essential to the dying Hamlet that his story be faithfully told: it is the words which record his story, rather than the arrival of a vaguely defined Fortinbras, on which he depends for the longed-for 'renovatio' to take place.

THE BRUNIAN CORE OF *HAMLET*

If from these comparisons between leading themes and concepts of language, we now concentrate on tracing precise Brunian echoes in the text of *Hamlet*, we must notice at once what may be called the Brunian core of the play. This is centred in the long Act II, scene ii, which starts with the arrival at Court of the spies, Rosencrantz and Guildenstern, welcomed by the Queen and King, and finishes with the arrival of the actors, welcomed by Hamlet. The complex development of the scene between these two poles adds nothing at all to the play in terms of plot, if by that we mean direct action, except for the brief episode of the return of the ambassadors from Norway with news that Fortinbras has decided to invade Poland rather than Denmark, thus getting him out of the way until his appearance in the final scenes. The entire action here is in terms of dialogue which represents clashes of opinions and ideas. Action has become words, and it is through action conceived in these terms that Hamlet reveals his true heroic fury, rising above the other characters who surround him and assuming control, at least temporarily, of the action itself. By the end of the scene he has penetrated the foolishness and dishonesty of Polonius and the falsity of Rosencrantz and Guildenstern, while the arrival of the actors offers him the weapon ('the play 's the thing') with which to penetrate the treachery of the King.

Some of the passages of this dialogue, particularly those with Polonius (already considered), demonstrate the similarities between Shakespeare's use of dialogue form in this scene and Bruno's in his Italian works. The linguistic cut and thrust of what becomes at the same time an exhilarating and dangerous game is directed towards two main ends, first of all the revelation of the essential foolishness and falsity of a prevailing and dogmatic culture, and secondly the clarification, against the prevailing philosophy, of a new cosmic vision involving at the same time a new vision of man and a new vision of the universe. The nucleus of Shakespeare's scene which appears to adopt Brunian dialogue as a model does not cover the whole of Act II, scene ii, but begins with Polonius's reading of Hamlet's letter and covers the whole of the hero's own presence on the stage in this scene from his entrance 'reading on a book' until the arrival of the players.

Hamlet's poem read by Polonius acts as an important and also explicit prologue to the dialogue proper. For it indicates quite clearly not just a Copernican, heliocentric universe, but one which has already been extended in what were peculiarly Brunian terms to a vision of a homogeneous infinity in which the innumerable stars are no longer conceived of as made of fire, and therefore constituting a purer and more ethereal substance than centric earth; instead the whole universe unites in a pattern of recurring variations and vicissitudes of a single infinitely extended matter. It is unlikely that Shakespeare had in mind here the English exponents of the theory of an infinite universe such as Digges, for their vision was dictated by a basically religious impetus and never challenged the whole range of premises of the dominating Christian-Aristotelian philosophy, as Bruno's did. It is Bruno's dramatic sense of the necessity to turn a whole culture on its head which Shakespeare is echoing when he makes Hamlet write 'Doubt truth to be a liar'; while his insistence on the necessity, beneath and beyond all these debates, of an act of love clearly places the whole letter in the context of Bruno's *Furori* where love is seen as an impetus of the mind involving both intellect and imagination which seizes, in its final phases, a vision of an infinite cosmic whole and of the 'sommo bene' as harmony and happiness in that whole.

If Hamlet's letter suggests the subversion of a whole cosmic vision and prevailing philosophy, subjecting it as Bruno did to 'doubt' in terms which make of doubt a philosophical method and principle,[52] the following passages of dialogue between Polonius and the King and Queen establish quite clearly their positions as the by now rather desperate upholders and repositories of an Aristotelian, hierarchical cosmos centred on earth. Polonius clarifies their communal position in a revealing metaphor where, just before his meeting with Hamlet, he assures the King and Queen: 'If circumstances lead me, I will find/ Where truth is hid, though it were hid indeed/ Within the centre'.[53] Behind the political and moral clash represented by Hamlet's refusal of Claudius's Court, lies thus a cosmic vision which needs redefining in new and daring terms. Only when this metaphysical context of the duel between Hamlet and the Court has been established does Hamlet himself enter 'reading on a book' to begin his linguistic 'play' which will lead to the breakdown of the certainties on which the Court is established.

The first reference to Brunian thought in Hamlet's skirmish with Polonius lies in the idea of the sun breeding maggots in a dead dog, or, as Hamlet at once clarifies, of spontaneous conception through the heat of the sun.[54] Recent studies have pointed out that this idea had ancient precedents, and was widespread in the sixteenth century, linked as it was to the cult of the sun and its power, at times approaching sun-worship, which had grown in the wake of the Florentine development of Neoplatonic doctrine.[55] Copernicus had incorporated the idea in his revolutionary cosmic theory as a means of rendering more acceptable the idea of the sun as 'centre'. In Bruno, with his yoking together of Copernicanism and aspects of Neoplatonic doctrine, the idea assumes particular importance as part of the vision of a universe in which life is continual vicissitude in all its parts, birth and death becoming not beginnings and ends so much as transitory moments of a universal life-process. That Shakespeare had the Brunian conception of vicissitude in mind seems probable, given the concept of death which he will later develop in the graveyard scene. It was above all this aspect of Bruno's thought that the German philosophical critics of the nineteenth century underlined, seeing Hamlet as a mouthpiece for Bruno in this sense.[56]

The thesis became particularly persuasive when the following exchange between Polonius and Hamlet with respect to the book he is reading was identified with a specific passage of Bruno's *Candelaio* in which the pedant Manfurio (a forerunner of the later Polinnio) has the following exchange with Ottaviano who is ridiculing him:

OTTAVIANO. What is the matter of your verses?
MANFURIO. Litterae, syllabae, dictio et oratio, partes pro-
             pinquae et remotae.
OTTAVIANO. What I mean is, what is the subject and matter?
MANFURIO. Do you mean: de quo agitur? materia de qua?
             circa quam? It's about the throat, the saliva and
             the gastric juices of that glutton Sanguino.[57]

There are striking similarities between this passage and Hamlet's replies to Polonius:

POLONIUS. What do you read, my lord?
HAMLET. Words, words, words.

POLONIUS. What is the matter, my lord?
HAMLET. Between who?
POLONIUS. I mean the matter that you read, my lord.
HAMLET. Slanders, sir.[58]

Shakespeare, if he did have the Brunian passage in mind, inverts the roles making Hamlet play the pedant consciously to Polonius's unconscious pedantry. But above all he calls to mind, with Hamlet's weary insistence on 'Words, words, words', the Brunian reaction against a culture conceived in primarily 'grammarian' terms as quantity and refinement of words rather than attention to things. Once again the thesis of a precise relationship between the passage in *Hamlet* and the one in *Candelaio* derives its force from the probability that the very next passage in the Hamlet-Polonius dialogue echoes a page of the *Spaccio*:

HAMLET. For the satirical rogue says here that old men have gray beards, that their faces are wrinkled, their eyes purging thick amber and plumtree gum, and that they have a plentiful lack of wit, together with most weak hams.[59]

JUPITER. Look, my body is wrinkling and my brain getting damper; I've started to get arthritis and my teeth are going; my flesh gets darker and my hair is going grey; my eyelids are going slack and my sight gets fainter; my breath comes less easily and my cough gets stronger; my hams grow weaker and I walk less securely.[60]

Bruno's treatment of the ageing Jupiter in satirical terms links up with a literary tradition of mockery of old age from Juvenal to Erasmus. Both Juvenal's Xth *Satire* and Erasmus's *Praise of Folly* have been suggested, with numerous other candidates, as the book Hamlet was reading; and it was inevitable that the critics who first noticed these similarities between Bruno's ageing Jupiter and this speech in *Hamlet* should have suggested that the book was the *Spaccio*. The hypothesis is obviously gratuitous given that Shakespeare chose not to specify the book. None the less, it is important to notice the context in which Jupiter's self-description occurs in the *Spaccio*, in pages which emphasize the theme of universal vicissitude to such an extent that not only the gods, including Jupiter himself, are seen as involved in the processes of time and change, but Truth herself and Virtue are presented as subject to vicissitude at least as far as the human intellect can conceive them. Bruno's placing of a traditional satirical 'topos' like that of the ageing body within this universal concept of relativity and vicissitude in the categories of time and space helps to clarify and explain Hamlet's remarks immediately after the cruel description of old age in which he hypothetically envisages a young Polonius in relation to his own old age: 'For yourself, sir, shall grow old as I am – if like a crab you could go backward'.[61]

Bruno's doctrine of eternal vicissitude within an infinite universe underlined the relativity of the individual life process in both time and space. Bruno himself defined the problem by conceiving of his philosophy as the product of a 'here' and 'now': himself as an 'eye' situated at a precise point in space and time with infinity and eternity stretching out both before and beyond him. From the point in space and time, or monad, derives multiplicity of points or moments which are only relative to the point of departure which has been defined.[62] All such points lie within Bruno's concept of infinite time and space. This was expressed in three-dimensional, Euclidean terms as a sphere of infinite diameter; so that to project him too far into a modern age as a forerunner of Einstein would be unwise. Nevertheless, he understood the contradictions involved in the concept of the infinite sphere, and realized the exciting potentialities of a mind whose finite nature had now to be measured in relation to unbounded quantities of space and time. The prospect which Hamlet picks up is the same as that which has fascinated post-Einsteinian writers of science fiction: the possibility of reversing the time process and travelling backwards instead of forwards between two moments in time seen as relative to a process of eternal vicissitude. The metaphor of the crab has complex meanings, for the suggestion that by reversing their positions in time, Polonius would become the younger of the two underlines Hamlet's sense of his own superior experience and wisdom at the same time as it expresses the idea of Polonius's dried-up and ungenerous humanity. As for Polonius himself, he is, once again, capable of appreciating Hamlet's acuteness and wit, or the 'method' in his 'madness', but unable to follow its complex subtleties. The full irony of the scene is developed by the fact that it is quite unconsciously that Polonius in fact continues the spiral of Hamlet's thought. For when Hamlet mischievously interprets his innocent invitation, 'Will you walk out of the air, my lord', as an invitation to walk to his death (which Polonius in all probability is scheming for) the reference to death is capped, again quite innocently, by Polonius with a reference to birth: 'How pregnant sometimes his replies are'. He thus quite unconsciously completes Hamlet's train of thought, to be picked up again in the graveyard scene, where birth and death are seen together, in Brunian terms, as momentary gatherings and dissolvings of individual formations in the eternal processes of time. It is thus Polonius who has happily hit on an expression 'which reason and sanity could not so prosperously be delivered of', becoming himself the 'fool' he takes Hamlet to be. The reversal of their roles is now complete, and is rendered explicit by the comment with which Hamlet greets the exit of Polonius: 'These tedious old fools'.[63]

The departure of Polonius and the immediate entrance of Rosencrantz and Guildenstern far from exhaust the densely packed passage of Brunian references. Rather, they are increased, as soon as the brief space dedicated to student joking is over, by Hamlet's reference to Denmark as a prison, followed by Rosencrantz's refusal to accept this definition which sparks off Hamlet's 'Why, then 'tis none to you: for there is nothing either good or bad but thinking makes it so'. Behind this comment lies the whole question of the possibility of making absolute ethical judgements which Bruno had tried to clarify in the *Spaccio*. His position is not that there are no ethical absolutes, but that the intelligence is unable to perceive absolute truth precisely because of its involvement in the process of universal vicissitude. Hence his insistence on the fact that his ethical philosophy must not be considered 'assertive'. His Jupiter, ageing and tired, is not making the final and irrevocable reform, but only doing his best, though with imperfect eyesight, to clean up a situation for which he himself is largely responsible. The continual witty objections of Momus to Jupiter's decisions, and his ridicule at times of the whole enterprise, serve to keep this aspect of Bruno's 'total reform' in mind. Hamlet's awareness of his own limitations, and particularly of the implications of his mortality, as he meditates on them in the great speech on man which ends this section of the drama, indicates that he too is considering the relativity of 'good' and 'bad' in a wide metaphysical context which has clearly Brunian connotations. These become even more evident when the question of the relativity of moral judgements is immediately followed by an overt reference to Bruno's proposal of an infinite universe peopled by atoms or monads:

HAMLET.   O God, I could be bounded in a nutshell and count myself a king of infinite space – were it not that I have bad dreams.[64]

Here the concept of an infinite universe, already briefly hinted at in Hamlet's love-letter, is taken up and qualified by reference to the minimum quantity or atom: the nutshell, and infinity, *unitas* – quantity – the maximum. Though neither atomism nor the infinite universe were ideas which only Bruno was aware of and embraced, his particular recovery of Epicurean-Lucretian cosmology and its application to the new Copernican universe had developed into one of the most complete and articulate philosophical messages of the period, radically subverting many of the metaphysical, cosmological, ethical, cultural, and linguistic assumptions of the European culture of his time. Taken piecemeal many of the ideas found in Bruno's works, including those referred to by Shakespeare in this part of *Hamlet*, were held by other thinkers of the time. Welded together into an organized whole they became not, as Bruno himself underlined, a definite and totally defined 'system' of thought, but certainly a new 'philosophy' centred above all on the autonomous activity of the mind in its continual redefinitions of its own powers and of the nature of the universal whole. It was primarily because of his stand for intellectual independence and dynamism that Bruno, at the precise moment of time in which Shakespeare was writing, was being (or was about to be, or had just been) burnt at the stake. For his philosophy as a whole could be judged, and was judged, as an act of ambition which recognized no external authority outside that of the mind in its contemplative act. Rosencrantz and Guildenstern point out just such a characteristic in Hamlet, for whom Denmark is a prison: 'Why, then your ambition makes it one: 'tis too narrow for your mind'.[65] Hamlet's bad dreams are quite clearly connected to his ambition in this sense as well as to the subversive doctrine of an infinite universe which he will only refer to hypothetically in the presence of his 'jailors', Rosencrantz and Guildenstern. The dreams are, of course, quite justified in view of the ease, and even the eagerness, with which Rosencrantz and Guildenstern will soon accept the King's orders to take Hamlet to England and have him killed there. To see Hamlet's dreams simply in the light of contemporary theories of melancholy, as in Bright,[66] is to undervalue the intense intellectual drama being played out in this scene. They are far nearer the dreams of John Dee, who tells us in his Private Diary of the dream he had on the night of 24 November 1582:

> Saterday night I dreamed that I was deade, and afterwards my bowels wer taken out I walked and talked with diverse, and among other with the Lord Thresorer who was com to my house to burn my bokes when I was dead, and thought he looked sourely on me.[67]

GUILDENSTERN.	Which dreams indeed are ambition; for the very substance of the ambitious is merely the shadow of a dream.
HAMLET.	A dream itself is but a shadow.
ROSENCRANTZ.	Truly, and I hold ambition of so airy and light a quality that it is but a shadow's shadow.
HAMLET.	Then are our beggars bodies, and our monarchs and outstretched heroes the beggars' shadows. Shall we to th' court? For by my fay, I cannot reason.[68]

The repeated play here on the theme ideas-shadows-dreams is a reference in fairly overt terms to the debate on memory which had been stimulated in Elizabethan England by the publication of Bruno's *De umbris idearum*: a debate we have already seen reflected in *Dr Faustus*. Not only Alexander Dicson with his Brunian-inspired *De umbra rationis* but also the well-known Puritan divine and Cambridge don William Perkins were involved. The controversy had been waged in strong terms with

Perkins accusing Dicson of spreading the dangerous doctrine of 'the impious artificial memory'. The 'impiety' of the Brunian memory doctrine was related to his vision of the material universe as a system of 'umbrae' or images which represented not a divine creation made in a moment of time and subsequently corrupted by the Fall, but eternal shadows of the light of the divine mind. The possibility, which Bruno's art of memory intended to open up for the human mind, of penetrating the truths of the divine intelligence through a correct ordering or remembering of the shadows, vestiges, and seals made, at least potentially, of the contemplative spirit what Hamlet defines it: 'a king of infinite space'. The subversive implications of such a philosophy, particularly with respect to the traditional hierarchical vision of the universe and of monarchical power impersonated by Claudius, are what Shakespeare underlines in Hamlet's words and what Guildenstern and Rosencrantz immediately perceive as 'ambition'. The whole evocation of the subject of 'shadows' is linked to the importance of memory within Hamlet's search for knowledge of the truth of his world. At the same time, the concluding exchanges of this brief piece of dialogue recall a page of the *Spaccio* in which Poverty and Riches are seen leaving the heavens, neither of them having been judged true virtues fit to take the place of constellations. Between them, as they leave, Momus sees a shadow which appears to link them, and wonders how two figures can possess only one shadow between them. Later he realizes that the shadow which joins them is Avarice or Ambition, a shadow of the shades represented by Riches and Poverty alike. The shadow of Avarice plays over both Poverty and Riches, but as Momus watches it, it moves away from Poverty to envelop Riches, which thus becomes not rich but overshadowed by fear of Poverty, while Poverty, untouched by Avarice, is no longer Poverty but an autonomous body without a shadow.[69] Precisely the same reversal of values is operated by Hamlet's play on the shadows of beggars and monarchs: 'Then are our beggars bodies, and our monarchs and outstretched heroes the beggars' shadows'.[70] It is an important corollary to this piece of dialogue that only seven lines later Hamlet identifies himself as a beggar.

With this complex reference to the Brunian concept of shadows, the passage of what appears to be an organized and almost overt evocation of Brunian philosophical concepts is brought to a close. It is noticeable that the shadows passage develops directly from the reference to the minimum-maximum theme based on the idea of an infinite universe, thus picking up the best-known aspects of Bruno's philosophy as they had already been obliquely introduced in the love-letter to Ophelia read by Polonius. It seems irrelevant to object, as critics of the Brunian thesis have always done, that Shakespeare's play elaborates no clearly organized philosophical vision. Shakespeare was writing a drama, not a philosophical treaty, and his form required above all the unfolding of an action or plot. His references to Brunian thought constitute not the elaboration of an organic philosophical vision, but a reminder to the public of a philosophy which was an aspect of the times and which, by calling all in doubt, was subverting many of the assumptions on which the world of the play and the audience alike was constructed. Hamlet is associated with that philosophy in the precise moment of his play in which he uses the dialogue form as a means of 'taking up arms' against the ethical, cultural, and linguistic distortions of his world in ways which clearly recall Bruno's use of dialogue in his Italian works. It is at this formal level that the identification between Hamlet and Bruno is, in this passage of the play, suggested most fully. At the conceptual level what we have is a closely packed series of hints and reminders which serve to identify Hamlet as a type of the contemplative hero or furious intellect operating at the most daring and advanced poles of thought for that period. At the same time, the reference to peculiarly Brunian philosophical concepts would have served to remind the most cultured part of the public that the Brunian *mens* had already been dramatically captured and crushed. The drama of Hamlet's position with respect to his Court, and particularly here to the spies, Rosencrantz and Guildenstern, who will obviously refer all to the King, is clarified and given a precise dramatic-historical meaning by the reminder of Bruno's tragic story.

Shakespeare's treatment of Brunian philosophical themes here is thus completely original and subservient to the ends of the tragedy he is creating. The precise metaphysical context of thought in which Hamlet has been placed no longer serves him, at least as a central theme, once the actors make their appearance to trigger off, in brilliantly unexpected terms, a plot of revenge. The great speech on man which bridges the two sequences, as well as standing out on its own as an anthology piece, serves to break up the sequence of specifically Brunian references in a treatment of the figure of man which crystallizes in unforgettable poetic images a commonplace of Renaissance thought. At the same time it contains, although in far more hidden and muted terms than the preceding dialogue, Brunian implications which suggest that the reference is not to be considered as exhausted but will continue to lie behind much of the conceptual aspect of the tragedy up to its closing scene.

The specific reference here is to man as a quintessence of dust. On a surface level this is nothing more than a dramatic reduction, in terms of crude mortality, of the great Renaissance image of man as a god which has just been evoked. However, the terms of that reduction are philosophically significant, for the Brunian vision of the universe denied the existence of the Aristotelian fifth-essence, or the ultimate refinement of matter which Aristotle had placed, in his hierarchical pattern, above the elemental spheres. Bruno's universe was seen as infinitely extended matter assuming infinite forms according to a process of eternal vicissitude: a vision which, considered from one point of view, ennobled man by conceding him a new autonomy and divinity as a shadow of the divine intelligence reflected in all things, while from another point of view it reduced all things, including man himself, to passing patterns in the eternal play of matter and form. Hamlet's paradoxical image of man as 'quintessence of dust' can be seen as a poetical expression of Bruno's philosophical concept. It was a vision of the universe which included in a general process of common vicissitude realities traditionally looked up to as higher expressions of purer and more spiritual being. The heavens themselves as crystalline spheres were one of those traditional realities. The other was woman, to whom Bruno's philosophy denies any less material existence than man himself. Bruno was quite aware of the crisis in traditional vision which his philosophy implied and laboured to present his new universe as more rich and varied and fine than the traditional one it replaced. The *Furori* is a development of precisely this theme. It starts with an introductory letter, again to Sir Philip Sidney, which adapts an anti-Petrarchan attitude, already present in sixteenth-century culture, to a reduction of woman, the poetical divinity, to a thoroughly flesh and blood phenomenon. Man too, with respect both to woman and to the universe as a whole, appears as little more than Hamlet's 'sterile promontory'. Through a long and complicated process built around the traditional Neoplatonic idea of love as an impetus towards new knowledge of being, Bruno then leads his reader to a final vision in which, through a pattern of music and dance, contemplative man perceives his identity as a part of the divinely ordered whole. It is not clear whether what we are faced with here is a divinization of the universe, or the first stage in its total materialization. The dilemma which was Bruno's was Hamlet's too, and it is significant that the great speech which terminates the Brunian core of the play introduces at the same time an aspect of his philosophy which is about to be picked up and developed, in later scenes, in particularly dramatic terms: the denial of that special divinity in woman which had been such a rich source of poetical and spiritual inspiration in European culture for so many centuries. 'Man delights not me – nor woman neither, though by your smiling you seem to say so'.

MEMORY AND THE CALM SPIRIT

Apart from urging Hamlet to revenge his murder, the Ghost is most remarkable for his insistence that Hamlet remember his visitation and his message: 'Adieu, adieu, adieu. Remember me'. It is in fact this aspect of the Ghost's visit which most strikes Hamlet himself:

> Remember thee?
> Ay, thou poor ghost, whiles memory holds a seat
> In this distracted globe. Remember thee?
> Yea, from the table of my memory
> I'll wipe away all trivial fond records,
> All saws and books, all forms, all pressures past
> That youth and observation copied there,

> And thy commandment all alone shall live
> Within the book and volume of my brain,
> Unmix'd with baser matter.[71]

When he swears to the Ghost to obey his command, it is not so much the command to revenge as that to remember which Hamlet emphasizes: 'Now to my word./ It is "Adieu, adieu, remember me". I have sworn it'.[72] And when the Ghost briefly reappears on the stage during Hamlet's scene with his mother, it is with a plea to remember him that he opens his speech: 'Do not forget'.[73]

The subject once again takes us to the text of Bruno's *Spaccio*, for of all his writings on memory, it is here that he most closely associates acts of memory with a movement towards universal reform. The subject is developed in a crucial passage which closes the first Dialogue. It is introduced by Mercury, traditionally associated with rhetoric, who has been describing to the earthly Sophia the initial stages of Jupiter's reform, which have already operated the return to the heavens of Truth, Prudence, and the Law. Delighted by such a 'renovatio', the earthly Sophia announces her intention of requesting Jupiter to sit in judgement against 'the great wrongs which have been done to me by divers sorts of men on earth'. Mercury promises to hand in her plea to the gods, but only if she will present it in writing, for a new command has been given that 'all decisions, whether civil or criminal, be registered in their place, including all their causes, means, and circumstances'. Such a new order, Mercury assures Sophia, will oblige the gods to exercise a true justice:

> for the registration which renders eternal the memory of acts will cause the gods to fear eternal shame, and to risk perpetual blame with the condemnation which is to be expected from the absolute justice which reigns above all rulers, and presides above the Gods.[74]

The careful registration of acts is thus seen as closely linked to the concept of Prudence who, in the new celestial order of Bruno's universe, sits next to the Law. But it is further connected to an even higher concept which is that of absolute justice or, as Bruno had called it earlier, 'the eye of eternal truth'. Memory of acts committed not only ensures a sense of history, seen as an aid to the formation of correct judgements on human conduct; but it submits that history to the larger, all-seeing 'eye' of an eternal and absolute justice. A similar idea lies behind the fact that it is the Ghost who, in Shakespeare's *Hamlet*, insists on the necessity to 'remember me'. Hamlet is thus enjoined not only to remember what, according to the Ghost's story of his death, had historically happened, but more importantly still to 'remember me': the spirit who has visited him from beyond the sphere of history with a message of absolute justice and eternal truth. Hamlet is perfectly aware of the sense of the Ghost's command, and accordingly writes on his tablet his 'word': 'It is "Adieu, adieu, remember me"./ I have sworn 't.'

In the *Spaccio*, Mercury's reference to the new command in heaven to proceed to the 'registration which eternalizes the memory of acts' is preceded by an account to the earthly Sophia of the kinds of acts which interest the gods. Mercury has been sent by them down to earth to Nola, Bruno's home town, where he has to check on a series of tiny, apparently unimportant facts which, in Bruno's fantasy in far-away London, are happening there: whether the melons in somebody's garden are ripening as they should, or whether Bruno's father's fruit trees have given thirty ripe fruit and let fall seven worm-eaten ones as the gods had decreed. Mercury's account of peasant life is related with an abundance of witty details which, in the structure of the Dialogue as a whole, create a delicate and lively parenthesis: a brilliant contrast to the grandiose acts of celestial politics which are the main theme of the work, and an ironic counterpoint to the aristocratic premises on which (symbolically in the figure of Bruno's protector, Sidney) the work is based. Yet, as Mercury points out to the surprised Sophia, his mission is not really a parenthesis, but rather an essential part of the gods' concern for the incessant and apparently inexplicable vicissitudes which make up the history of the universe. At this point Mercury launches into a speech which returns, in a context different from those we have so far examined, to Bruno's philosophical concept of the identity between the infinitely large and the infinitely small, the Maximum and the Minimum, the One and the Whole:

> Everything, then, however small, is under an infinitely great providence, every smallest and most vilely minute happening

is of the greatest importance within the order of the whole universe, because great things are composed of the small, the small of the smallest, and these of the individuals and minimums. In such a way I intend things of great substance, together with their great powers and effects.[75]

The sense in which Bruno's Mercury insists on the importance of 'eternalizing acts' in the places of memory clarifies the sense of the inner play of *Hamlet*. It is precisely the 'eternalizing' of his act within a play he is forced to watch which finally causes Claudius to 'fear eternal shame' as Bruno's Mercury had predicted for such cases. At the same time, the importance accorded by Hamlet to the actors, in spite of their being, within the order of the period, social 'minima' (thus arousing the indignation of Polonius) corresponds to the importance accorded to their function; for they, like Bruno's Mercury, are the 'abstract and brief chronicles of the time'.[76]

Following such reasoning, clearly it is not just the inner play which is linked to the function of memory. Rather the play as a whole becomes a complex memory system, chronicling the times and thus eternalizing their acts, submitting them to the eye of absolute justice and eternal truth. The theme opens the way to an expansion of the Brunian associations within the graveyard scene, for example, where we find one of Shakespeare's most intense meditations on the sense of death: the transformations of the dust of Alexander ('the dust is earth, of earth we make loam, and why of that loam whereto he was converted might they not stop a beer-barrel?').[77] Here we are clearly reminded of Bruno's treatment of death, particularly in the *Spaccio*, as part of a process of continual mutation and transformation. Within this process of eternal vicissitude, it is memory which creates a sense of time and order, leading to knowledge, and through knowledge to justice and truth. In this sense the skull of Yorick which sparks off Hamlet's meditations becomes a memory object or symbol in classical memory-tradition terms. Memory of the being whose lips had been kissed 'I know not how oft' and whose jibes, gambols, songs, flashes of merriment 'were wont to set the table on a roar' is conducted back to the object in Hamlet's hands, the rotting skull 'abhorred' in his imagination, giving him the measure of man's life and transience. At the same time the gravediggers, who literally offer Hamlet his memory 'object', may also be seen as 'minima' in the Brunian sense: figures of apparently little significance within the order of society of the times who nevertheless, with their earthly wit and their vulgar but acute philosophy of death, play an essential part in the vicissitudes of the story contributing in important ways to things of 'great substance, together with their great powers and effects'.

Yet of all the references to memory in the play, the most pregnant is Hamlet's own instructions given to Horatio with his dying breath. For in his last moments before death, Hamlet is above all possessed by the anxiety that his story should not be forgotten: that it should, in its entirety, be told or 'registered'; and he personally appoints his only true friend, Horatio, to perpetuate his memory:

> Absent thee from felicity awhile,
> And in this harsh world draw thy breath in pain
> To tell my story.[78]

The appointment of Horatio to this function could be surprising, for although his loyalty to Hamlet as a friend has been underlined throughout the drama, it has also been made clear that, especially with respect to Hamlet himself, his vision of things in its limited, sceptical rationality leaves him unaware of much that Hamlet is projected towards discovering and knowing. In fact when, at the end of the play, he accepts Hamlet's charge, he makes no claim to 'interpret' fully what he will tell (which is, of course, the play of *Hamlet* itself), but rather vouches, in his love for his friend, to 'record' his story faithfully, thus 'eternalizing' it, in Brunian terms, in the tables of universal memory which recall the eternal vicissitudes of time:

> So shall you hear
> Of carnal, bloody, and unnatural acts,
> Of accidental judgements, casual slaughters,
> Of deaths put on by cunning and forc'd cause,
> And, in this upshot, purposes mistook
> Fall'n on th' inventors heads. All this can I
> Truly deliver.[79]

The contrast which Shakespeare creates here may be considered as that between the philosopher (Hamlet's meditations, enquiries, and analyses indicate that he thinks of himself in such terms) and the historian in what is already a modern conception of the figure. In this context, Horatio's role appears as essentially connected to that of Hamlet himself, not in terms of a secondary function, but rather as complementary to the efforts of philosophy to penetrate beyond the appearances of reality into the inner truths of being.

One of the questions which the play poses is thus that of the ideal nature of this new narrator-historian. Shakespeare does not avoid the question; rather, he clarifies it in extremely specific terms through Hamlet's praise of Horatio just before the staging of the inner play. During its performance, significantly, Horatio becomes something more than the loyal and loved friend, starting a direct collaboration with Hamlet in the unmasking of the hidden truth. Horatio appears to Hamlet the ideal figure for this role for characteristics which we continue today to appreciate in the historian-narrator: his impartiality, his balanced independence of judgement, his calm rationality. Hamlet also heavily underlines the importance of Horatio's position as an independent observer with respect to the political intrigues of the Court, considering it an essential part of his worth as both friend and collaborator that he has kept himself financially independent of the prevailing power-complex as Rosencrantz and Guildenstern, for example, the paid spies, have not: 'no revenue/hast but thy good spirits/To feed and clothe thee' –

> Dost thou hear?
> Since my dear soul was mistress of her choice,
> And could of men distinguish her election,
> Sh' ath seal'd thee for herself; for thou hast been
> As one, in suffering all, that suffers nothing,
> A man that Fortune's buffets and rewards
> Hast ta'en with equal thanks; and blest are those
> Whose blood and judgement are so well commeddled,
> That they are not a pipe for Fortune's finger
> To sound what stop she please. Give me that man
> That is not passion's slave, and I will wear him
> In my heart's core, ay, in my heart of heart,
> As I do thee.[80]

Hamlet's choice of Horatio as friend, and later as recorder of his 'story', relates in interesting ways to the final section of the *Spaccio* where Bruno deals with the merits of what he calls 'the Calm Spirit'. Bruno too is developing here the final stages of his process of universal reform or 'renovatio' which take place in the third part of the heavens. The precise moment in which Bruno introduces the theme of the Calm Spirit is when Jupiter consults Neptune as to the correct way of dealing with the constellation known as the Cetus or the Maritime Monster. As usual Momus wants to have his say, and butts into the discussion to identify the Maritime Monster as a whale, associating it with the biblical story of Jonah. Jupiter accepts the connection with the Old Testament fable, and accordingly decides to send the Cetus off to Salonicca, a Greek town famous as a hospitable centre for the Jews and counting a large Jewish community. The question to be faced is then what kind of virtue to promote to the seat vacated by the Maritime Monster. It is here that Jupiter summons to the skies the virtue which he calls the Calm Spirit. The whale itself, Jupiter claims, may be associated with the idea of rest or calm, for 'when this animal makes its appearance above the high waves of a boiling and tempestuous sea, it announces the arrival of future calm, if not on that same day, at least on an approaching one'. This episode of the reform thus announces the coming end of the convulsive working out of the new order. But the virtues of the Calm Spirit are also considered by Bruno as important accompanying factors of the final stages of the reform itself:

> It is to be desired – said Jupiter – that this sovereign virtue, called Calmness of Spirit, appear in the heavens, as it is that which balances men against the upheavals of the world, renders them constant against the buffets of fortune, keeps them away from the care of governments, prevents them from pursuing every novelty, makes them of little annoyance to enemies and of little trouble to friends, quite untouched by pride or conceit, unperplexed by the vagaries of chance, not irresolute at the prospect of death.[81]

There are striking similarities between this speech of Jupiter's in praise of the Calm Spirit and Hamlet's praise of Horatio.

These similarities become even more striking if we examine them within their particular contexts. The importance of the episode in the *Spaccio* is due to the fact that it immediately precedes the discussion over the removal of Orion. It is through the symbol of Orion that Bruno represents the Christ figure in what he conceives as its oppressive historical function; and it is with the removal of Orion from the skies that Bruno's reform reaches its most provocative and dramatic climax, challenging the cultural and philosophical premises of the European cultures, both Catholic and Protestant, of his times. For it is Orion, in Bruno's view, who makes men believe

that white is black, that the human intellect, where it appears to see clearest, is in fact blind; and that what, according to reason, appears excellent, good, and wisest is in fact vile, wicked, and extremely bad; that nature is an insolent whore, the law of nature mere ribaldry; that nature and divinity cannot act together towards a single good end, and that the justice of one is not subordinate to the justice of the other, but that they are direct contraries, like shadows and light.[82]

It is debatable if *Hamlet* can be subjected to such a militantly anti-Christian interpretation, particularly in view of the muted and oblique theology of the play with respect to its evident and obtrusive political and historical dimensions. It is primarily in political or historical terms that Shakespeare develops his 'revenge tragedy' theme, transposing his northern-pagan source story into the context of a Renaissance Court dominated by an assassin-Prince as its familiar tyrant. The fact that the Prince claims a divine right in traditional theological as well as political terms is intimated but not insisted on, and anyway appears as a dimension of his 'Machiavellian' political realism rather than a genuine religious argument. There is no simple identity between Bruno's triumphant beast and Shakespeare's. There is, however, a remarkable identity in vision and development with respect to the fundamental movement of total reform; and it is this which applies in the case of the parallel between Bruno's Calm Spirit and the figure of Horatio. For he too appears in the story as a specifically defined character of Hamlet's particular choice in the moment previous to the unmasking, through the inner play, of the essential principle of confusion and deception in a negative-Silenus world: in this case the figure of Claudius, the tyrant.

It is thus the function both of the Calm Spirit and of Horatio, within their respective 'plays', to accompany, as a factor of balance and rationality, the moment of recognition of the triumphant beast, to be present through the inevitable catastrophe, but also to announce the coming end with the return of calm and silence. Their function in this sense is clearly related to elements of Stoical moral philosophy which are being picked up by both Bruno and Shakespeare. But more interesting and more complex is the relationship between the theme of the Calm Spirit and the biblical sources to which each writer relates it.

Bruno develops his reference to the book of Jonah in terms which demonstrate a rich but ambiguous use of biblical material.[83] For on the one hand the fable is ridiculed as such by Momus, while on the other the reference to the book of Jonah continues to run throughout this passage of the *Spaccio* adding to it multiple and complex meanings. For the corrupt city of Nineveh was not destroyed by the anger of the Lord as Jonah, carried there through the various vicissitudes of his dark journey in the bowels of the whale, had predicted. Jonah, who was expecting the city's destruction, was obliged to learn the patience associated with the Calm Spirit through the lesson of the gourd under which he was waiting to witness the catastrophe but which God caused to be shrivelled up by the action of a worm, thus exposing Jonah to the violent rays of the midday sun (see Plate 10). To the indignant Jonah, God explained that it was contradictory to be angry at the violent withering of the gourd and at the same time to be angry because the city, a far more precious object, had been saved through repentance. It must be enough to know that his prophecy had been the cause of the gradual return of the city to the ways of divine truth. The question which Bruno's biblical source allows him to raise here is thus the question of the *means* by which the total reform may be implemented: whether by an act of force and wrath, or through the patience of the Calm Spirit prepared to act within the revolutions of vicissitude and time. In the following pages of his text, the question becomes explicit in a discussion between

Plate 10 A sixteenth-century engraving of the prophet Jonah by Adamo Scultori (*c.* 1530–85) after Michelangelo. Reproduced by courtesy of the Istituto Nazionale per la Grafica, Rome, cat. no. F.C. 50647.

Minerva and Jupiter about the virtues which should succeed to the space vacated by Orion. The severe goddess warmly proposes the introduction of warlike exercise and the military art; for, she argues, wisdom is not sufficient in itself to convince a barbarian age corrupted by crime to return to civil living and humane conversation. It is necessary to persuade with 'the point of a lance'. To this argument, Jupiter opposes the virtues of patience and the Calm Spirit, making his own, within the terms of his different fable, the message of the biblical Jehovah. 'Wisdom is sufficient, my daughter, for such things. They wither of their own accord, fall and are devoured and digested by time, for they are things based on weak foundations.' However, Minerva sticks to her point, and although Jupiter's authority prevails, it is she who has the last word of the exchange: 'but in that while', said Pallas, 'there must be resistance and protestation, so that all things are not destroyed before we can reform them'.[84]

It is through tensions of a very similar kind that the final acts of *Hamlet* move to their resolution. In the play the tensions are represented by Fortinbras (military arts), Horatio (the Calm Spirit), and Hamlet himself (wisdom united to resistance and protestation with, when necessary, the point of a lance). Seen within the context of the kind of discussion which Bruno had developed around the theme of the Calm Spirit, it is possible to consider in terms based less on individual psychology and more on conflicts of ideas such crucial problems of the play as Hamlet's hesitations in front of the prospect of violent justice, his apparent indifference towards the deaths of Polonius or Guildenstern and Rosencrantz ('they are not near my conscience') which represent his 'point of a lance', and above all the increasing sense of patience and the waiting on time and Providence which dominate the final stages of the tragedy. The 'divinity that shapes our ends' and the 'special providence in the fall of a sparrow'[85] derive, as Bruno's meditations on the same theme did, from biblical sources, although Shakespeare's overt references are to the New rather than the Old Testament. This has sometimes been taken to indicate that the tragedy moves towards a peculiarly Protestant sense of predestination, particularly as the 'sparrow' passage from St Matthew 10:29 followed by the further echo of Matthew's 'Be ye also ready' (which becomes Hamlet's 'the readiness is all') were texts well known to have been particularly dear to Calvin. But the emphasis changes when we realize that these two New Testament echoes contain between them a passage which has been related to a quite non-Christian page of Bruno's *Candelaio*. We are at the end of his brief dedication to his play where he addresses a lady, named Morgana, outlining to her the essence of those things in which he believes but which he must refrain from teaching. The address culminates in an intense meditation on the meaning of the passage of time and the moment of death:

> Time takes away all and gives all, everything changes, nothing dies; only one is void of change, eternal, and can remain eternally one, like to itself. – With this philosophy my soul is enlarged and my intellect magnified. Yet, whatever be the moment of evening that I wait for [that is, the moment of death], if the mutation is true, I who am in the night wait for the day, and those who are in the day expect the night: *everything which is, either is here or there, either near or far, either now or to come, either early or late.*[86]

Hamlet's 'If it be now, 'tis not to come; if it be not to come, it will be now; if it be not now, yet it will come',[87] inserted between the two quotations from Matthew, suggests that Shakespeare is following a complex scheme of juxtapositions which allow the possibility of Christian interpretations of the play while leaving the way open for alternative philosophical visions of the divinity, time, and death. That such alternatives are not to be considered of marginal importance is further suggested by the fact that Hamlet, at the moment of death, shows no proper Christian concern for the fate of his soul or the nature of his after-life, but appears entirely preoccupied with the question of ensuring a correct recording of his story in words which will both illuminate the future ages of the world and satisfy Bruno's 'eye of eternal truth'. It is in this aspect of his ending that Shakespeare elaborates the theme of the Calm Spirit with masterly dramatic originality, allowing Horatio to emerge in the final sequence of the play as the voice of memory itself, appointed by Hamlet as the means of eternalizing his story within the perplexing vicissitudes of fortune and time.

Through the image of the whale, Bruno had connected the Calm Spirit with the completion of the drama of total reform: the return to universal justice and silence. Earlier on in the *Spaccio*, he had dwelt on the importance of eternalizing acts in memory, connecting this function with the figure of Mercury, traditionally associated with rhetoric. To Mercury, the gods gave the task of ascertaining the vicissitudes of time down to the barest minimums and also of recording those vicissitudes in the tables of memory. The particularly dramatic power of the final sequences of *Hamlet* derives from Shakespeare's brilliant perception of the identity of these two apparently dissimilar moments. For the whole concept of the Calm Spirit, as it had already been developed in the play around the balanced and dependable presence of Horatio through the drama of the 'renovatio', lends him a special weight and dignity at the moment of his final emergence as the voice of memory or history itself.

Bruno more than once describes the working out of the 'renovatio' in terms of the gradual creation of a work of art. In his 'Proprologo' to *Candelaio* he says of his own play: 'This is a kind of canvas whose order and weaving coincide'. And in his later philosophical works he uses the form of the dialogue with dramatic intensity, allowing the dilemmas and conflicts of an era to emerge through the clashes of a dramatic debate. In Shakespeare the 'play' is not only metaphor but 'the thing'. It is the play which catches the conscience of mankind, which reveals the intimate elements of corruption and which traces the course of the heroic intellect in its impetus towards 'renovatio', ending in death and silence. It is entirely appropriate that Horatio, the Calm Spirit who accompanies and counterbalances the heroic intellect through the convulsive process of moral, intellectual, and historical reform, should emerge at the end of that process as the voice of memory: the historian of the drama which has been played out. It is even more appropriate that he should announce his function as a theatrical undertaking:

> give order that these bodies
> High on a stage be placed to the view,
> And let me speak to th' yet unknowing world
> How these things came about.[88]

WORDS FOR POSTERITY

The circular ending of *Hamlet*, with its almost obsessive return to its own point of departure, signals the end of an epoch, the apocalyptic destruction of the Renaissance Court which had been, at its zenith, the brilliant centre of a new concept of man and his works, a new flourishing of his intelligence and his arts. Now bloodstained and corrupted, the villainous Prince has come to his deserved end, while the future cycle of history is left, perhaps deliberately, undefined. The answer to the question 'Who is Fortinbras?' is made over to the coming times. The new Prince will reveal his nature to the new century which, for the Shakespeare of *Hamlet*, seems to begin in anger at the betrayal of past ideals rather than hope for the future to come.

The new century would in fact move away from both Bruno and Shakespeare, not forgetting them but losing much of the sense of their complex messages in which the enquiring intellect always plays a primary part, but permeated with the impetus of the passions and the visions of the imagination. For with all their interest in human reason (an interest which was almost a faith), neither Bruno nor Shakespeare were spirits of the Enlightenment. Their sense of myth and of the symbolic quality of the material world, their insistence on the creative powers of the mind, their complex sense of forms of language which move in indirect, circular or even more complicated patterns towards ultimate forms of truth which continually elude the human mind make of them exponents of the Renaissance imagination rather than the Enlightened reason. It is no coincidence if a rediscovery of their works in their manifold layers and meanings starts with the advent of Romanticism, with its revaluation of the creative powers of the imagination and its vision of human history as a dynamic force of human making. In the course of the nineteenth century both Bruno and Shakespeare would become standard-bearers of a new ideal of liberty – intellectual, political, and artistic – assuming the role not just of great artists and thinkers, but also of figure-heads of special significance in the progress of man towards a fuller freedom and completion. On a philological level, which is clearly a consequence of this new enthusiasm, it is in the nineteenth century that we find both the first modern critical editions of Shakespeare (a watershed being Furness's New Variorum Edition) and the first editions ever of Bruno's works since their original publication. Yet often, in both cases, the enthusiasm and editorial activity which increasingly surrounded their work was less well matched by a careful and documented investigation into the overall substance of their messages. What still appeared as their more abstruse aspects, such as their references to magic or the art of memory, their ideas on language, or their use of myth, were often misunderstood or ignored.[89]

Perhaps it is rather to our own day that both men speak with a particular relevance: to a civilization which is predominantly scientific, but which in its post-Einsteinian enquiries is becoming increasingly aware of the relativity of its own scientific truths, of the uncertain frontiers and continually changing patterns of human knowledge itself; to an age which is gradually understanding what Bruno and Shakespeare knew so well, that the human intelligence creates continually and then destroys to recreate in different shapes and modes its intuitions – metaphysical, scientific, and artistic – of an absolute truth which remains beyond the borders of the languages man is capable of elaborating; above all to an age aware, as Bruno and Shakespeare were so acutely, of its own profound historical crisis, the sense of living with much that has perhaps been noble, but with time and betrayal has become antiquated and rotten, consumed in the armed conflicts and ideological contrasts of a bloodstained and confused century; while the emergence of a new cycle and new values remains, like the ambiguous figure of Fortinbras, shadowy and undefined. The Renaissance drama of knowledge which this book has attempted to study and define through the influence of Giordano Bruno on the English culture of the time is a historical phenomenon of the end of the sixteenth and beginning of the seventeenth centuries. Yet the way it was lived through and expressed by the figures considered in these pages makes such a study useful, perhaps, and relevant to our own crises, our own intellectual uncertainties and debates.

APPENDIX I 'SAXON BRUNO'

There is a possible piece of evidence of a direct reference to Bruno in the text of *Dr Faustus*. This occurs in the so-called B-text among the episodes of Faustus's anti-papal jokes in the much-debated central scenes of the play. Here we find the appearance, with the name of 'Saxon Bruno', of an anti-Pope, appointed by the Emperor, who goes to Rome in an attempt to conquer the papal throne. The Pope succeeds in humiliating him and imprisons him in Castel Sant'Angelo from which Faustus's magic rescues him and sends him back to Germany 'on a furies back'. The source for this episode has been traced to John Foxe's *Acts and Monuments* where the humiliation of the anti-Pope, Victor IV, at the hands of Pope Alexander III is related in words almost identical to those used in the B-text of *Dr Faustus* (see Leslie M. Oliver, 'Rowley, Foxe, and the Faustus additions', in *Modern Language Notes*, LX, 1945, pp.391-4). In the earliest discussion I know of tracing an influence of Bruno on *Dr Faustus*, E.G. Clark claims that the name in the play was intended to permit a reference to Giordano Bruno who could be considered a 'Saxon' Bruno on the strength of his relationship with the German academies, in particular with Wittemberg where Marlowe's Faustus begins and ends his story (see Eleanor G. Clark, *Ralegh and Marlowe: a Study in Elizabethan Fustian*, New York, 1941, Chapter 18, 'Atheism and the Bruno scandal in *Dr Faustus*', pp.338–89).

The suggestion has had little following among Marlowe's critics, although some commentators, like Harry Levin, are prepared to concede that the reference was 'possibly in honour of Giordano Bruno' (see *Christopher Marlowe: The Overreacher*,

London, 1954, p.142). More recently, the question has been discussed once again by R.T. Eriksen who makes the interesting suggestion that the 'furies' who carry Saxon Bruno back to Germany are intended as a direct reference to the *Heroici furori*, where the heroical frenzies are sometimes compared to the torments inflicted by the mythical furies (see 'Giordano Bruno and Marlowe's *Doctor Faustus* B', *Notes and Queries*, December 1985, pp.463–5).

Eriksen's further assumption that the reference was made by Marlowe himself, or at least authorized by him, depends on Greg's proposal of an early date for the B-text (1592–3: see W.W. Greg, *Marlowe's Dr Faustus 1604–1616: Parallel Texts*, Oxford, 1950, pp. vii–viii). To justify this suggestion, Eriksen points out that Bruno was arrested in Venice in May 1592, the likely year of composition of *Dr Faustus*: 'the news about Bruno's imprisonment may well have prompted Marlowe to insert the episode with the mock-trial and the escape of "Saxon Bruno" into his play'.

Although I believe it is possible that the news of Bruno's arrest and imprisonment sparked off Marlowe's final tragedy, it seems unlikely that the Saxon Bruno episode was written by Marlowe himself. Bowers's recent arguments against Greg's textual suppositions seem to be valid, for they take into account the evident inferiority in the level of dramatic and poetic writing of episodes such as these with respect to the indisputed Marlovian parts of the play (see n. 2 to Chapter 4). The fact that this episode is the only one in the play to depend on a source outside the *Faust-book* also suggests that it represents an addition with respect to the main text. Bowers places it among the Rowley-Birde additions which it is known, on documentary evidence, were made in 1602. This date would justify the unexpected emphasis placed on Castel Sant'Angelo as the dreaded papal prison in a text which ignores the other monuments in Rome. Bruno, it must be remembered, was arrested on 23 May 1592, in Venice, where the first part of his trial took place. The final hearing of the Venetian part of the trial was held on 30 July 1592, followed by a complicated administrative process which led to his extradition and transfer to Rome where he arrived on 27 February 1593. Marlowe died in London on 1 June 1593, only three months later, so that on his part it would have been a very last minute insertion.

If, on the other hand, as Bowers conjectures, this scene was written in 1602, it is probable that the author was making a direct reference to Bruno's long Roman imprisonment, and to his death on 17 February 1600. But the tone of the passage, in the context of the magical tricks and practical jokes of the central Roman scenes of the drama, seems to make of the reference something less than a memorial 'in honour of Giordano Bruno'. Rather it appears as a deliberate reduction of his name and reputation in the light of what is clearly, at this point of the play, a negative presentation of Faustus himself and the sense of his intellectual enquiry. But why bring Bruno into the picture at all? Was there, perhaps, in some lost Marlovian original of the central part of the play, a direct reference to Bruno in quite different terms which it was thought prudent, in those dark years of the turning century, to substitute with what is basically a sneer at his memory? In the present uncertainty of the textual status of this part of the play, and the unlikelihood of new documentary evidence emerging to solve the problem, such a question seems bound to remain without an answer. All that can be said is that the 'Saxon Bruno' scene does appear to be making a direct reference to the Italian philosopher, and that it was almost certainly written after his Roman imprisonment, and his death at the stake, by an author other than Marlowe who appears to be presenting him in an unfavourable light.

APPENDIX II BRUNO-SHAKESPEARE CRITICISM

The following bibliographical survey is composed of a chronological description, with a few personal considerations, of the
main critical contributions to the Bruno-Shakespeare relationship, with particular reference to *Hamlet*. The discussion of this
relationship develops in three main phases, in its initial stages
largely outside the sphere of English culture. It starts and for
half a century continues in Germany followed, though in more
hesitant tones, by Italy. In recent years, in the wake of the
influential Yatesian interpretation of Bruno in Hermetic terms,
it has made a limited entry into English Shakespearian criticism
with reference, above all, to the occult or magical elements in
Shakespearian drama.

Christian Bartholmess, *Jordano Bruno*, Paris, 1846, 2 vols

Bruno's first serious biographer makes a number of references
to a possible relationship with Shakespeare, both in vol.I, *Vie*,
and in vol. II, *Travaux*. They are, however, only passing
references relegated to the notes. On p. 352 of vol. II, note 2
refers to the text of *Hamlet*, IV. iii and V. i on the theme of vicissitude and the sense of death as a process of passage from one
state to another. Hamlet's meditations on death in this sense are
put in relation to the Second Dialogue of Bruno's *De la causa*
where he traces the passage of animated matter through the
seed to the grain of corn, bread, blood, animal seed, embryo,
man, carcass, earth, and once again vegetation. This parallel will
be frequently taken up and developed throughout the nineteenth century by the German critics interested in the relationship.

Ferdinand Falkson, *Giordano Bruno*, Hamburg, 1846

In the same year as Bartholmess's biography, Falkson published in Germany his study of Bruno which suggests in the text itself (p. 289) a parallel between Bruno's thought on matter and the same scenes in *Hamlet* (IV. iii and V. i) as those indicated by the French scholar. The coincidence seems strange enough to suggest that both may have been referring to some preceding source which I have been unable to trace. What appears clearly from these early references is a primary interest in Bruno's vitalistic concept of matter in its continual process of transformation which is clearly stimulated by similar philosophical and scientific concepts being developed during this period.

Moriz Carrière, *Die philosophische Weltanschauung der Reformationzeit*, Stuttgart und Tübingen, 1848, p. 446

In his section on the philosophy of Bruno, during a discussion of the Italian dialogues written in London, Carrière draws attention to the affinity between passages in *De l'infinito* where Bruno describes the travail of nature in the moments of tension between matter and form, and a passage from *1 King Henry IV*, III. i. 27–33:

> Diseased nature often times breaks forth
> In strange eruptions: oft the teeming earth
> Is with a kind of colic pinch'd and vex'd
> By the imprisoning oft unruly wind
> Within her womb; which, for enlargement striving,
> Shakes the old beldame earth, and topples down
> Steeples, and moss-grown towers.

Carrière's status as a highly respected historian of philosophy lent considerable weight to his textual parallel, which is referred to by both Beyersdorff (see pp. 172–4) and Croce (see pp. 178–9), although both were intent on proving the differences rather than the similarities between Bruno's and Shakespeare's thought.

Benno Tschischwitz, *Shakespeare Forschungen*, Halle, 1868

In a long section dedicated to Bruno and *Hamlet* Tschischwitz calls attention to the philosophical crisis caused by the gradual acceptance of the Copernican theory, and to the importance of Bruno as a thinker who developed a new philosophy around a pantheistic concept of the universe which would influence more modern philosophers such as Spinoza and Leibniz. He underlines the importance of Bruno's visit to England, and the publication in London of his Italian dialogues which were read by the most distinguished minds of the time. Memory of Bruno was not erased by his departure in 1586 (the date is erroneous: Bruno left England in the autumn of 1585) but was kept alive by a number of English scholars who followed him to Wittemberg, such as Fynes Moryson who was there in 1590–2 and would have heard of Bruno's lectures there. Hamlet, who is supposed to have studied at Wittemberg, is portrayed more as a student of the Elizabethan period than a Prince of ancient Denmark. Tschischwitz does not see Shakespeare as wanting to reproduce Bruno's thought as a system, but rather as wanting to present Hamlet as an intellectual familiar with abstract thought: a mind which has climbed the highest peaks of thought of his time. Tschischwitz supports this thesis by a densely packed series of parallels, some of them referring to other Shakespearian works, but most of them to *Hamlet*. Apart from a number of important particular parallels, Tschischwitz stresses the numerous echoes in *Hamlet* of Bruno's atomic philosophy of matter, in particular in Hamlet's meditations on death. He also develops an interesting discussion of Bruno's cultural pedants in relation to Shakespeare's portrait of Polonius.

This study represents the most extended, detailed, and frequently quoted discussion of the Bruno-Hamlet relationship to appear in the nineteenth century.

Wilhelm König, 'Shakespeare und Giordano Bruno', in *Shakespeare Jahrbuch*, XI, 1876

König's essay refers to all the works of Shakespeare and not *Hamlet* in particular, although this play is often singled out as one in which Shakespeare shows himself interested and well prepared in philosophy. Tschischwitz's study is used and quoted with approval. The biography by Domenico Berti, *La vita di Giordano Bruno*, Turin 1868, is also used for the details of Bruno's English experience and the links with English culture which he formed there. Following Berti, König claims that Hamlet would have been a student at Wittemberg when Bruno was teaching there. Although König does not think it possible to ascertain how far Shakespeare was influenced by Bruno's thought as compared with others, like Montaigne, who also certainly influenced him, he is convinced that Bruno's Italian dialogues published in London (which he lists and comments on, p. 107) were important for Shakespeare's thought. König then goes on to develop three main arguments:

1 the influence on Shakespeare of Bruno's atomic-materialist philosophy, particularly in his vision of death (pp. 108–26);
2 the influence of Bruno's drama, *Candelaio*, on numerous aspects of Shakespeare's dramas (pp. 127–34);
3 the influence of the poetry of the *Heroici furori* on Shakespeare's sonnets (pp. 135–7).

König concludes that Shakespeare does not take Bruno as his only or even his ultimate philosophical model, but he can find no other poet or thinker among his contemporaries, or even earlier, who had a greater influence on his cultural formation.

H.H. Furness (ed.) *Hamlet*, New Variorum Edition (1877), republished New York, 1963, vol. II, pp. 331–2

In his Appendix to his edition of Shakespeare's text, in which he gives a panorama of the main critical developments to his day, Furness offers a brief summary of Tschischwitz drawing particular attention to the textual parallels indicated by the German critic. Furness himself, however, is sceptical: 'To me this similarity of phrases, or of the principles of philosophy is of the faintest. More importance might attach to it had Shakespeare written no play but *Hamlet*; and if we did not know that he was myriad-minded' (p. 332). A year earlier König's essay had in fact undermined the last part of Furness's objections by extending the arguments of Tschischwitz, which primarily regarded *Hamlet*, to many of Shakespeare's other works, and also by stressing that to suggest the influence of Bruno did not mean excluding the possibility of other influences. However, König's essay was never translated into English, and Furness's edition, which is still consulted by modern editors and scholars, must have had a dampening effect on the reception in the English-speaking world of the Shakespeare-Bruno hypothesis.

Robert Prolss, 'Shakespeare, Montaigne und Giordano Bruno', *Shakespeare's Hamlet*, Leipzig, 1878, pp. 222–31

In a chapter of his book which discusses together the influence on Shakespeare of Montaigne and Bruno, Prolss expresses his conviction that 'the enthusiastic Nolan dreamer' with his profoundly serious and at the same time provocatively satirical Italian dialogues must have attracted the British playwright. He then offers a scrupulous summary of the main parallels adduced by Tschischwitz, which he appears to find interesting and convincing although 'exaggerated'. Prolss accepts the validity of the relationship although he prefers to think of it as influencing Hamlet's general behaviour and attitudes towards a corrupted Court rather than depending on the particular echoes and parallels pointed out by Tschischwitz. Like most of the German critics interested in the relationship, Prolss gives particular importance to Hamlet's links with Wittemberg in the light of Bruno's important stay there in the late 1580s.

I. Frith, *Life of Giordano Bruno, the Nolan*, London, 1887, Chapter V, pp. 104–7

In the first English biography of Bruno, Frith refers to the theory of a Shakespeare-Bruno relationship with moderate interest. The works of Falkson and Tschischwitz are quoted as having first given rise to the idea and most of the main textual parallels proposed in these works are referred to. The doubts voiced by Furness are also reported without being fully accepted.

Robert Beyersdorff, 'Giordano Bruno und Shakespeare', *Shakespeare Jahrbuch*, X, 1888

Beyersdorff's long and at times repetitive essay develops a heavy attack on the theses advanced by Tschischwitz and König. In the first part of the essay the arguments used are mainly external to the texts themselves. It is emphasized that little is known of Shakespeare's education, which was not a formal one. He absorbed his ideas from the people he met and conversed with, and was not a philosopher but a poet. Beyersdorff concludes that he is more likely to have been influenced by other literary works such as Montaigne's *Essays* (1580, Florio's English translation, 1603) or Lyly's *Anatomy of Wit* than by a philosopher like Bruno. He points out that it is doubtful if Shakespeare ever met Bruno, and that anyway they moved in different and at times rival circles, Bruno being linked to Sidney as a patron and Shakespeare to Southampton. He is further doubtful if Shakespeare would have had good enough Italian to read Bruno's difficult and complex dialogues. As far as Bruno is concerned, Beyersdorff doubts if his influence persisted in London after his departure, for he left no philosophical school behind him and was only of real importance for his fight against the Aristotelian-Ptolemaic world system. Beyersdorff further contends that Bruno's stay in London was a relatively unimportant episode, as is proved by the fact that no contemporary documents refer to him, while his books circulated in very small numbers (these last considerations have been largely disproved by modern research: see the relevant information given in *Bib. Salvestrini* and *Bib. Sturlese*).

Coming to the texts, Beyersdorff doubts if Shakespeare knew the *Candelaio* and is sceptical of its influence on him. He finds the various parallels proposed by Tschischwitz and König unconvincing and only apparently similar. The similarity claimed between Bruno's pedants and Polonius is particularly criticized on the grounds that the pedant was a stock figure of fun in the literature of the time, and that Shakespeare was more likely to have chosen models from English texts such as the Old Man in Lyly's *Euphues*. More generally, Beyersdorff emphasizes the differences between Bruno's philosophy and Shakespeare's thought, and particularly between the cynicism and world-weariness of Hamlet and Bruno's more optimistic pantheism. He considers Hamlet's meditations on death to be supported by a purely materialistic philosophy which he sees as quite different from Bruno's particular form of animistic atomism. Beyersdorff concludes that the arguments used by Tschischwitz and König to prove Bruno's influence on Shakespeare are based on a misunderstanding of the Italian's philosophy, which is discussed in the final pages of the essay with ample references to most of his major works, both in Italian and in Latin.

Beyersdorff's essay represents a powerful and authoritative attack on the Bruno-Shakespeare thesis. In the absence of any objective proof that Shakespeare knew, or did not know, Bruno's works, it nevertheless rests ultimately on a question of interpretation. This was not always recognized, and in the following half-century or more a number of scholars, some of them distinguished, considered Beyersdorff's contribution as having 'proved' that the Shakespeare-Bruno parallel is a groundless one. Today a new and more flexible approach to the whole question of cultural influences, added to many new developments in the study of both Shakespeare and Bruno, deprive Beyersdorff's arguments of much of their authority. Even so, a modern scholar venturing into the uncertain territory of Bruno's thought with respect to Shakespeare does well to bear Beyersdorff's detailed and at times penetrating study in mind.

Ruggiero Bonghi, in *La cultura*, X, Rome, 1889, pp. 541–2

The first extended Italian comment on the question of a Bruno-Shakespeare relationship appears in the form of a review of Beyersdorff's negative study of the question. Bonghi is in total agreement with Beyersdorff's negative thesis. The arguments of Tschischwitz and König are presented as useless 'soap bubbles' which Beyersdorff has happily burst. Bonghi makes no attempt to enter into the field himself, or to offer a comment of his own apart from his enthusiastic endorsement of every aspect of Beyersdorff's study which, he claims, is to be considered completely persuasive.

George Brandes, *William Shakespeare: a Critical Study*, London, 1898, 2 vols (first published Copenhagen 1895)

Bruno's influence on *Hamlet* is discussed by Brandes in the second volume of his book with reference to the work of Tschischwitz, König, and Beyersdorff. Brandes does not appear to have a first-hand knowledge of Bruno's work. His attitude to the relationship is on the whole sceptical although he allows that certain passages of Bruno's, in particular on fortune and on the theme of vicissitude and the negation of death, are close to some of Hamlet's meditations. In particular the parallels suggested between the 'fall of a sparrow' passage in *Hamlet*, V, and Bruno's 'tutto quel ch'è o è qua o là' in his dedication to *the Candelaio*, as well as the theme of relativity of moral judgements, seem to Brandes to carry some conviction. He is also convinced by the links, developed in particular by König, between some of Bruno's ideas and Shakespeare's sonnets. He ends up, however, by judging the influence of Montaigne to be more direct and central than that of Bruno.

J.M. Robertson, *A History of Freethought Ancient and Modern*, London, 1899

In vol. II, Chapter XIII of his *History*, where he discusses the rise of modern free-thought, Robertson gives extensive and sympathetic treatment to Bruno, particularly in his account of the rise of modern scientific thought where Bruno is considered together with Copernicus, Vanini, Galileo, Vives, Ramus, Descartes, and Gassendi. His influence on Elizabethan culture, both scientific and literary, is recognized as probably extensive, although Robertson advances some reserves on the literary influence which he will develop in his later study of Shakespeare and Montaigne (see pp. 176–7).

O. Elton, 'Giordano Bruno in England'

Elton's essay was first published in the *Quarterly Review*, 196, October 1902, pp. 483–508, as a review of a number of works on Bruno including Beyersdorff's. The same essay in an expanded and revised form was republished in the volume *Modern Studies* in 1907. This final version is divided into sections, the first five of which discuss the nature of Bruno's thought and the story of his stay in England. The sixth section raises the important question of the silence of English records concerning Bruno's stay and rapidly reviews the question of his influence on Shakespeare and Spenser, as well as the few allusions to be found in seventeenth-century English writers. The final section discusses briefly eighteenth-century interest in Bruno centred on the figure of John Toland. The essay as a whole is to be regarded as a finely written and authoritative contribution to the study of Bruno in England, complementing the more factual biographical account offered in the same years by J. Lewis McIntyre in his book *Giordano Bruno*, 1903, pp. 21–47. Unfortunately the weakest part of the whole essay is represented by the few pages of comment on the Bruno-Shakespeare relationship (pp. 26–8) in which Elton simply refers approvingly to Beyersdorff's negative judgement of the whole question without adding any personal contribution of his own.

J. Lewis McIntyre, *Giordano Bruno*, London, 1903

On p. 34 of his book, McIntyre dismisses the idea of a Bruno-Shakespeare relationship as 'entirely fanciful'. He supports this view with references to Beyersdorff, Furness, and Elton who, in McIntyre's opinion, succeed in completely demolishing the theses of Tschischwitz and König. Although McIntyre makes no direct contribution to the discussion, his adoption of a negative attitude is to be considered particularly influential in view of the high esteem in which his book was for long held, particularly as regards questions relating to Bruno in England. It is frequently quoted by Italian scholars such as the first editor of Bruno's Italian dialogues, Giovanni Gentile, and by Benedetto Croce (see p. 178).

J.M. Robertson, *Montaigne and Shakespeare*, London, 1909

In Chapter V, 'Shakespeare and Bruno', Robertson here follows Beyersdorff in a violent attack on the theses of Tschischwitz. His sympathetic attitude to Bruno expressed in his *History of Freethought* (see p. 175) is completely overturned in what appears to be a fundamental conviction that any concession to the Shakespeare-Bruno thesis would invalidate his argument in favour of an influence of Montaigne. No new concrete arguments are developed, however, and it is never made clear why

Shakespeare could not have read and admired both Bruno and Montaigne except on the basis of Robertson's unproved claim that he was unable to read any foreign language. Florio's translation of Montaigne thus makes the work of the Frenchman available to him, while the lack of English translations of Bruno destroys any credibility in the Bruno- Shakespeare thesis.

P. Orano, *Amleto è Giordano Bruno?* Lanciano, 1916

The first Italian work to give extended treatment to the Bruno-Shakespeare relationship was written, as the author himself reveals in his opening pages, by a nephew of Domenico Berti, the first Italian biographer of Bruno. Berti himself had mentioned the possibility of a Shakespeare-Bruno relationship with extreme caution, referring to what seemed to him basic differences, which he omitted to define, between the thought of Shakespeare and that of Bruno. Orano at once announces his intention of defying his uncle's caution. Unfortunately he proceeds to develop his subject in over-dramatic and at times almost frenzied terms which soon reveal an exalted sense of national pride in Bruno's Mediterranean 'Latinity' which he is anxious to present as the main, if not exclusive, germ and inspiration of Shakespeare's genius. In doing so he manages to arrive at an ingenuous equation of 'identity' between the figure of Hamlet and that of Bruno. Throughout the work no proper distinction is maintained, either in the case of Bruno or of Shakespeare, between author and work; or, more strangely in a nephew of Berti, between biographical facts and convenient fictions. A number of textual parallels are proposed, but the most convincing remain those already put forward by Tschischwitz, who is acknowledged by Orano. He appears not to have known, or preferred to ignore, the later stages of the German controversy. This strange, confused hotchpotch of ideas, which does little to credit a serious hypothesis of a Bruno-Shakespeare relationship, was nevertheless noticed by Sir Isaac Gollancz who included a rather more sober two-page summary, prepared by Orano himself, in his *A Book of Homage to Shakespeare*, 1916, published to celebrate the 300th anniversary of Shakespeare's death.

Thomas Whittaker, 'Shakespeare and the world order'. *The Hibbert Journal*, XVII, April 1919, pp. 473–9

Whittaker's essay is a discussion of Bradley's book on Shakespearian tragedy and Robertson's on Shakespeare and Montaigne (see. p. 176). The discussion picks up the subject of a possible influence of Bruno on contemporary English literature already mentioned (although with reference to Spenser's *Cantos on Mutability* rather than to Shakespeare) in his *Essays and Notices: Philosophical and Psychological*, London, 1895. Whittaker repeats his observation already made in this earlier work that 'it is often difficult to decide between a possible influence from Bruno and the influence of Renaissance Platonism on Bruno and his English contemporaries alike'. In this later essay Whittaker tends to play down Robertson's enthusiasm for a wide influence of Montaigne, whom he sees as a Lucretian materialist, so not the particular influence on Shakespeare that Robertson claimed. Bruno on the contrary is considered as near to Shakespeare's thought on the relation of nature to art: 'here nature becomes again divine because living with a life that includes the life of man'.

Benedetto Croce, 'Shakespeare, Napoli e la commedia napoletana dell'arte', *La critica*, XVII, 1919

In a brief article so entitled, Croce, in his most brilliant vein, advances the thesis that Shakespeare's comedy, and in particular *The Tempest*, contains elements of the Neapolitan 'commedia dell'arte'. In his opening page, Croce at once denies the necessity that this idea involves any reference to Bruno as 'Neapolitan philosopher'. He recognizes the attraction of the idea that Shakespeare, particularly in his creation of *Hamlet*, was indebted to Bruno's works; but is not prepared to concede to what he calls the 'Bruno-hypothèse' any serious credit. Croce is, needless to say, well versed in the critical history of the discussion, He refers to all the major sources from Carrière to Beyersdorff, accepting without qualification the negative thesis of the latter. Croce supports this position with reference to Brandes, Furness, and Elton, without himself entering directly into the discussion. He maintains that the negative position with respect to the Bruno thesis is at that time the generally accepted one. In a long note (p. 255) or digression with respect to his main argument, Croce bitterly attacks the book of Orano, whom he describes as a well-known Italian purveyor of nonsense, who presents the theses of others as his own to the admiration of an ignorant public. In the final note of his essay (p. 263), Croce nevertheless returns to the 'Bruno-hypothèse' to remark on the similarity between the name of Berowne in *Love's Labour's Lost* and the name of Bruno, claiming that references in Shakespeare's works to the anecdotes of Bruno's London life are more likely than references to his philosophy. He, however, leaves to 'another and better researcher' the task of following up such references – a challenge which will be later picked up by Frances Yates in her first book dealing with Shakespeare and Bruno in which she acknowledges the suggestions made in Croce's essay (see p. 182).

Giuseppe Toffanin, *La fine dell'umanesimo*, Padua, 1920

A discussion in rather different terms from those so far considered: Toffanin, a distinguished professor of Italian literature of a militant Catholic persuasion, is more concerned with establishing a relationship between Bruno and Shakespeare in general theological and philosophical terms than with tracing textual parallels or precise influences. He starts off from Orano's thesis, which he says much excited him, in order to bend it to his own interests, claiming that Shakespeare did not portray Hamlet as Bruno, but rather as a disciple of Bruno's whose tragedy is precisely that of having been led astray by Bruno's pagan and immoral 'furies'. Toffanin sees Hamlet's dilemma as an internal struggle between the logic of his thought, which leads him into forms of frenzied rebellion against the established political and religious orthodoxy, and a fine moral sensitivity which leads him to satirize and repent of his choice of Brunian metaphysical and ethical assumptions. To support his thesis, Toffanin claims, on the basis of the play's references to purgatory and the divine decree against suicide, that Shakespeare himself was a Catholic. Rather than a tragedy, Toffanin sees *Hamlet* as a kind of morality play, or dramatic illustration of the dangers of Bruno's heretical ideas. Shake-speare thus becomes a major representative of Toffanin's title, 'The end of humanism', by demonstrating the tragic conse-quences of the loss of a Christian faith and ethic, which, throughout his work, Toffanin considered as a central compo-nent of the true humanistic movement. It is interesting to notice the points of contact between this thesis and T.S. Eliot's irritated reaction against Hamlet's supposedly 'adolescent' rebelliousness in his famous essay on the play. Both these discussions are products not just of the same historical period, but of similar religious and political stances of 'high orthodoxy'.

Giuseppe di Lorenzo, *Shakespeare e il dolore nel mondo*, Bologna, 1921

Di Lorenzo's book, which offers a wide and at times intelligent panorama of Shakespeare's works, makes frequent mention of Bruno throughout, although the most extended reference is in the chapter on *Hamlet.* Here the connection with Wittemberg is particularly underlined through a reference to Hamlet's evo-cation of the pains of life in the 'To be or not to be' monologue ('the whips and scorns of time, the proud man's contumely', etc.) in the light of Bruno's *Oratio valedictoria*, pronounced at Wittemberg on the eve of his departure, where he complains of 'the whips and scorns of vile and foolish men who, although they are really beasts in the likeness of men, in the pride of their good fortune, are full of evil arrogance'. Other references include some interesting remarks on Falstaff as a comic character in the light of Bruno's comic techniques in *the Candelaio*, and also references to some of Shakespeare's major meditative charac-ters, such as Prospero, in the light of the dedicatory poem of the *De monade* where Bruno claims that the true sage does not climb into the dim sky aided by external forces such as the wings, fire, wind, clouds, spirit, etc., imagined by prophets, but, if he will allow himself to be guided by Bruno's counsel, ascends the stair securely erected within his own breast. Also underlined is Shakespeare's and Bruno's harsh treatment of the vulgar mob. The author makes no references to the German or the Italian history of the Bruno-Shakespeare thesis, but as he evidently knew and admired Brandes's book he must have heard of the critical discussion. He appears to know Bruno first-hand and his parallels are often original. He may be approaching the subject with an unusual slant as he was producing work in the same period on Buddhist philosophy.

Vincenzo Spampanato, *Vita di Giordano Bruno*, Messina, 1921; and *Il candelaio di G. Bruno*, in *Opere italiane*, vol. III, Bari, 1923

Bruno's chief biographer could hardly ignore the possibility of a direct relationship with Shakespeare which he discusses on pp. 357–60 of his biography and again two years later in his introduction to the play *Il candelaio*, pp. lxi–lxiii. On both occasions Spampanato carefully weighs the evidence for and against as it had been emerging in Bruno criticism, opting in the end for a cautious interest similar to Croce's although, unlike Croce, he makes no original suggestions of his own and proposes no new textual parallels. In the biography Spampanato is particularly concerned to distance himself both from the conservative Catholicism of Toffanin and from the foggy idealism of Orano. However, in very general terms he expresses his conviction that some kind of reference to Bruno on the part of Shakespeare must be presumed: 'it is unthinkable that the Elizabethan playwright, a friend of Giovanni Florio's, completely ignored the life and works of a man who had excited the admiration and also the indignation of the highest and most cultured parts of contemporary London society'.

Piero Rebora, *L'Italia nel dramma inglese*, Milan, 1925

Rebora makes a number of references to Bruno and to his general influence on English culture, a problem which he defines as fascinating. In his discussion of *Hamlet* he dedicates several pages to the Bruno thesis, claiming that it represents one of the most interesting and important recent contributions to critical discussion of Shakespeare. But then he appears unable to take the subject any further, probably because he is overawed by the negative standpoints not so much of Beyersdorff as of Elton on the English front and Croce on the Italian. However, he is not particularly enthusiastic about the Berowne-Bruno suggestion put forward by Groce, preferring the thesis of an influence of Bruno on Ben Jonson's comedy, in particular of the *Candelaio* on *The Alchimist*.

Frances A. Yates, *A Study of 'Love's Labour's Lost'*, Cambridge, 1936

Here Frances Yates makes her first attempt to link her work on Bruno, already developed through her researches into the figure of Florio, with Shakespearean drama. The approach is one which underlines Bruno's stay in London and the presence in the play of continual contemporary references to Florio and the circles in which he moved through the satire directed against the figure of Holofernes who is identified with Florio: in this sense the discussion picks up the suggestion made by Croce and his hypothesis that Berowne could be a synonym of Bruno (see p. 179). What is envisaged is an interpretation of the drama as anti-Brunian and anti-Copernican satire which includes the suggestion that Shakespeare may have been a Catholic sympathizer. Chapter V on 'Bruno and the School of Night' approaches Bruno through Florio's dialogues of the *Second Fruits* (1591) where Bruno is introduced with his name of Nolano and reminders of the *Cena*. Florio's text contains some strong criticisms of England, as Bruno's own Italian dialogues did; and the suggestion is that Shakespeare replies by satirizing the whole 'School of Night' group as mathematical and astronomical 'fantastics' who have to learn, through the development of the comedy, the sense of true and realistic human love.

J.C. Whitebrook, 'Fynes Moryson, Giordano Bruno and William Shakespeare', *Notes and Queries*, October 1936

This long note raises the question of possible links between Shakespeare and Bruno through the mediation of Fynes Moryson, whose *Itinerary*, which included an account of his journeys to Italy from 1593 to 1594, was published in 1617 but was certainly known to many in manuscript form during Shakespeare's lifetime. Whitebrook himself raises the question only to claim there is no evidence of such a link because Moryson makes no mention of Bruno in spite of the fact that he followed fairly closely on his heels throughout Europe: Moryson visited

Wittemberg only just after Bruno's departure, reached Padua and Venice in 1593 just after his trial by the Inquisition there, and arrived in Rome in 1594, where he claims to have met Cardinal Bellarmino, who was to become one of Bruno's principal accusers in the final stages of his trial. Whitebrook, after describing Moryson as a simple-minded Protestant gentleman, thinks that had he heard of Bruno he would probably have regarded him as a 'foul mountebank'. It is certainly possible that he had heard of him and refrained from mentioning him for reasons of antipathy and prudence. Whitebrook, who is not always accurate in his dates and information, nevertheless supplies some interesting facts which suggest possible links of some kind between Bruno, Shakespeare, and Marlowe. He quotes a mildly obscene epigram dedicated to 'Brunnus' in the collection by John Davis published in 1590 together with Marlowe's translations of Ovid's *Amores*. Whether this refers to Bruno, or simply to some other 'Brown' who remains unidentified, it is impossible to say. But two other epigrams dedicated to 'Faustus', which would seem to refer to Marlowe himself, suggest that Bruno might have had contacts with the libertine circles in which Marlowe is known to have moved. A final point of contact, of a different character, is Moryson's acquaintance with Alberigo Gentile, a well-known scholar and professor of civil law whom Bruno is known to have met at Oxford and who was instrumental in obtaining for him the teaching post at Wittemberg which he held from 1586 to 1588. Moryson mentions having met Gentile both in England and abroad: an acquaintanceship through which he would almost certainly have heard something of Bruno. On the whole Whitebrook's note must be considered untidy and inconclusive; but it nevertheless suggests a number of possible channels which, on a biographical level at least, would seem to link the names of Bruno, Marlowe, and Shakespeare through the figure of Fynes Moryson. It must, however, be noted that none of the channels suggested amounts to any secure proof of such links.

Walter Clyde Curry, *Shakespeare's Philosophical Patterns*,
Baton Rouge, 1937

It is curious that in a book which in many ways made a notable contribution to clarifying Shakespeare's thought, Clyde Curry shows very limited interest for just those areas which were about to be picked up and developed in a number of important new studies on the Bruno-Shakespeare relationship. In Chapter V of his book, entitled 'The age: Platonism', mention is made of the efforts made in the past to show Shakespeare's direct dependence on the pantheistic doctrines of Bruno. However, after claiming correctly that it is not possible to determine with absolute certainty whether Shakespeare had personally studied Bruno's works, it is further asserted that there is no important motive for determining Shakespeare's immediate relationships to any writers in the Neoplatonic tradition. With this surprising statement, Clyde Curry dismisses the 'Bruno-hypothèse' as essentially uninteresting, backing up his claim with reference to Brandes (see p. 174).

Frances A. Yates, 'Shakespeare and the Platonic tradition', *University of Edinburgh Journal*, autumn 1942; repr. in *Collected Essays*, vol. II, *Renaissance and Reform: The Italian Contribution*, London, 1983

In direct contradiction to Clyde Curry's position, this essay is concerned with establishing the channels which link Shakespeare's thought to the continuous European Platonic tradition which survived through the Middle Ages to be picked up and developed by the Neoplatonic Florentine school, above all by Marsilio Ficino and Pico della Mirandola. Hamlet's letter to Ophelia is selected as the text which demonstrates most fully Shakespere's rejection of Aristotelian cosmology and his acceptance of a cosmological view which finds its original source in Plato's *Timaeus*. A central figure in the European development of this view is indicated in Nicolas of Cusa, who is known to have been deeply indebted to Neoplatonic influences. However, Shakespeare's channel of knowledge of these views is seen more probably to have been the early group of English humanists such as Thomas More and John Colet, who had studied deeply the Florentine Neoplatonists. Bruno is introduced in the final pages of this discussion as the terminating figure of Renaissance Neoplatonism who defends the contemplative tradition of Platonism from the contempt of the Tudor church and universities, introducing it into the sphere of art through the spiritual imagery of the *Furori*. Rather than Bruno's supposed 'modernity', it is his strong links with the spirituality of the Middle Ages which is emphasized here, and which is considered a basic influence particularly on the figure of Hamlet.

Lorenzo Giusso, 'Barocco: Bruno e Shakespeare', *Il Giornale di Sicilia*, June 1948.

This newspaper article, which is more a brief literary essay, makes no attempt to prove any biographical or precise artistic 'influence' between Bruno and Shakespeare. It is concerned rather to make, in what are advanced terms for the period, a stylistic comparison of elements of baroque which in both writers lead to a taste for formal irregularities and supposed aberrations. Both Bruno and Shakespeare are associated with esoteric enquiries particularly in the field of magic which 'makes of the universe an ever-changing metaphor'. Hamlet is seen as a major figure or expression of this type of world-vision: 'what awes Hamlet is the secret of universal transformation and the ever-changing movement of the universe'; a sense of universal vicissitude and vitality which is equally a characteristic of Bruno and leads towards the metaphysic and aesthetic of the baroque movement.

Nigel Alexander, *Poison, Play and Duel: a Study in Hamlet*, London, 1971

This stimulating study of *Hamlet* reintroduces Bruno into modern Shakespeare criticism through the theme of memory in a discussion of the appearance and meaning of the Ghost in the light of Frances Yates's *The Art of Memory* (see also N. Alexander, '*Hamlet* and the art of memory', *Notes and Queries*, XV, 1968, pp. 137–9). The discussion starts out from Hamlet's references to his 'tables of memory' and his vow to cancel everything written in them other than the Ghost's image and command. Hamlet thus establishes a 'doctrine of remembrance' which will eventually destroy Claudius's consciously developed 'rhetoric of oblivion'.

The author treats the question of Shakespeare's direct link with Bruno through a reading of the *Heroici furori*, although no claim is made that Shakespeare had necessarily read his work. All that is aimed at is a demonstration of the way in which they use similar imagery to describe similar emotional situations. The third sonnet of the first dialogue of the *Furori* is given particular attention. Here we have the image of the captain of a ship putting to death the 'traitor' thoughts which refuse to be controlled by reason: an image which is used to illuminate Hamlet's conflict between his rational self and his passionate self, particularly evident in his reactions to the appearance of the Ghost.

In later sections of the book, the Bruno reference is extended to the play-within-the-play seen not just as a 'mirror' of the times (Hamlet's own image) but also as a mnemonic aid or memory system. The particular reference made here is to Part II, dialogue 1 of the *Furori* where Bruno discusses an Egyptian emblem of prudence: the god in the Temple of Serapis at Alexandria with its three heads, one looking into the past through memory, another tormented by the things of the present, a third looking ahead for better things in the future. *Hamlet*'s inner play in the light of this discussion becomes an 'intricate memory image which is certainly closely associated with the operation of prudence and the passage of time'.

Chapter 5, 'The power of beauty: Hamlet and Ophelia', refers to Bruno's much-discussed treatment of the myth of Acteon in Part I, dialogue 2, and Part II, dialogue 2, of the *Furori*.

> In this context the dogs which pursue Acteon are not simply the lusts of the flesh which destroy him. They are a desire and passion for a divine harmony which make him indifferent to the 'thousand natural shocks/ That flesh is heir to'.

What we have in this book is an articulate reference to Bruno which is used to illustrate various aspects of Shakespeare's tragedy in some new and convincing ways. It is a pity that Bruno's work is represented directly only through a reading of the *Furori*, although ample use is made of Yates's work as a secondary source.

Frances A. Yates, *Shakespeare's Last Plays: a New Approach*, London, 1975

This distinguished book brings the whole Yatesian study of the Hermetic tradition as the core of Renaissance Neoplatonism to bear on the plays of Shakespeare's final period which are seen not so much as Jacobean, but as revivals of an Elizabethan world-vision centred on the figure of the young Prince Henry. In accordance with the final Yatesian view of Elizabethan Hermeticism, Bruno's influence tends to give way to what is seen as a more dominating presence of John Dee, particularly as far as the interpretation of Prospero's magic is concerned. However, Bruno's influence on the magical elements in *The Winter's Tale* is considered to be direct and crucial, particularly in the scene in which Pauline pretends to use magic arts to make the supposed statue of Hermione come to life. Furthermore the 'profundities about "nature"' which are a characteristic of this play are seen as directly linked to Bruno's interpretation of Renaissance Hermeticism as a return to moral law and a restoration of the religious values inherent in nature herself. The book represents the application of an idea to the last plays rather than a detailed analysis or discussion of the plays themselves: 'a beginning not an end' as the author herself puts it; and stimulates the question of whether it is only the Hermetic element in Bruno's thought which is relevant here. As far as that element is concerned, however, there can be no doubt that a resonance is struck between his thought and the magical dimension of the last plays.

A. Buono Hodgart, '*Love's Labour's Lost* di William Shakespeare e il *Candelaio* di Giordano Bruno', *Studi Secenteschi*, XIX, 1978

This essay starts with a brief comment on the central moments of the Bruno-Shakespeare literature referring to Tschischwitz, König, Beyersdorff, and Croce (see pp. 169, 170, 172, 178). It then accepts the traditional suggestion that Florio acted as the main link between Bruno and Shakespeare. The central section of the essay is a discussion of the three-part plot which can be found both in Shakespeare's play and Bruno's where the satire, in each case, is directed: a) against false forms of debased neo-Petrarchan love; b) against false forms of scientific enquiry; c) against the pedantries of latter-day humanism. This discussion of the similarities in tripartite theme is the most convincing part of the essay. A further section attempts to establish similar linguistic concerns in the two playwrights, both of them in search of meaningful forms of language in contrast with empty and pedantic linguistic formulas. Images of light and darkness are considered essential in each play. The final section takes up the cosmological visions of Shakespeare and Bruno, considering this as the point of contrast between the two authors. Bruno is seen as primarily a modern post-Copernican in his cosmology whereas Shakespeare appears as still linked to an orthodox cosmology of a vaguely medieval character: in both cases the cosmological discussion, to be convincing, would have needed a wider and more detailed study of the thought of the authors both in the particular plays discussed and in their other works.

Frances A. Yates, *The Occult Philosophy in the Elizabethan Age*, London-Boston, 1979

Following her studies of the Hermetic tradition, seen by her increasingly, and more and more emphatically, as the fundamental element of Renaissance culture, Yates here presents the Elizabethan age as founded on Christian cabbalist Neoplatonism. The relationship between Bruno and Shakespeare is only occasionally touched on. In Chapter VI, 'The occult philosophy and melancholy', Yates refers to the page on inspired melancholy in Agrippa's *De occulta philosophia*, which Bruno certainly knew: a page which is interesting in reference to Hamlet's 'furies' or his 'prophetic soul'. But the main Shakespearian section of the book is Chapter XIV, 'Shakespearean fairies, witches, melancholy: King Lear and the demons', where there is a discussion of the occult elements in *Hamlet*, particularly in relation to his father's Ghost and to Hamlet's own melancholy or black humour.

My thanks to Ivan May and Edita Imperatori-Spinosi for the help they have given me in drawing up this bibliography.

NOTES

1 THE BRUNIAN SETTING

1 See *Op.lat.*, II, ii, pp.76–8.
2 *Dial.ital.*, I, pp.26–32.
3 The three items of the Frankfurt Trilogy were published in two volumes in 1591. The first volume to appear was the *De triplici minimo et mensura* followed shortly afterwards by a second volume containing the *De monade numero et figura* and *De innumerabilibus, immenso et infigurabili.* Bruno's dedication to the Duke of Brunswick appeared originally in the form of a Preface to the *De innumerabilibus, immenso et infigurabili* (generally known as the *De immenso*) due to confusion engendered by his hurried departure from Frankfurt. It is, however, known that he intended it as a preface to the whole trilogy, and modern Bruno scholarship accepts it in these terms. For the original text, see *Op.lat.*, I, i, pp.193–9.
4 See the much-discussed passage in Dialogue I of the *Cena* (*Dial.ital.*, I, p.39) where Bruno, under the name of Teofilo, values the learning of the modern sage rather than his antique counterpart 'because we are older and more aged than our predecessors . . . in certain judgements'. Although G. Gentile's interpretation of Bruno in terms of the principle *Veritas filia temporis* has been much criticized, especially by Garin, for its exaggerated exaltation of the spirit as the creative impulse of modern history, Aquilecchia has seen in this passage a progress from an antique providentialist concept of knowledge towards an experimentalist scientific one. See Giovanni Gentile, *Giordano Bruno e il pensiero del rinascimento*, Florence, 1925, chap. VII: 'Veritas filia temporis', pp.225–9; Eugenio Garin, 'La storia nel pensiero del rinascimento', in *Medioevo e rinascimento*, Florence, 1955, pp.192–210, and Giovanni Aquilecchia, 'Introduction to the *Cena*', Turin, 1955, pp. 56–7.
5 *Op. lat.*, I, iii, pp.137–8. Translation of Bruno's Latin works into English is limited to occasional excerpts, while those of the Italian dialogues are of uneven quality, lacking in any unifying

editorial criteria. To ensure consistency all translations in the book are mine, unless specified.

6 There is no recent full-scale biography of Bruno. The fullest biographical account is V. Spampanato, *Vita di Giordano Bruno, con documenti editi e inediti*, 2 vols, Messina, 1921, later completed by the volume of *Documenti*. Spampanato's work has been incorporated into the works of Dorothea Waley Singer, *Giordano Bruno, His Life and Thought, with Annotated Translation of His Work on the Infinite Universe and Worlds*, New York, 1950, and Frances Yates, *Giordano Bruno and the Hermetic Tradition*, London, 1964. G. Aquilecchia has published a brief biographical profile, incorporating recent research, *Giordano Bruno*, Rome, 1971.

7 See *Documenti*, pp. 34–5.

8 *Dial.ital.*, II, p.570. Critical discussion of Bruno's religious views in the light of the *Spaccio* has been developed by Alfonso Ingegno in *La sommersa nave della religione: studio sulla polemica anticristiana del Bruno*, Naples, 1985, and Michele Ciliberto in *La ruota del tempo*, Rome, 1986.

9 The movement from east to west delineated here by Bruno evokes the historical rise of Christianity to the eastern side of Europe, while the journey to the west was still associated with the 'barbaric' territories of the New World. The movement also corresponds to the rising and setting of the sun, an important metaphor for Bruno in the expression of his cyclic view of historical religions. For Bruno's sceptical attitude to the New World see Fulvio Papi, 'Il nuovo mondo – una polemica libertina', in *Antropologia e civiltà nel pensiero di Giordano Bruno*, Florence, 1968. For his cyclic concept of historical religions, A. Ingegno, 'Ermetismo e oroscopo delle religioni nello "Spaccio" bruniano', *Rinasc.*, 7, 1967, pp.157–74.

10 Bruno's relationship to Epicurean philosophy, and particularly to Lucretius, has not yet received the full-length study it needs. However, see the interesting pages on Bruno's debt to Democritean and Epicurean materialism in Irving Louis Horowitz, Chapter 2, 'The heritage of Greek and medieval philosophy', *The Renaissance Philosophy of Giordano Bruno*, New York, 1952; also Papi, *Antropologia*, and the Introduction by Carlo Monti to his Italian translation of the Frankfurt Trilogy, *Opere Latine di Giordano Bruno*, Turin, 1980, pp.61–2.

11 For detailed accounts of Bruno's philosophical method, see Horowitz, Chapter 4, 'Dialectics and reality', *Renaissance Philosophy*, pp.69–80, and the section on Bruno in Paul Kristeller, *Eight Philosophers of the Italian Renaissance*, Stanford, 1964.

12 I shall not be discussing in detail here or elsewhere the story of Bruno's clash with the Oxford dons. It has already been the subject of much attention, particularly since the discovery of George Abbot's first-hand description of the interruption of Bruno's Oxford lectures. See the section 'Bruno in England' and n.38.

13 Particular attention is paid to Bruno's German experience by I.
Frith (Isabella Oppenheimer) in Chapter VII of her early English
biography, *Life of Giordano Bruno*, London, 1887. For the
Marburg episode, see pp.164–7. I use Frith's translation of
Nigidius's account which remains among the documents of the
University of Marburg. (See *Documenti*, pp.49–50.)

14 *Op.lat.*, I, i, pp.1–25. Yates treats the Wittemberg period at some
length, above all in a discussion of the *Lampas triginta statuarum*
first published from the Noroff MS, in *Op.lat.*, III, pp.3–258, but
probably written at Wittemberg. The work is connected to the
Oratio in its three-partite distinction of truth and wisdom, but
here the theme is stated in more mystical terms through a use of
Neoplatonic and Hermetic imagery: see Yates, *The Hermetic
Tradition*, pp.307–11. It is perhaps significant that Bruno decided
to publish the *Oratio* of which seventeen known copies remain
(see *Bib. Sturlese*, 19) but not the *Lampas triginta statuarum*. For
an important comment on the concept of knowledge which
Bruno is developing in texts such as the *Oratio*, see Kristeller,
Eight Philosophers, p.138: 'the more we are inclined to extol the
role of imagination in the sciences, alongside that of empirical
observation and logical deduction, the more we should appreciate
the contribution made by such thinkers as Bruno'. See also L.
Spruit, *Il problema della conoscenza in Giordano Bruno*, Naples,
1988.

15 From Luther's review of Erasmus's Preface to *The Freedom of the
Will*. See *The Bondage of the Will*, translated by J.I. Packer and
A.R. Johnston, London, 1957, pp.66–7. The negative aspects of
the relationship of Bruno to Luther have recently been the
subject of extended comment by M. Ciliberto. See the
introduction to his edition of the *Spaccio*, Milan, 1985, and his *La
ruota del tempo*, above all Chapter IV, 'Angeli nocentes'.
Ciliberto's work on this theme must be considered an original
contribution, particularly in his discovery of and comments on
the exact passages in Luther's work which Bruno uses to attack
and contradict. It could, however, be argued that Ciliberto has
not taken due account of the complexity of Bruno's relationship
with Luther and the Reformation generally. To do this, he would
have had to allow more space to Bruno's German experience,
and to his increasing concern with philosophical liberty: a theme
which Ciliberto tends to ignore.

16 See *The Yale Edition of the Complete Works of St Thomas More*, vol.
IV, *Utopia*, ed. Edward S. Surtz and S.J. and J.H. Hexter, New
Haven and London, 1963, p.57: 'From the monarch, as from a
never-failing spring, flows a stream of all that is good or evil over
the whole nation'.

17 The classic study of this aspect of sixteenth-century European
history is the opening chapter of Frances Yates's *Astraea: the
Imperial Theme in the Sixteenth Century*, London, 1975.

18 See, for example, David Scott Kastan, 'Proud majesty made a

subject: Shakespeare and the spectacle of rule' in *Shakespeare Quarterly*, Summer 1987, pp.459–75.

19 The terms of Bruno's participation in this cult of the French monarchy have been argued by Frances Yates, 'Considérations de Bruno et de Campanella sur la monarchie française' in *L'art et la pensée de Léonard de Vinci*, Communications du Congrès . international, Paris-Algiers, 1954, pp.409–22. See also Yates's *Astraea*.

20 *Dial.ital.*, II, p.826.

21 *Cena*, Dialogue II, *Dial. ital.*, I, pp.69–70.

22 ibid., p.68.

23 For the exchange between Bruno and the Venetian Inquisitors over his praise of the 'Diva' Elizabeth, see the relative documents reproduced in *Dial.ital.*, I, p.67, n.2. The passage is translated and discussed by Frances Yates in *The Hermetic Tradition*, p.288.

24 Carew travelled in Italy between 1613 and 1616 and is known to have learned Italian well. His masque, which was among the last of the Stuart reign, was composed by royal command and staged on 18 February 1633.His use of the *Spaccio* as a source was first pointed out by Robert Adamson in his article on Carew in the ninth edition of the *Encyclopaedia Britannica* (1875–9). The fullest discussion of the problem is still that developed by Rhodes Dunlap in the introduction to *The Poems of Thomas Carew*, Oxford, 1949.

25 The importance of this dedication as Bruno's most articulate appeal for free thought and expression has been pointed out by Guido Calogero in 'La professione di fede di Giordano Bruno', *La cultura*, 1963, pp.1–14. For the original text see *Op.lat.*, I, iii, pp.3–8.

26 For Dee's and Kelley's stay in Prague, see Peter French, *John Dee: the World of an Elizabethan Magus*, London, 1972, pp.110–25.

27 *Op.lat.*, I, i, pp.29–52.

28 ibid., pp.193–9. See also n.3 to this chapter.

29 ibid., I, ii, p.358.

30 F. Bacon, *Works*, ed. J. Spedding, R.L. Ellis, and D. D. Heath, London, 1858–68, vol. III, pp.261–4.

31 Notes of these lectures were published by Bruno's disciple Raphael Egli in 1595 when Bruno was already on trial in Rome. Thirteen known copies of the first edition survive: see *Bib. Sturlese*, 28.

32 The thesis is developed at length by Frances Yates in *The Hermetic Tradition*, Chapter XIX, 'Return to Italy'. She develops arguments already put forward, as she acknowledges, by A. Corsano in *Il pensiero di Giordano Bruno*, Florence, 1940, pp.267 ff., and L. Firpo in *Il processo* (see Abbreviations, p. xvi), pp.10 ff.

33 See the Introduction to Giordano Bruno, *Praelectiones geometricae e Ars deformationum*, ed. G. Aquilecchia, Rome, 1964.

34 See E. Garin, *Rinascite e rivoluzioni: movimenti culturali dal XIV al XVIII secolo*, Bari-Rome, 1975, pp.279–81.

35 *The Complete Prose Works of John Milton*, vol.II, *Areopagitica*, ed. E. Sirluck, New Haven, 1959, p.538.
36 ibid., p.492–3.
37 *Dial.ital.*, I, p.223.
38 Although this letter has been frequently discussed by all of Bruno's major critics, it received adequate comment and attention only in the essay by L. Limentani, 'La lettera di Giordano Bruno al Vicecancelliere della Università di Oxford', *Sophia*, 1, 1933, pp.317–54. Limentani's suggestion that the letter was intended purely as a literary device without reference to a specific moment of his Oxford experience is not accepted by modern comment on the problem which stems from the discovery by Robert McNulty ('Bruno at Oxford', *Renaissance News*, XIII, 1960, pp.300–5) of Abbot's references to Bruno in *The Reasons which Doctour Hill Hath Brought, for the Upholding of Papistry*, 1604. Abbot's account definitely speaks of two separate visits of Bruno to Oxford in the early summer of 1583, and it is now generally thought that the letter was published between the first visit, when Bruno, according to the testimony of Gabriel Harvey (see *Marginalia*, ed. C.C. Moore Smith, Stratford, 1913, p.156) was involved in a violent theological debate with John Underhill, who would become Vice-Chancellor in 1584, and his second visit as a lecturer which was interrupted in the terms described by Abbot. The whole question of Bruno's Oxford experience has recently been reviewed on the basis of the known documentation by Ernan McMullen, 'Giordano Bruno at Oxford' in *ISIS*, 77 (286), March 1986, pp.85–95.
39 See in particular the detailed discussion developed by Ciliberto in *La ruota del tempo*, and also, with reference to the *Spaccio*, Ingegno, *La sommersa nave della religione*. A further interesting contribution to this recent Italian discussion, although without a particular reference to Protestant doctrine, is offered by Nuccio Ordine in *La cabala dell'asino: asinità e conoscenza in Giordano Bruno*, Naples, 1987.
40 A tantalizingly brief annotation in this sense is made by Aquilecchia in his biographical profile, *Giordano Bruno*, p. 14. See also A. Ingegno, 'Per uno studio dei rapporti tra il pensiero di Giordano Bruno e la Riforma' in *Magia, astrologiae religione nel rinascimento*, Warsaw, 1974, pp.130–47. But although Ingegno distinguishes acutely the aspects of Catholicism which Bruno rejects from those which he continues to admire, he tends, like most Italian commentators, to see the attitude to the Reformation as completely consistent and entirely negative. See, however, more recently by the same author *Regia pazzia: Bruno lettore di Calvino*, Urbino, 1987, where Bruno's reading of Calvino is shown to have represented an important stage in his rejection of the whole Christian concept of the divine.
41 The principal text here is Ingegno, *La sommersa nave della religione*.

42 Interesting in this context is Ciliberto's claim of a direct relationship between certain pages of the *Spaccio* and the Machiavelli of the *Discorsi*: see *La ruota del tempo*, pp.176–8.

43 See n.15.

44 *Dial.ital.*, I, p.70. Curiously, no mention has been found of Bruno among the public or private papers of Sidney or of Fulke-Greville. It is, however, accepted by Bruno scholars that the volume containing *De la causa*, *De l'infinito*, the *Spaccio*, and the *Cena*, which would later be bought by John Toland and its contents divulged by him throughout modern Europe, originally belonged to Queen Elizabeth herself. For information about the Queen's copy of these dialogues see G. Aquilecchia, 'Nota su John Toland traduttore di Giordano Bruno', in *English Miscellany*, 9 (1958), pp.77–86; M.R. Pagnoni Sturlese, 'Postille autografe di John Toland allo "Spaccio" di Bruno', in *Giornale critico della filosofia italiana*, LXV, 1986, pp.27–41; and the comments on Bruno first editions in Great Britain in *Bib. Sturlese*, pp.XXIV–V.

45 *Dial.ital.*, I, p.33.

46 For all the above quotations see the relevant texts and notes of the following chapters.

47 *Dial.ital.*, II, p.618. For a recent treatment of Bruno's *Spaccio* as a special form of Renaissance Utopia, see F.E. Manuel and F.P. Manuel, *Utopian Thought in the Western World*, Oxford, 1979, pp.222–42.

2 THE NORTHUMBERLAND TEXTS

1 See John William Shirley, 'The scientific experiments of Sir Walter Ralegh, the Wizard Earl, and the three Magi in the Tower 1603–1617', *Ambix*, IV (1–2), 1949, pp.52–66.

2 *The Poems of George Chapman*, ed Phyllis Bartlett, London, 1941, p.19. An idea of the contemporary interest aroused by Northumberland's intellectual enquiry can be gained from the portraits painted of him. These have been studied by J. Peacock in 'The "Wizard Earl" portrayed by Hilliard and Van Dyck' in *Art History*, 8 (2), June 1985, pp.139–57.

3 See James Spedding, *The Letters and the Life of Francis Bacon* (*Works*, XI), London, 1868, p.63. In a letter written to Northumberland shortly after the accession of James I, Bacon had tried to attract his favour with these words:

> And to be plain with your Lordship, it is very true, (and no wind or noises of civil matters can blow this out of my head or heart), that your great capacity and love towards studies and contemplations of an higher and worthier nature than popular (a nature rare in this world, and in a person of your Lordship's quality almost singular), is to me a great and chief motive to draw my affection and admiration towards you. (*Works*, X, p.58)

4 *Advice to his Son*, ed G.B. Harrison, London, 1930 (hereafter *Advice*), contains two of Northumberland's three compositions addressed to his son, printed with modernized spelling from a private MS. The third (*Instructions for the Lord Percy, in his Travells*) was published from the original MS in the possession of the Earl of Egremont, in *The Antiquarian Repertory*, ed. Francis Grose, IV, 1809, pp.374–80. The 'Essay on Love' was published as an Appendix in Frances Yates, *A Study of Love's Labour's Lost*, Cambridge, 1936, pp.206–ll, and is discussed on pp. 137–51.

5 *Advice*, Chapter 3, p.116.

6 ibid., p.67.

7 *Dial.ital.*, I, p.426.

8 *Advice*, p.70.

9 See Jean Jacquot, 'Harriot, Hill, Warner and the New Philosophy', in *Thomas Harriot: Renaissance Scientist*, ed. J.W. Shirley, Oxford, 1974, pp.l07–28. Jacquot discusses Hill's reference to Bruno on p.110.

10 For a detailed description of these texts and for the annotations to the copy of the *Heroici furori* see Appendices I and II to my essay in *JWCI*, 46, 1983, pp.63–77. This group of texts has now been integrated into *Bib. Sturlese*. A valuable reconstruction of the Ninth Earl's library was attempted by G.R. Batho in 'The library of the "Wizard" Earl: Henry Percy Ninth Earl of Northumberland', *The Library*, 5th series, XV, 1960, pp.246–61.

11 *Advice*, p.69.

12 See E. Garin, 'La rivoluzione copernicana e il mito solare', *Rinascite e rivoluzioni: movimenti culturali dal XIV al XVIII secolo*, Rome-Bari, 1975, p. 258.

13 See Yates, *A Study of Love's Labour's Lost*, Chapter V, 'Bruno and the School of Night' and Chapter VII, 'The Earl of Northumberland and "Stella's" sister'.

14 See *Gesta Grayorum or the History of the High and Mighty Prince Henry Prince of Purpoole* (1594, first published 1688), ed Desmond Bland, Liverpool, 1968, pp.46–7 and 55. In a note on p.100 the editor refers to the claim made by James Spedding in *The Letters and the Life of Francis Bacon* (*Works*, VIII), London, 1861, p.342, that Bacon wrote the speeches of the six counsellors. The text of the *Gesta* itself (see p. 35) mentions Northumberland as among the 'Great and Noble Personages' present on this occasion, as Frances Yates underlines in her *Study of Love's Labour's Lost*.

15 This quotation is taken from 'A study of *Love's Labour's Lost* revised', an unpublished revised version of her book among the Frances Yates papers kept at the Warburg Institute. The manuscript passage quoted amalgamates passages on pp. 147 and 149 of the printed version of the book, developing a particularly clear statement of the antithesis between Northumberland's essay and Shakespeare's play. I am grateful to the Warburg Institute for allowing me to consult the Yates papers relating to her study of *Love's Labour's Lost*.

16 Quoted in Yates, *A Study of Love's Labour's Lost*, p.207.
17 *Dial. ital.*, II, pp.928-9.
18 In a passage on the dating of the play in the revised 'Study' Frances Yates underlines even more firmly than in the printed version (p.169) her conviction of the chronological link between the Gray's Inn revels, Northumberland's 'Essay', and *Love's Labour's Lost*: 'the play was therefore probably written some time during 1595 when the revels and Northumberland's reply to them were both recent history'. As she specifies in the Appendix of the printed *Study*, where the 'Essay on Love' was first published, the text of the 'Essay' appears in a volume of the State Papers Domestic (S.P.14, XI, no.9) written in a secretary hand and endorsed in a different contemporary hand 'My lo. of Northumberland'. The only suggestions for a date, made in modern pencil endorsements, are '1605, 1604? James I?'. Frances Yates was of the opinion that these dates probably correspond to the entry of the 'Essay on Love' among the State Papers, possibly during the searching and confiscations of Northumberland's possessions after the Gunpowder Plot; and she points out that the 'Essay' could well have been written before that date. In fact the collocation of the 'Essay' among the State Papers appears to offer no secure indication as to dating. *The Calendar of State Papers, Domestic, 1603-10* gives volume S.P. 14, XI, as '1604? UNDATED', and indicates its contents in a group of miscellaneous documents none of which has any apparent connection with the Gunpowder Plot. The fact that Northumberland's 'Essay' finished among the State Papers at all is almost certainly due to the suspicions surrounding him during and after his trial; but as he must have been subject to control of some kind throughout his imprisonment (it may be remembered that in 1611 investigations into his case were reopened after allegations made by a discharged servant, Elkes), there seems no way of ascertaining the date of composition or of entry into the State Papers through the Papers themselves, which offer no precise indication on the subject.
19 John Florio, *Queen Anna's New World of Words*, London, 1611.
20 John Florio, *A Worlde of Wordes*, London, 1598.
21 The definition is obviously derived from Bruno's own use of the word. It is interesting to note that Bruno's works are not listed by Florio in his first edition among 'The names of the Bookes and Auctors, that have bin reed of purpose, for the accomplishing of this Dictionarie', whereas in the much enlarged list prefaced to the second edition all Bruno's Italian dialogues appear except for the *Cabala del cavallo pegaseo*.
22 In the 1598 edition: 'a little torch or linke, or any burning light, a little brande'.
23 The other examples are: 'fracasso'='a noyse' (definition present in

Florio 2 but not in Florio 1); 'guai'='griefes or lame[n]tatie[n]s' (both definitions present in Florio 2 but neither in Florio 1); 'scelse'='lett loose' (Northumberland has confused 'scelse', past tense of 'scegliere', to choose, with 'sciolse', past tense of 'sciogliere' defined as 'to loose' in Florio 1 but 'to let loose' in Florio 2); 'straviare'='to wander' (not listed in Florio 1, but defined 'to wander' in Florio 2); 'scorger'='to discover a far of' (defined 'to perceive or to be aware of, to guide, to leade, to direct, to shew' in Florio 1, but 'to perceive, to ken a farre off, to discerne' in Florio 2). In general, Northumberland often accepts one or two only of Florio's multiple definitions, but 'only once or twice does he venture a definition outside Florio's suggestions.

24 De Fonblanque, *Annals of the House of Percy*, II, Appendix XIX, London, 1887, pp.626–30.

25 Filippo Venuti *Dittionario generale volgare & latino*, Venice, 1568; Frosino Lapini *Institutionum Florentinae linguae libri duo*, Florence, 1569; Scipio Lentulus *An Italian Grammar written in Latin by Scipio Lentulo a Neopolitan: and turned into Englishe by Henry Grantham*, London, 1587. There was also a copy of the bilingual dialogues: John Florio, *Florios Second Frutes to be gathered of divers but delightsome tastes to the tongues of Italians and Englishmen*, London, 1591. It is also interesting to note that a Syon House Roll of Accounts dated 6 February 1609– 6 February 1610 indicates among the rewards: 'To Francesco Petrozani, for reading Italian to the Earl, 7£'. See *Historical Manuscripts Commission*, Appendix to Sixth Report, London, 1877–8, p.229.

26 *Le osservationi del Dolce dal medesimo ricorrette, et ampliate.* Quarta edizione con privilegio. In Vinegia appresso Gariel Giolito de' Ferrari, e fratelli. MDLVI. The volume does not carry the Ninth Earl's book-badge, but it does have his two-number classification for cataloguing, 2.33, written in ink and heavily crossed out. The later classification number of the period of the Tenth Earl is J.7.21.

27 Northumberland was released from the Tower in the summer of 1621, and spent the rest of his life in retirement at Petworth.

28 *Advice*, p.73.

29 Yates, *A Study of Love's Labour's Lost*, p.145.

30 *Advice*, p.208.

31 ibid., p.210.

32 ibid., p.211.

33 In the first edition of the *Furori*, p.42; *Dial.ital.*, II, p.964.

34 In the first edition, pp.41–2; *Dial.ital.*, II, p.963.

35 Yates, *A Study of Love's Labour's Lost*, pp. 209–10.

36 ibid., p.208.

37 *Op.lat.*, I, iii, pp. 300–1.

3 THE NORTHUMBERLAND CIRCLE: HARRIOT'S PAPERS

1 See A. Koyré, *From the Closed World to the Infinite Universe*, Baltimore, 1957, p.54. For Koyré's full discussion of Bruno's thought, see pp. 39–55.
2 See, for example, the few dismissive lines dedicated to Bruno in Marie Boas Hall, *The Scientific Renaissance 1450–1630*, London, 1962, pp.122–5. But see also n.5 to this chapter.
3 F.A. Yates, *Giordano Bruno and the Hermetic Tradition*, London, 1964. See, in particular, Chapter VIII, 'Renaissance magic and science'.
4 'The truth is that for Bruno the Copernican diagram is a hieroglyph, a Hermetic seal hiding potent divine mysteries of which he has penetrated the secret' (ibid., Chapter XIII, 'Giordano Bruno in England: the Hermetic philosophy', p.241).
5 In 'Problems of the scientific Renaissance' (*The Renaissance, Essays in Interpretation*, London and New York, 1982, pp.273–96), Marie Boas Hall underlines the extent of the reaction against mysticism as a dominant force in the evolution of modern science, particularly as it was manifested in the symposium *Reason, Experiment and Mysticism in the Scientific Revolution* (ed. M.L. Righini Bonelli and W.R. Shea, New York, 1975): 'not that the historians concerned wished in any way to minimize the existence of mystic, even Hermetic thought, but they were inclined to reject it as a principal, or even very strong causative factor' (p.283). That this general revaluation has been accompanied by a renewed interest in some of the more scientific aspects of Bruno's work is pointed out in the same essay ('Problems of the scientific Renaissance') with a reference to the reconsideration of his Copernicanism by R.S. Westman (see 'Magical reform and astronomical reform: the Yates thesis reconsidered', *Hermeticism and the Scientific Revolution*, Los Angeles, 1977, pp.1–91). Work on Bruno in Italy in recent years has also been much concerned with a substantial revaluation of Bruno's scientific enquiry. See in particular the essay by E. Garin, 'La rivoluzione copernicana e il mito solare (*Rinascite e rivoluzioni: movimenti culturali dal XIV al XVIII secolo*, Rome-Bari, 1975, pp.255–97) which underlines the importance of the complex naturalistic physics of Bruno. Garin sees Bruno as the philosopher who made explicit all the general theoretical possibilities inherent in the vision of Copernicus (p.280). In one of the most recent full length studies of Bruno's thought, A. Ingegno (*Cosmologia e filosofia nel pensiero di Giordano Bruno*, Florence, 1978) begins with a chapter on his enquiry into the behaviour of stars and comets, to support the claim that he cannot be dismissed as an epigone, however illustrious, of the Florentine Neoplatonic magi (p.XII). A similar position is developed by C. Monti in his introduction to the first complete Italian translation of Bruno's great Frankfurt Trilogy (*Opere latine di Giordano Bruno*, Turin, 1980). The outcome of Bruno's enquiry

is seen by Monti as neither purely mystical nor religious, but rather as the unveiling of ever more precise knowledge of the structure of reality (p.37).

6 See J. Jacquot, 'Thomas Harriot's reputation for impiety', in *Notes and Records of the Royal Society*, IX, 1952, pp. 175–6; J. Jacquot, 'Harriot, Hill, Warner and the New Philosophy' in J.W. Shirley (ed.) *Thomas Harriot: Renaissance Scientist*, Oxford, 1974, pp. 107–28. A more tenuous connection between Bruno's atomism and that of the Northumberland group is suggested by R.H. Kargon in *Atomism in England from Harriot to Newton*, Oxford, 1966. See in particular Chapter II, 'The Wizard Earl and the new science', pp.5–17. For Harriot's story as a member of Northumberland's circle, see G.R. Batho, *Thomas Harriot and the Northumberland Household*, The Durham Thomas Harriot Seminar, Occasional Paper no. 1, London, 1983.

7 There is no evidence available to indicate when Northumberland acquired the Frankfurt Trilogy. The first volume of the trilogy, containing the *De triplici minimo*, was published for the spring book fair of 1591, while the second volume, containing the *De monade* and the *De immenso*, appeared for the autumn book fair of the same year, together with Bruno's last published work, the *De imaginum, signorum et idearum compositione*. The presence of all these works in the Northumberland library suggests a purchase made at the autumn book fair of 1591 when the trilogy and the *De imaginum* together constituted one of the novelties of the moment. As Northumberland's copies of all these works carry the early cataloguing number used in his library, it is reasonably certain that they were part of the collection when the cataloguing of his books was carried out in 1602. For evidence concerning the date of cataloguing see G.R. Batho, 'The library of the "wizard" Earl: Henry Percy Ninth Earl of Northumberland (1564–1632)', in *The Library*, 5th series, XV, 1960, p.252.

8 See Felice Tocco, *Le opere latine di Giordano Bruno esposte e confrontate con le italiane*, Florence, 1889, pp.318–22.

9 See BL Add. MS 6788, fol.67^v. Harriot's note of Bruno's title appears to have been discovered by Ethel Seaton, who discussed it in a lecture given to the Elizabethan Literary Society in 1933. The lecture is unpublished, but reference to it was made by Frances Yates in her early discussion of the relationship between Bruno and the Northumberland circle in *A Study of Love's Labour's Lost*, Cambridge, 1936, pp.92–3. Referring directly to the lecture, Frances Yates gives the note as 'Nolanus de immenso et mundi' accepting Ethel Seaton's suggestion that Harriot had confused the titles of two of Bruno's works, the *De immenso* and the Italian dialogue *De l'infinito universo et mondi*. However, close examination of the page in the original manuscript reveals Harriot to have written quite clearly 'Nolanus de universo et mundis'. In BL Add. MS 6785, fol.310^v, Harriot appears to have had in mind Bruno's

concept of motion in space and time, for he writes: 'Interpretatio NOLANI De Motu elementares propositiones T. Tempus/S. Spatium/G. Gradus'.

10 The book list (See Plate 4, p.52) contains the following items:
a. *Valverde Anatomia nova. Venetiis.* [Juan de Valverde, *Anatomia del corpo umano* . . . nuovamente ristampata. Venetia. 1586.]
b. *Piccolomini* [probably Alessandro (1508–79) or Francesco (1523–1607), both from Siena, and both translators and commentators of Aristotle. Francesco, who operated at the School of Padua, is perhaps the most likely candidate.]
c. *Telesisus* [sic] *9 lib et De Cometis de iride etc.* [Telesius (Bernardino Telesio of Cosenza), *De rerum natura iuxta propria principia*, libri IX, Naples, 1587. *Varii de naturalibus*, ed. Antonio Persio, Venice, 1590, contains nine pamphlets including *de Cometis et lacteo circulo* and *de Iride.*]
d. *Nolanus de universo et mundis.* [Giordano Bruno, *De innumerabilibus, immenso et infigurabili, seu de universo et mundis*, published in the same volume as *De monade numero et figura*, Frankfurt, 1591.]
e. *De imaginibus – Juliani epistola.* [These two final items, linked by a stroke of the pen, appear one under the other immediately below the reference to 'Nolanus de universo et mundis'. In view of the fact that no new author's name is indicated, it may be that Harriot was still thinking of Bruno. In this case the first reference could be to the *De imaginum, signorum et idearum compositione*, also in the Northumberland library, which Bruno himself sometimes refers to as the *De rerum imaginibus.* If the second reference also remains in the context of Bruno's works, the only possibility seems that Harriot was thinking of the important introductory letter to Duke Henry Julius of Brunswick, prefixed to the *De monade* but intended by Bruno as a preface to the whole Frankfurt Trilogy, although the genitive case is perhaps not appropriate for a letter to Julius written by Bruno.]

11 See, for example, G. Rees, 'Matter theory: an unifying factor in Bacon's natural philosophy', *Ambix*, XXIV, 1977, pp.110–25.

12 Nicolas Hill (1570?–1610), *Philosophia Epicurea, Democritiana, Theophrastica proposita simplicitur, non edocta*, Paris, 1601. The second, slightly revised, edition of Hill's work published in Geneva in 1619 does not include the marginal note to aphorism 434, which names 'Hermes, Cusanus, Nicetus, Copernicus, Nolanus, Gilbertus, Franciscus patricius' as the inspirers of a heliocentric theory. The close relationship between the central philosophical ideas developed in Hill's book and the related aspects of Bruno's thought has been discussed by Daniel Massa in 'Giordano Bruno's ideas in seventeenth-century England', *Journal of the History of Ideas*, XXXVIII, 1977, pp.227–42.

13 Walter Warner died in the early years of the 1640s, outliving the other members of the Northumberland circle and forming an

important link between them and a later generation of scientific enquirers such as Sir Charles Cavendish, Hobbes, and Mersenne. His position in the Northumberland household has been described by J. Shirley as something between a trusted personal servant and a kind of literary assistant to the Ninth Earl (see *Thomas Harriot: a Biography*, Oxford, 1983, pp.367–71). Warner's papers are in BL Add. MSS 4394–96 and 6754–56. For an attempt to classify them according to subject, see Jacquot, 'Harriot, Hill, Warner', p.127, n.47. The task is rendered extremely difficult by the repetitive nature of Warner's thought, as well as by the fact that some papers appear more than once. Reflections on the nature of space occur on almost every page of Warner's papers. The page to which I refer here is Add. MS 4395, fol.204^v, headed 'Space, Locus, Ubi' (see Plate 5, p.55).

14 *De immenso*, bk II, chap.II. See *Op.lat.*, I, i, p.253. The ancient philosophers named here with approval by Bruno are Parmenides, Xenophanes, and Melissus.

15 *Deimmenso*, I, viii. See *Op.lat.*, I, i, pp.231–2.

16 See A. Koyré, *Etudes galiléennes*, Paris, 1966. The importance of Bruno's concept of space is underlined in a number of passages, especially in Chapter III which discusses Galileo and the principle of inertia.

17 *Op.lat.*, I, i, p.321.

18 'Me thinkes my diligent Galileus hath done more in his three fold discoverie then Magellane in openinge the streightes to the South sea'. This letter was first printed in full by S. Rigaud in his *Supplement to Dr. Bradley's Miscellaneous Works*, Oxford, 1832, pp.25–6. It was reprinted by Henry Stevens of Vermont in his biographical study *Thomas Harriot, the Mathematician, the Philosopher and the Scholar*, London, 1900, pp.116–18. The original is in BL Add. MS 6789, fols 425–6.

19 The letter is actually dated by Lower 'the longest day of 1610'.

20 Kepler's arguments against an infinite universe and Lower's objections to them have been analysed in detail by Jacquot in 'Thomas Harriot's reputation for impiety', pp. 175–6. The discussion involved the opinions of Sir William Gilbert, whose *De magnete* had appeared in 1600, as well as Bruno's.

21 *Op.lat.*, I, ii, p.69.

22 My translation. Hasdale's letter, which is in Italian, was published by Favaro in vol. X of the *Opere di Galileo*, Florence, 1900 (repr. 1968), pp. 314–15.

23 A detailed discussion of Kepler's objections and Galileo's hesitations in front of Bruno's thesis of an infinite universe can be found in Koyré, *From the Closed World*, Chapters III and IV respectively.

24 Harriot's telescopic observations of sunspots, which some commentators claim preceded Galileo's, have been the cause of much recent discussion. See J. North, 'Harriot's telescopic

observations of sunspots' in Shirley, *Thomas Harriot: Renaissance Scientist*, pp. 129–65.

25 The papers are in BL Add. MS 6782, fols 362–74^v. No complete and detailed description of or comment on their contents has so far been published. Partial discussion of some aspects of them can be found in Jacquot, 'Thomas Harriot's reputation for impiety', pp. 177–9, and Kargon, *Atomism in England*, pp.24–6. No exact date has so far been suggested for them, but it is probable that they belong to the period of intense philosophical speculation which followed the publication of Gilbert's *De magnete* and saw Harriot's correspondence with Kepler: i.e. the first decade of the seventeenth century. Harriot died in 1621.

26 R.C.H. Tanner, 'The ordered regiment of the minus sign: offbeat mathematics in Harriot's manuscripts', *Annals of Science*, XXXVII, 1980, p.153. The passage quoted by Tanner here to support her assertion is to be found in BL Add. MS 6782, fol.374^r (see Plate 6, p.73), and reads:

> Of contradictions that spring from diverse suppositions it cannot truly be said that the one parte [erasure] or other is false, for they are true consequences from there suppositions & in that respect are both true. but that which followeth; is, that one of the suppositions is necessarily false, from whence one of the partes of the contradiction was inferred. As in the reason Achilles & other reasons of Zeno & c:.

27 *Op.lat.*, I, iii, pp.119–361.

28 See the passage where Bruno presents the victory of the new cosmology over the old in terms of light vanquishing darkness, with apocalyptic overtones, as, for example, during his critique of the Aristotelian orbs still accepted by Copernicus (*De immenso*, III, x).

29 See BL Add. MS 6782, fol.374^v. Harriot himself supplies the reference for his quotation, Revelation 20. The idea of the Aristotelian vision of the universe as a gigantic deceit foisted on history is used by Bruno himself, although without the biblical quotation, in a page of strong attack at the beginning of the *De triplici minimo* (I, vi), see *Op.lat.*, I, iii, pp. 150–1. Aristotle is not mentioned by name here, but the chapter is entitled: 'Ad eos qui continuum in infinitum divisibile accipiunt', and the arguments under attack are clearly those exposed by Aristotle in the *Physics*, bks III and VI. For an exposition of Aristotle's arguments on these points, see the relevant sections of Sir Thomas Heath, *Mathematics in Aristotle*, Oxford, 1949. The complex attitudes of Renaissance thinkers towards Aristotle are discussed in C. Schmitt, *Aristotle in the Renaissance*, Princeton, 1983. For a discussion of the philosophical problems relating to seventeenth-century atomism, see T. Gregory, 'Studi sull'atomismo del seicento' in *Giornale critico della filosofia italiana*, 1964, pp.38–65; 1966, pp.44–64; 1967, pp.529–41. On Bruno's atomism, besides the already mentioned commentary of

Tocco, see the two studies by Paul-Henri Michel: 'L' atomisme de Giordano Bruno' in *La science au seizième siècle*, Paris, 1960, pp.249–64; and 'Les notions de continue et de discontinue dans les systèmes physiques de Bruno et de Galilée', in *Mélanges Alexandre Koyré*, vol.II, Paris, 1964.

30 See the *Physics*, bk III, and in particular 5–8, 206ᵃ–08ᵃ. (References to Aristotle's *Physics* are to the text printed in *The Works of Aristotle Translated into English*, ed W.D. Ross, Oxford, vol.II, 1930.)

31 *De triplici minimo*, I, ii. See *Op.lat.*, I, iii, pp. 138–40.

32 *De triplici minimo*, I, iv. See *Op.lat.*, I, iii, pp. 144–9.

33 Bruno's judgements on the outcome of his enquiry in the three books of the trilogy are expressed in the letter of introduction to Duke Henry Julius of Brunswick discussed in Chapter 1.

34 *De triplici minimo*, I, vi. See *Op.lat.*, I, iii, pp. 152–3.

35 *Physics*, bk V, 3, 226ᵇ–27ᵃ and bk VI, 1, 231ᵃ–31ᵇ.

36 *De triplici minimo*, I, vii. See *Op.lat.*, I, iii, pp.158–62.

37 *De triplici minimo*, II, x. See *Op.lat.*, I, iii, p.223.

38 See BL Add. MS 6782, fol. 374ᵛ and also the page subtitled *De continuo*, fol.362, where Harriot refers to 'the 26th text of the 5th booke' of Aristotle's *Physics*, and the beginning of the 6th book as the texts he is specifically discussing.

39 See BL Add. MS 6782, fol.374ᵛ and Add. MS 6785, fol.436ʳ. It is in such a context of thought, which shows Harriot's awareness of the capacity of minimum and maximum quantities to resolve logical contradictions ('In the minimum, the monad, all contraries are resolved', Bruno had written: see *Op.lat.*, I, iii, p.147), that we find his statement 'omnia fiunt ex nihilo & ex nihilo nihil fit non contradiciunt' (see fol.374ᵛ). Such speculations derived from Cusanus through Bruno, give a new and subtle twist to the theological controversy over the divine creation which so preoccupied Harriot's contemporaries, and had such a harmful effect on his reputation (see Jacquot, 'Thomas Harriot's reputation for impiety'), as indeed on Bruno's too. The influence of Cusanus on Bruno is discussed in Hélène Vedrine, 'L'influence de Nicolas de Cues sur Giordano Bruno', in *Nicolò Cusano agli inizi del mondo moderno*, Florence, 1970, pp.211–23.

40 *Op.lat.*, I, iii, pp.152–3.

41 BL Add. MS 6782, fol.363ʳ.

42 For bibliographical information on the recent studies of Harriot's mathematical enquiries see the bibliography of work on Harriot since 1900 in Shirley, *A Biography*, pp.483–90.

43 For some interesting comments on this subject, see Hélène Vedrine, 'L' obstacle réaliste en mathématique chez deux philosophes du XVIᵉ siècle: Bruno et Patrizi', in *Platon et Aristote à la Renaissance*, Paris, 1976, pp.239–48.

44 See K. Atanasijevich, *The Metaphysical and Geometrical Doctrine of Bruno*, St Louis, Mo., 1962, p.96 (first published in French in Belgrade, 1923). More recent comments on the richness but also

the ambiguities of Bruno's concept of number and the infinite are in A. Deregibus, *Bruno e Spinoza: La realtà dell'infinito e il problema della sua unità*, Turin, 1980, vol. I, Chapter 6.

45 See Tocco, *Le opere latine di Giordano Bruno*, pp. 157–64.

46 *The Elements of Geometrie . . . translated by H. Billingsley. . . . With a very fruitfull Praeface made by M.I. Dee specifying the Chief Mathematicall Sciences, what they are, and whereunto commodius: where, also, are disclosed certaine new Secrets Mathematicall and Mechanicall, vntill these our daies greatly missed.* London, 1570, sig.ij. A modern reprint of Dee's *Preface* has been edited by Allen G. Debus, Science History Publications, New York, 1975.

47 Giordano Bruno, *Praelectiones geometricae e Ars deformationum*, testi inediti a cura di G. Aquilecchia, Rome, 1964.

48 See BL Add. MS 6782, fol.369^r.

49 See BL Add. MS 6785, fol.436^r.

50 For Warner's conception of *vis*, see in particular BL Add. MS 4394, fols 389^v and 397^r. On Bruno's concept of the atom as a 'centre de vie', see P.H. Michel, 'L'atomisme de G. Bruno', p.263, and the relevant sections of his study, *La cosmologie de Giordano Bruno*, Paris, 1962.

51 Jacquot, in 'Harriot, Hill, Warner', touches on the importance of this link. See pp.112–13.

52 See *Op.lat.*, II, iii, pp.87–322.

53 Paolo Rossi, *Clavis universalis: Arti mnemoniche e logica combinatoria da Lullo a Leibniz*, Milan-Naples, 1960.

54 Frances A. Yates, *The Art of Memory*, London, 1966.

55 ibid., Chapter 13, 'Giordano Bruno: last works on memory', p. 297. See also Luciana de Bernart, *Immaginazione e scienza in Giordano Bruno: L'infinito nelle forme dell'esperienza*, Pisa, 1986, which takes Yates's comments on Bruno's memory works as a starting-point from which to elaborate an extended analysis of his complex concept of scientific method.

56 *De triplici minimo*, I, i. See *Op.lat.*, I, iii, pp.137–8.

57 Besides the works on the memory tradition already referred to, see, for example, F. Papi, *Antropologia e civiltà nel pensiero di Giordano Bruno*, Florence, 1968, pp.291–3.

58 Distinguishing between different planes of truth Bruno writes in the *De compositione imaginum* (*Op.lat.*, II, iii, p. 94): 'Idea sunt causa rerum ante res, idearum vestigia sunt ipsae res seu quae in rebus, idearum umbrae sunt ab ipsus rebus seu post res'. In a page of the *Cabala del cavallo pegaseo* which develops similar distinctions, Bruno had specified: 'La prima [verità] ha nome di causa, la seconda ha nome di cosa, la terza ha nome di cognizione' (see *Dial.ital.*, II, p.872). For Bruno's concept of simplicity as associated with the highest form of truth, resembling, in its uniformity, the aspect of divinity, see the *Spaccio* (*Dial.ital.*, II, p.707): 'Lo aspetto della Simplicità piacque a tutti gli dei, perché per la sua uniformità in certa maniera rapresenta ed ha la similitudine del volto divino'.

59 BL Add. MS 4395, fol.194^r. The same diffidence towards words as

insufficient instruments of scientific discourse is developed more
fully as a central theme by Bacon, particularly in the *Novum
organum*, I, aphorisms LIX-LX, where his treatment of the Idols of
the Market Place closely echoes Bruno's passage on the danger of
received linguistic formulas. See *Bacon's Works*, ed. Ellis and
Spedding, London, 1857–9, I, pp.170–2.

60 See Henry Percy, Ninth Earl of Northumberland, *Advice to His Son
(1609)*, edited and with a biographical introduction by G. B.
Harrison, London, 1930, p.73.

61 ibid., p.68. From such a definition of universal grammar it is clear
that Northumberland is thinking not only of language as a means of
expression, but also of pictorial images, signs, gestures, or any other
possibility of communication provided by 'the whole variety of
means sensible'. His reflections on communication are thus closely
linked to the tradition of works on memory, which had always
underlined the importance of finding adequately clear images both
for the communication of the truths of nature and for
remembering those truths. Northumberland was clearly interested
in the memory works of the period, for besides Bruno's *De
compositione imaginum*, we know he had read the work of Filippo
Gesualdo, *Plutosophia: nella quale si spiega l'Arte della Memoria*,
published in Padua in 1592 and again in Vicenza in 1600 (see the list
of Northumberland's books sent back to Syon House from the
Tower in l614, published in E. de Fonblanque, *Annals of the House of
Percy*, London, 1887, vol. II, Appendix XIX, pp.626–30).

62 *Advice*, p.69.

63 It is in precisely such terms that Harriot was valued in his own
century by John Wilkins, a strenuous supporter of the search for a
universal language, and as such much interested in the invention of
mathematical symbols. In his *Vindiciae Academiarum* (1654,
reprinted in Allen G. Debus, *Science and Education in the Seventeenth
Century*, London, 1970, pp.193–261) Wilkins points out how it is
through the management of mathematical symbols that

> we are enabled to behold, as it were, with our eyes, that long
> continued series of mixt and intricate Ratiocination, which would
> confound the strongest fancy to sustaine it, and are with ease let
> in to the Abstrusest, and most perplexed depths, wherein the
> contemplation of quantity is concerned. p.19, Debus p.213)

Shortly afterwards, the 'symbolicall way' is claimed to have been
'invented by Vieta, advanced by Harriot, perfected by Mr
Oughtred and Descartes' (p.20, Debus p.214). In an appreciation of
Harriot's achievements in the field of mathematical symbolism, Dr
Tanner has underlined how 'Harriot's manuscripts confirm that
symbols for him were a medium for mathematical thinking, not a
mere means of avoiding tedious repetition'. See R.C.H. Tanner,
'Thomas Harriot as mathematician', *Physis, Rivista internazionale di
storia e delle scienze*, IX (2–3), 1967, p.290.

64 Quoted by Papi, *Antropologia*, pp.290–3, in his discussion of this
text.

65 'In prospettiva, nello sfondo, si profilavano una nuova logica, alla convergenza fra "ragioni vive" e "ragioni calculatorie", e una nuova cosmologia unitaria, senza separazioni o fratture fra cielo della perfezione e mondo della corruzione'. See the page synthesizing the essential aspects of Bruno's development of Copernicanism in Garin, 'La rivoluzione copernicana e il mito solare', in *Rinascite e rivoluzioni*, p.265.

66 See BL Add. MS 4394, fol.385ᵛ.

67 See *De monade*, vii. *Op.lat.*, I, ii, p.424.

68 The surviving documents relating to Bruno's long and complicated trial are presented and discussed in *Il processo*.

69 *De immenso*, VII, xi. *Op.lat.*, I, ii, p.269. For this passage the Latin text edited by Tocco and Vitelli has been collated with the first edition in the Biblioteca Nazionale at Florence (pressmark, Guicc. 2.4².72). Some of the changes in punctuation introduced by Tocco and Vitelli have been maintained, as well as their correction of the verb 'opperit' (1.2) to 'oppetit', while the 'n' of 'torquentis' and the 's' of 'compactasque', which had dropped out in the Tocco-Vitelli edition, have been reintroduced. For the important but complex relationship between Bruno and Lucretius, see Papi, *Antropologia*, *passim*, and Monti, Introduction to *Opere latine*, especially pp.56–9.

70 Shortly after James's accession, Dee pleaded with him, on 4 June 1604, to be tried for sorcery, hoping that a trial would clear his name from scandals fomented by his 'Brainsicke, Rashe, Spitefull, and Disdainfull Countrey men'. James ignored him and in 1608 Dee died in obscurity and poverty. See Peter J. French, *John Dee: the World of an Elizabethan Magus*, London, 1972, p.10.

71 Harriot appointed the mathematician Torporley (1564–1632), an Anglican priest associated with the Northumberland circle, as the 'overseer' of his unpublished mathematical papers (see the copy of Harriot's will published in Stevens, *Harriot, Mathematician*, pp.193–203). Torporley behaved ambiguously, collaborating on work which led to the very partial publication of Harriot's mathematical papers in the *Artis analyticae praxis*, 1631, while at the same time dissociating himself from Harriot's philosophical views. Torporley prepared, in direct contradiction to the views of T.H. (evidently Harriot), 'A synopsis of the controversie of atoms', which remained in manuscript. It has been printed by Jacquot as an appendix to 'Thomas Harriot's reputation for impiety', pp.183–7. Torporley's work as the 'overseer' of Harriot's papers has been discussed in R.C.H. Tanner, 'Nathaniel Torporley and the Harriot manuscripts', *Annals of Science*, XXV (4), December 1969, pp.339–49.

72 A detailed presentation of the documents relating to Northumberland's trial and Harriot's imprisonment can be found in Shirley, *A Biography*, Chapter VIII, 'From the Court to the Tower – Northumberland', pp.327–57.

73 Harriot's correspondence with Kepler in the years 1606–8 has been

discussed by Jacquot in 'Thomas Harriot's reputation for impiety', pp.180–2, and also in Shirley, *A Biography*, pp.385–8. The translations from Harriot's Latin are those given in these texts.
74 BL Add. MS 6782, fol.374^r.

4   BRUNO AND MARLOWE: *DR FAUSTUS*

1 See J.W. Smeed, *Faust in Literature*, Oxford, 1975, Chapter 9, 'Faust and science in the nineteenth and twentieth centuries'.
2 For all problems concerning dating and textual criticism, and for quotations from the drama, my references are to the edition of *Dr Faustus* published in F. Bowers (ed.) *Christopher Marlowe: the Complete Works*, Cambridge, 1981, II (Textual introduction, pp. 123–59; text, pp.160–228).
3 See F.A. Yates, *The Occult Philosophy in the Elizabethan Age*, London, 1979, pp.92–3. The suggestion that Bruno was somehow behind Marlowe's drama has been made by E.G. Clark in *Ralegh and Marlowe*, New York, 1941, pp.338–89.
4 The complex problem of which parts of the drama were written by Marlowe himself and which by various collaborators is largely a question of hypothesis, on which not all commentators are agreed. I accept as valid the breakdown of the parts of the drama according to probable authorship offered by Bowers, *Christopher Marlowe*, pp. 155–8.
5 See, in particular, F.S. Boas, *Christopher Marlowe*, Oxford, 1940.
6 The early texts establishing a group of unorthodox thinkers around Ralegh and the Ninth Earl of Northumberland are M.C. Bradbrook, *The School of Night*, Cambridge, 1936, and F.A. Yates, *A Study of Love's Labour's Lost*, Cambridge, 1936. Subsequent research on this group, which has modified and clarified this early picture, is summed up in J.W. Shirley, *Thomas Harriot: a Biography*, Oxford, 1983, Chapter V, 'Years of transition, 1590–1600', pp.175–240.
7 Chapman's poem to Harriot was published in 1598 as an accompaniment to *Achilles Shield*, part of his translation from Homer. See *The Poems of George Chapman*, ed P. Bartlett, London, 1941, pp.381–4. The Baines note is given in full in Shirley, *Harriot*, pp.182–3.
8 For the documentary evidence relating to Bruno's trial, see *Il processo*.
9 See J. Jacquot, 'Thomas Harriot's reputation for impiety', *Notes and Records of the Royal Society*, IX, 1952, pp.170–1.
10 F. Papi, *Antropologia e civiltà nel pensiero di Giordano Bruno*, Florence, 1968, pp.96–7. Bruno's reference to the Virginia expeditions is in the *De immenso*, VII, xvi.
11 See *Dial.ital.*, II, pp.798–9.
12 See *Il processo*, sections 10–11.
13 See *Dial.ital.*, II, pp.791–2.
14 See *Op.lat.*, II, ii, p.183.

15 Magic, far from being a superstitious and sinful art is: 'una cognizione dei segreti della natura con facoltà d'imitare la natura nell'opere sue e far cose meravigliose agli occhi del volgo'. See *Il processo*, p.56.

16 *The Historie*, p.2.

17 G. Pico della Mirandola, *Oratio de hominis dignitate*, ed. E. Garin, Florence, 1946, I, p.l28. For the long and complex history of the eagle image in both eastern and western cultures, see K. Wittkover, *Allegory and the Migration of Symbols*, London, 1977, pp.15–45.

18 See *Op.lat.*, I, iii, p.8.

19 *Dr Faustus*, Chorus I, p.161.

20 See I. Ribner, 'Marlowe and the critics', *Tulane Drama Review*, 8, 1964, pp.211–24.

21 See Pico della Mirandola, II, pp.160–2.

22 I refer here to the commentary of Francisco Sanchez of Salamanca on Alciati's *Emblemata*, printed at Lyons in 1573.

23 See *Dial.ital.*, II, p.999. E. Cassirer quotes this sonnet in the concluding pages of *Individuum und Kosmos in der Philosophie der Renaissance*, Leipzig-Berlin, 1927. Cassirer's perception of the way in which new concepts of knowledge developed in Renaissance thinkers through their use of certain key mythological symbols has deeply influenced my reading of Marlowe's tragedy.

24 Some good comments on Bruno's mythological writing, and particularly on his use of the myth of Circe in the *Furori*, can be found in A. Gareffi, *La filosofia del manierismo: la scena mitologica della scrittura in Della Porta, Bruno e Campanella*, Naples, 1984, Chapter 2, 'Anteriorità della memoria e scrittura mitologica di Giordano Bruno'.

25 *Cabala del cavallo pegaseo*, Dialogue I, in *Dial.ital.*, II, p. 878:

hanno inceppate le cinque dita in un'unghia, perché non potessero, come l'Adamo, stender le mani ad apprendere il frutto vietato dell'arbore della scienza, per cui venessero ad essere privi de frutti de l'arbore della vita, o come Prometeo (che è metafora di medesimo proposito), stender le mani a suppurar il fuoco di Giove, per accendere il lume nella potenza razionale.

26 See *Francis Bacon (Works, VI)*, ed J. Spedding, London, 1887–92.

27 Kepler's autograph comment was written in Latin in a Commentary of Alciati's *Emblemata*. The original is in BL Egerton MS 1234, fols 242b–243a.

28 See Rosamund Tuve, *Elizabethan and Metaphysical Imagery*, Chicago, 1947, in particular Chapter XII, 'Ramist logic: certain general conceptions affecting imagery'. On Ramus's method in its historical context, see W.J. Ong, SJ, *Ramus: Method and the Decay of Dialogue*, Harvard, 1958, and the relevant sections in C. Vasoli, *La dialettica e la retorica dell'Umanesimo*, Milan, 1968. On Ramus's influence in England, see W.S. Howell, *Logic and Rhetoric in England, 1500–1700*, Princeton, 1956, pp.146–282, and, more recently, G.

Oldrini, 'Le particolarità del ramismo inglese' in *Rinasc.*, 1985, pp.19–80.

29 *Dr Faustus*, I, i, pp.162–3.
30 See A.G. Debus, *The English Paracelsians*, London, 1965.
31 *Dr Faustus*, I, i, pp.162–3.
32 The religious aspects of Marlowe's thought and learning are given particularly thorough treatment in P.H. Kocher, *Christopher Marlowe: a Study of his Thought, Learning and Character*, Chapel Hill, 1946.
33 For an analysis of Faustus's use of Aristotelian and Ramist logical doctrine, see A.N. Okerlund, 'The intellectual folly of Dr Faustus', *Studies in Philology*, 74, 1977, pp.258–78. I do not, however, agree with the conclusion that Marlowe is necessarily censuring Faustus for his misuse of Ramist concepts.
34 *Dr Faustus*, I, i, pp.162–3.
35 D.P. Walker, *The Decline of Hell. Seventeenth Century Discussions of Eternal Torment*, London, 1964, outlines the historical terms of the discussion in which I think Marlowe is participating here.
36 Marlowe's knowledge of Luther's and Calvin's works is discussed in Kocher, *Christopher Marlowe*. The Hermetic conception of the Renaissance magus has been outlined by F.A. Yates in Chapters I–X of *Bruno and the Hermetic Tradition*, London-Chicago, 1964, although in *The Occult Philosophy*, she argues that Marlowe was condemning the magus. The clash between the Hermetic conception of the magus and orthodox Protestant views of man is well illustrated in G.F. Waller, ' "This Matching of Contraries": Bruno, Calvin and the Sidney circle', *Neophilologus*, 56 (1972), pp.331–43.
37 See Chapter 44, 'Of witchinge magicke', in the English translation, ed C.M. Dunn, California, 1974, p.129. The introduction to this edition has some interesting remarks on the relationship between this work of Agrippa's and 'the legend of Faustus, which in many ways symbolizes the intellectual crisis of the sixteenth century' (p.xxii).
38 Harriot's interest in Arminianism has been deduced from the list of books, for which he still owed money on his death, printed by R.C. Tanner, 'Henry Stevens and the associates of Thomas Harriot', in J.W. Shirley (ed.) *Thomas Harriot, Renaissance Scientist*, Oxford, 1974, pp.91–100.
39 See *Dial.ital.*, I, pp.211–12.
40 For Bruno's attack on Ramus, see *Dial.ital.*, I, pp.260–1. For the conflict between Brunian and Ramist doctrines of memory in Elizabethan England, see F.A. Yates, *The Art of Memory*, London, 1966, pp.260–78.
41 See the introduction to *De la causa, principio et uno*, ed. G. Aquilecchia, Turin, 1973.
42 Yates, *The Art of Memory*, p.271. There can be no doubt of the

knowledge of this controversy in the Northumberland-Ralegh circles. Yates (p.277) points out that a copy of Dicson's *De umbris rationis*, republished in 1597 with the title *Thamus*, was in the Ninth Earl of Northumberland's library, while a *Diksonus de memoria* is listed among Ralegh's books. See W. Oakeshott, 'Sir Walter Ralegh's library', *The Library*, Vth s., XXIII, 1968, pp.285–327. The importance of the Bruno-Dicson relationship has recently been underlined by the discovery made by Rita Sturlese of a copy of the *De umbris idearum* held in the library of University College, London, which contains a personal dedication by Bruno to Dicson in his own hand: see R. Sturlese, 'Un nuovo autografo del Bruno con una postilla sul *De umbris rationis* di A. Dicson' in *Rinascimento*, 2nd series, vol. XXVII, 1987, pp. 387–91.

43 *Dr Faustus*, I, i, pp.162–3.
44 The fourth book of Agrippa's *De occulta philosophia*, generally considered spurious, appears to have been first published in the volume *Henrici Cornelii Agrippae Liber Quartus de Occulta Philosophia, seu de Cerimonyis Magicis, cui accesserunt Elementa Magica Petri de Abano Philosophi*, Marpurgi, 1559.
45 Cassirer, *Individuum und Kosmos*, Chapter II.
46 See E. Garin, 'Alcune osservazioni sul libro come simbolo', in *Umanesimo e simbolismo*, Padua, 1958, pp.91–102.
47 *Dr Faustus*, I, i, p.16.
48 See C. Defaye, 'Mephistophilis est-il un démon authentique?', *Etudes anglaises*, janvier-mars 1979, pp. 1–10, for some interesting comments on the peculiar nature of Marlowe's demon.
49 *Dr Faustus*, II, i, p.179.
50 The Oxford don in question was George Abbot whose sneering description of Bruno at Oxford was published in his book *The Reasons which Doctour Hill Hath Brought for the Upholding of Papistry*, 1604 (See Chapter 1, n.38). The hasty departure of Nundinio and Torquato from the Ash Wednesday supper is described at the end of Dialogue IV of the *Cena* (*Dial.ital.*, I, p.141). The page contains Bruno's famous misreading of Copernicus's description of the movements of the earth and moon, which repeats a similar error made by Pontus de Tyard in his French translation of 1552: see Aquilecchia's text of the *Cena*, Turin, 1955, p.201, n.19–n.20. The persecution suffered by Bruno after the publication of the *Cena* is hinted at in the *Proemiale epistola* and Dialogue I of the *De la causa*.
51 I agree with Kocher (see n.29) who refuses to consider as truly Copernican the verses in *Tamburlaine* sometimes considered as expressing a heliocentric universe. The critics who remain perplexed by Marlowe's apparent ignorance of Copernicanism are those who consider him an advanced Renaissance thinker, and include Kocher himself and Harry Levin in *The Overreacher*, London, 1954.
52 *Dr Faustus*, II, i, pp.179–82.

53 See 'Marlowe's "Imperial Heaven" ', *English Literary History*, XII, 1945, pp. 35–44 and 'Marlowe's astronomy and Renaissance skepticism', *English Literary History*, XIII 1946, pp.241–54.

54 In his discussion of Faustus's ceremonial magic in *The Invisible World: a Study in Pneumatology in Elizabethan Drama*, New York, 1969, Chapter VII, p.120, R.H. West suggests the possibility that Mephostophilis constantly lies to Faustus.

55 *Dial.ital.*, I, p.139. (Torquato's reply: 'Look, keep quiet, and learn: I am going to teach you Ptolemy'.)

56 I have made no attempt here to relate the Mephostophilis-Faustus relationship to Bruno's theory of 'linking' as a magical-erotic technique which allows one mind to control and dominate another. This theory was fully developed only in Bruno's late works on magic, unpublished in his life time.

57 See *Op.lat.*, I, iii, p.135.

58 There is, of course, no Chorus in the *Faust-book*. Marlowe is using a dramatic convention to express the sermonizing, disapproving tones of the anonymous, Lutheran *Faust-book* author. In the *Faust-book* it is Faust himself who describes his journey through the heavens in a letter to 'a friend in Liptzig' (see *The Historie*, Chapter XXI). Unfortunately, as Johnson pointed out, his description is based on an 'ignorant jumble of wholly unscientific astronomical lore'.

59 *Dr Faustus*, Chorus 2, p.186.

60 Song of Solomon 1:2 and 2:5. My quotations are from the English Authorized Version of 1611. Bruno, like Marlowe's Faustus, was probably quoting from the Latin of Jerome's Bible, where the sense is slightly different: 'Osculetur me osculo oris sui. . . . Fulcite me floribus, stipate me malis; quia amore langueo'; Psalm 132: 4–5: 'Si dedero somnum oculis meis dormitationem, Et requiem temporibus meis'.

61 See *Dial.ital.*, II, pp. 1011–12.

62 ibid., II, pp. 1012–13. For the classic comment on this page, see B. Spaventa, 'La dottrina della conoscenza di G. Bruno', in *Saggi di critica*, Naples, 1867, pp.252–5.

63 See Titi Lucreti Cari, *De rerum natura*, ed C. Bailey, Oxford, 1947, bk III, ll. 434–9.

64 See *De l'infinito, universo e mondi, Proemiale epistola. Dial. ital.*, I, p.360.

65 T. Nashe, *Pierce Penilesse his supplication to the devill*, London, 1592. See T. Nashe, *Works*, ed. R.B. McKerrow, Oxford, 1966, I, p.172.

66 Modern scholars underline the context of fierce religious polemic which stimulated Parsons's tract and point out that no historical evidence of the existence of such a 'school' supports his assertion. See E.A. Strathmann, *Sir Walter Ralegh: a Study in Elizabethan Skepticism*, New York, 1951, pp.25 ff., and Shirley, *A Biography*, pp.179–80.

67 The documents relating to the Ralegh enquiry were published in full by G.B. Harrison, *Willobie His Avisa*, London, 1926, Appendix III, pp.255–71. Ironside's report to the Commission is republished in Shirley, *A Biography*, pp. 194–6.
68 *Dr Faustus*, V, ii, pp.222.
69 Ibid., pp.225–7.
70 Idem.
71 See *Dial.ital.*, I, p.324.
72 *Dr Faustus*, V, ii, pp.225–7.
73 William Empson's brief discussion of Faustus's final verses as an example of his seventh and most conflictual type of ambiguity points out how the weight of Marlowe's verses here falls on the verbs 'gape' and 'come' rather than on the negatives, in which Faustus himself hardly seems any longer to believe. I agree with Empson's reading of the verses, although his conclusions from his reading seem to me arbitrary and unconvincing. See *Seven Types of Ambiguity*, London, 1930.
74 *Dr Faustus*, V, iii, p.227.
75 *Dr Faustus*, Chorus 4, p.228.
76 See *Il processo*, p.105.

5   BRUNO AND SHAKESPEARE: *HAMLET*

1 In S.T. Coleridge, *Shakespearean Criticism*, London, 1960, vol. II, p.150.
2 ibid. vol.I, p.16.
3 See *Hamlet*, The Arden Shakespeare, ed H. Jenkins, London, 1982, Introduction, pp.1–3 and Longer Notes, pp.470–2. All quotations from *Hamlet* in this chapter are from this edition.
4 See S. Schoenbaum, *William Shakespeare: a Documentary Life*, Oxford, 1975.
5 See S. Schoenbaum, *William Shakespeare: Records and Images*, London, 1981, 'The Stratford Monument', pp.156–66. Schoenbaum scrupulously gives both the positive and negative judgements which have been made of this monument, but is himself spurred to ask: 'What are we to make of the well-fed gentleman with his short neck, plump sensual cheeks, and vast forehead, who stares at us – rather stupidly, it must be granted – from his station?'.
6 The text was a polemical religious book by George Abbot, *The Reasons Which Doctour Hill Hath Brought for the Upholding of Papistry*, 1604. The discovery was made by R. McNulty, 'Bruno at Oxford', *Renaissance News*, XIII, 1960, pp. 300–5. See Chapter 1, n.38.
7 For Cobham's message from Paris, see V. Spampanato, *Vita di Giordano Bruno*, Messina, 1921, p.329, and for comments on what Bruno himself called the 'great and dangerous tempest' roused by the publication of the *Cena*, see *Dial.ital.*, I, pp.176–7.
8 Prof. G. Aquilecchia informs me that he has personally been through all these papers without finding a trace of Bruno's name.

9   For the heated discussion in Elizabethan England over Bruno's ideas on memory, see F.A. Yates, *The Art of Memory*, London, 1966, Chapter 12, 'Conflict between Brunian and Ramist memory'.

10 Bruno's remark on the importance of translations appears to have been made during his lectures given at the University of Oxford. It is picked up and referred to by the friend of Samuel Daniel who writes the Introductory Letter, signed 'N.W.', to Daniel's translation of Paolo Giovio's *Dialogo dell'imprese militari e amorose*, London, 1585, and is repeated by Florio in his Introduction to his translation of Montaigne's *Essays*. Both references are noted in *Bib. Salvestrini*.

11 Cartari's study was first published in Venice in 1576 and frequently republished for a century or more. At the end of the nineteenth century, Dowden wrote that 'a curious essay might be written upon the silences of some of the characters of Shakespeare'. This suggestion is quoted with approval in A. Thaler, *Shakespeare's Silences*, Cambridge, Mass., 1929, p.6. The subject is unfortunately discussed only briefly and superficially. The authoress appears to be unaware of a more eccentric but more imaginative treatment of the theme by Delia Bacon in *The Philosophy of the Plays of Shakespeare Unfolded*, with a Preface by Nathaniel Hawthorne, London, 1857. Although there is a lot of foggy verbiage in this book, which is among those seeking to prove that Shakespeare's works were really written by Bacon, it has some good remarks on the connections between the 'new learning' of the sixteenth century and Shakespeare's heroes and dramas. Of particular interest is Hawthorne's Preface to the book in which he quotes an unpublished page of manuscript by the same authoress which he appears to find more interesting than much in the book itself:

> it was a time when puns, and charades, and enigmas and anagrams, and monograms and cyphers, and puzzles, were not good for sport and child's play merely; when they had need to be close; when they had need to be solvable, at least, only to those who *should* solve them. It was a time when all latent capacities of the English language were put in requisition, and it was flashing and crackling, through all its lengths and breadths, with puns and quips, and conceits, and jokes, and satires, and inlined with philosophic secrets that opened down 'into the bottom of a tomb' – that opened into the Tower – that opened on the scaffold and the block.

Hawthorne quotes this passage with an approving comment on the authoress's ability to show 'how familiar the age was with all methods of secret communication, and of hiding thought beneath a masque of conceit or folly' (pp.ix–x).

12 *Dr Faustus*, Scene XVII, l. 1696.

13 ibid., ll. 1768–96.

14 *Hamlet*, I.V, ll. 167–8.

15 ibid., I.V, l. 195. The Hermetic and occult elements in *Hamlet* have been stressed by F. Yates in *The Occult Philosophy in the Elizabethan Age*, London, 1979.

16 *Hamlet*, I.V, ll. 196–7. Hamlet's mission in this sense has been seen in the light of sacrificial ritual in ancient Hellenistic terms and related as such to the *Oedipus Rex* of Sophocles in so far as both are plays in which 'the survival of the state is threatened by a specific disaster – plague or invasion – which has its source in some more obscure evil which has to be brought to light and eradicated'. See J.P. Brockbank, 'Hamlet the bonesetter', *Shakespeare Survey*, 30, 1977, pp.103–15.

17 *Dial.ital.*, II, p.554. There is now a vast literature on Renaissance astrological beliefs, but the seminal studies remain those by Aby Warburg and Fritz Saxl. See Aby Warburg, *La rinascita del paganesimo antico*, ed Gertrude Bing, Florence, 1966 and Fritz Saxl, *La fede negli astri*, ed Salvatore Settis, Turin, 1985.

18 All these references to the *Spaccio* are taken from the 'Epistola esplicatoria': see *Dial.ital.*, II, pp.549–70.

19 *Hamlet*, I, ii. 158–9.

20 ibid., V. ii. 363.

21 ibid., I. ii. 75–86.

22 See Plato, *The Symposium*, in *The Dialogues of Plato*, ed B. Jowett, Oxford, 1892, vol.I, p.586. Jowett in his analysis of *The Symposium* refers to these objects as 'the busts of Silenus, which have images of the gods inside them' (p. 523).

23 The Latin translation (the *Convivium*) was first published, together with Plato's other works, in Florence in 1484. Ficino's commentary on the text, completed in 1482, was first published together with the translation. Numerous editions of both Ficino's translations from Plato and his commentaries were published throughout the sixteenth century. There was no English translation of either, but Ficino's commentary was translated into French by Guy Le Fèvre de la Boderie and published in Paris in 1578.

24 Erasmus's extended treatment of the theme of the Sileni of Alcibiades was first published as no. 2201 of his *Adagia* by Froben in Basle, 1516. It was published again separately by Froben in 1517. The Biblioteca Erasmiana lists six other separate editions in Latin, three in Spanish, one in German, five in Dutch, and one in English. This last was printed by John Goughe, London, n.d. but probably 1543. For a modern English translation, see Margaret Mann Philips, *Erasmus on His Times: a Shortened Version of the Adages*, Cambridge, 1967, pp. 77–97. The Latin text of the Silenus adage in the modern collected works is in *Desiderii Erasmi Roterodami*, Ord. II, tom.V, Amsterdam–Oxford, 1981, pp. 159–90. A long note at the bottom of pp.159–61 sketches a history of the Silenus image in Renaissance literature. Besides Rabelais and Bruno's *Spaccio*, reference is made to a letter from Pico della Mirandola to Ermolao Barbaro in which he writes:

'L'esperienza stilistica del Bruno fra Rinascimento e Barocco', in
Atti del secondo Congresso Internazionale di studi italiani, Florence,
1958, pp.154–69. An interesting English study of Bruno's 'unusual
mode of exposition' is L. A. Breiner, 'Analogical argument in
Bruno's "De l'infinito" ', *Modern Language Notes*, 93, 1978,
pp.22–35.

45 In commenting on Bruno's relationship to Elizabethan culture,
Frances Yates wrote:

> An entirely new approach to the problem of Bruno and
> Shakespeare will have to be made. The problem goes very deep
> and must include the study, in relation to Bruno, of
> Shakespeare's profound preoccupation with significant
> language, language which 'captures the voices of the gods' – to
> use one of Bruno's marvellous expressions – as contrasted with
> pedantic or empty use of language.
>
> (*Giordano Bruno and the Hermetic Tradition*, London-Chicago,
> 1964, p.357)

46 *Hamlet*, II. ii. 173–89.
47 The only figure of a pedant in Bruno's work after the Polinnio of
the *De la causa* is Coribante in the *Cabala* (see n.40); but he is not a
major presence in the dialogue which is really a monologue of a
single character, Saulino, with occasional marginal remarks from
the other two characters present. M. Ciliberto has written on the
development of Bruno's figure of the pedant in *La ruota del tempo*,
Rome, 1986, pp.24–59.
48 *Dial.ital.*, II, p.591. The figure of Momus goes back to Hesiod who
writes of him in the *Theogony* that his mother was Night and his
father Sleep. He produces nothing of his own, but criticizes the
work of the other gods with caustic freedom. He was made use of as
a figure of satire by Lucian, where Erasmus, a translator of Lucian
with Thomas More, found and appreciated him. Erasmus includes
among his *Adages* (Iv74): 'Momo satisfacere, et similia', where after
sketching a history of the figure of Momus, he remarks
significantly:

> This god is not as popular as the others, because few people freely
> accept true criticism, yet I do not know if any of the crowd of
> gods in the poets is more useful. Nowadays, however, our Joves
> shut out Momus and only listen to Euterpe, preferring flattery to
> wholesome truth.
>
> (Erasmus, *Collected Works 31*, p.449)

On Momus as a symbol of the voice of humanism, see J.H.
Whitfield, 'Momus and the Nature of Humanism', in *Classical
Influences on European Culture A.D. 500–1500*, Cambridge, 1971,
pp. 177–83. Here the text primarily referred to is *Momus o del
Principe*, by Leon Battista Alberti (composed 1443–50, published
posthumously in Rome, 1520). Alberti's work is to some extent a

source for Bruno's *Spaccio*, for he too uses a mechanism of turning the gods into symbols of virtue and vice.

49 *Dial.ital.*, II, p.594.
50 *Hamlet*, V. ii. 221–35.
51 ibid., 252–5.
52 Bruno's clearest page in this sense comes in the first chapter of the *De triplici minimo*: see *Op.lat.*, I, iii, pp.137–8.
53 *Hamlet*, II. ii. 157–9. The rather ambiguous statement of Polonius's neo-Aristotelian cosmology here suggests that Shakespeare may have been conversant with the limited acceptance of the Copernican theory by the Danish astronomer Tycho Brahe, whom Bruno much admired although his sentiment was not reciprocated. The relationship between Bruno and Brahe has been recently studied by M.R. Pagnoni Sturlese: see 'Su Bruno e Tycho Brahe', *Rinasc.*, 1985, pp.309–33.
54 See *Hamlet*, II. ii. 181–2.
55 See Appendix II, pp.169–70, 172. Recent treatment of the theme tends to relegate Bruno to a marginal position with respect to this concept: see, for example, J.E. Hankins, *Backgrounds of Shakespeare's Thought*, Hassocks, 1978, pp. 161–71, where only a passing reference is made to Bruno on p.166.
56 Bruno's vitalism which sees all matter, even dead bones, as imbued with a vital principle which animates the entire universe is expressed with particular clarity in the second dialogue of *De la causa*: see *Dial.ital.*, I, pp.225–53.
57 *Candelaio*, II, i.
58 *Hamlet*, II, ii. 191–6.
59 ibid., 196–200.
60 *Dial.ital.*, II, pp.589–90. Quote from Dialogue I of the *Spaccio*.
61 *Hamlet*, II. ii. 202–4.
62 For these concepts see in particular the first two books of the *De triplici minimo*.
63 For the whole exchange see *Hamlet*, II. ii. 206–19.
64 ibid., 254–6.
65 ibid., 252–3.
66 *Hamlet*, p.250, n.256.
67 See John Dee, *The Private Diary and the Catalogue of his Library of Manuscripts*, ed J.O. Halliwell, London, 1842, pp. 17–18.
68 *Hamlet*, II. ii. 258–65.
69 See *Dial.ital.*, II, pp.679–80.
70 *Hamlet*, II. ii. 272. As well as completing the close identification in this part of the play between Hamlet's ideas and Bruno's, this parallel serves to illuminate a passage which has always appeared obscure in spite of the attempts to paraphrase it: see *Hamlet*, p.251, nn.263–4.
71 *Hamlet*, I. v. 97–104.
72 ibid., 110–12.

73 ibid., III. iv. 110. In one of the best books to appear on *Hamlet* (N.
Alexander, *Poison, Play and Duel: a Study in 'Hamlet'*, London, 1971)
Bruno is reintroduced into *Hamlet* criticism through the subject of
memory, underlining how Hamlet's mission to remember the great
wrongs done to his father contrasts with Claudius's deliberate
rhetoric of forgetfulness: the rhetoric of corrupt power. Alexander
appears to have based his thesis on a reading of the *Furori* in the
light of the Yatesian study of the *Art of Memory*. See Appendix II,
p.185.
74 *Dial.ital.*, II, pp. 644–5.
75 ibid., pp.633–43.
76 For a discussion of the inner play as a memory aid, see Alexander,
Poison, Play and Duel, n.73.
77 *Hamlet*, V. i. 178–86.
78 ibid., V. ii. 352–4. For a discussion of this episode within the
economy of the whole play, see W.T. Jewkes, ' "To tell my story":
the function of framed narrative and drama in *Hamlet*', in
Shakespearian Tragedy, Stratford-upon-Avon Studies no. 20,
London, 1984, pp. 31–46. The telling and retelling of things from
multiple points of view is also commented on by F. Kermode in the
section on *Hamlet* in his study *Forms of Attention*, London, 1985,
where *Hamlet* is discussed in the light of a play of mirrors: the
central image of the drama according to Kermode's reading.
79 See *Hamlet*, V. ii. 385–91. The contrast between the figures of
Hamlet and Horatio can be considered in terms of the contrast
between the philosopher and the historian developed by Sir Philip
Sidney in his *An Apology for Poetry*, ed K. Duncan-Jones and J. Van
Dorsten, Oxford, 1973, p. 85:

> For his [the philosopher's] knowledge standeth so upon the
> abstract and general, that happy is that man who may understand
> him, and more happy that can apply what he doth understand.
> On the other side, the historian, wanting the precept, is so tied,
> not to what should be but to what is, to the particular truth of
> things and not to the general reason of things, that his example
> draweth no necessary consequence, and therefore a less fruitful
> doctrine.

Sidney resolves this contrast in the figure of the poet: 'Now doth the
peerless poet perform both', a conclusion with which Shakespeare
no doubt agreed. Horatio's declaration concerning the things he
can 'truly deliver' should also be seen in the light of a wide
Renaissance meditation on the nature of the historical process: for
some comments on this question see n.86.
80 *Hamlet*, III. ii. 62–74.
81 *Dial.ital.*, II, p.803.
82 ibid., p.804.
83 Bruno's pages here correspond to a widespread interest in England

for this particular biblical book in the years of cultural crisis around the turn of the century. Nor is it a coincidence, perhaps, if we find the main references to the prophet Jonah in a series of figures who, in one way or another, may be directly linked to Bruno. The first figure to draw attention in this context is Peter Baro (Petri Baronis Stempani). This French Protestant theologian had fled to England during the anti-Protestant massacres in France, and was appointed a professor of divinity at Cambridge where he taught until the last years of the sixteenth century. Baro's tenure of his Cambridge post was not a tranquil one, for he stood firmly for some form of retainment of a doctrine of free will, and for the importance of human works as a factor in man's salvation. Baro's formulation of these opinions in his most radical writings led him to clash directly with the doctrine of salvation by faith alone. In his *A Speciall Treatise of Gods Providence*, for example, published in an English translation from Latin in 1588, Baro in one of his sermons provocatively makes his point of reference the Epistle of James rather than the Pauline epistles which had offered Luther his basic texts for his doctrine of salvation by faith. Through reference to James 2, Baro on the contrary defends what he calls a 'lively' faith, which includes good works, while attacking 'that idle and unprofitable faith' which he considers as dead and which disregards works as a means of man's salvation, Bruno, during his prolonged stay at the French Embassy in London in the 1580s, would almost certainly have heard about Baro, and would surely have appreciated his stand against extreme Protestant doctrines which he himself was criticizing in powerful terms in his Italian dialogues. If Bruno consulted Baro's weighty Latin commentary on the book of Jonah, published in 1579, he would have found there a particular appreciation of this biblical book for the clarity with which it exposes the problem of the divine will in relation to man's possibility of acting within the workings of providence. A second source to refer to the book of Jonah in a treatment of contemporary problems takes us to a date after Bruno's departure from England. It could be that the reference to Jonah here owes something to Bruno, for the drama concerned, *A Looking-Glass for London and England*, published in-quarto in 1594, was written by Thomas Lodge and Robert Green. We have seen that Greene was closely associated with Marlowe, while Lodge too is thought possibly to have had connections with Bruno. What is certain is that this play, which contains a number of clear echoes from *Dr Faustus*, makes a direct identification between the corrupt Nineveh of the book of Jonah and the London of the day. It was probably an analogous sense of the direct relevance to contemporary problems of this particular biblical book which led George Abbot, later to be Archbishop of Canterbury, to publish in English, at the beginning of the seventeenth century, a lengthy commentary on the same book. Abbot has already been encountered in this study as the figure who offers us the only written evidence we have of Bruno's débâcle at Oxford. His treatment of that episode, as we have seen, was sharply critical of Bruno; and it was not to be expected that his treatment of the Jonah story, which is orthodox and without elements of particular interest, should relate in any way to Bruno's own, far more polemical and complex reference. Nevertheless, to find the only person we know of who actually witnessed Bruno's performance at Oxford also paying particular attention to this book is perhaps something more than a mere coincidence. At the least, it confirms the relevance which the Jonah story seems to have assumed during the crisis years which saw the composition both of Bruno's *Spaccio* and Shakespeare's *Hamlet.*

84 *Dial.ital.*, II, p.807. For Bruno's anti-Christian polemic, see A. Ingegno, *La sommersa nave della religione*, Naples, 1985.

85 *Hamlet*, V. ii. 215–18. For the relative 'functions' of Fortinbras, Horatio, and Hamlet himself in the final scenes of the play, see R.M. Frye, *The Renaissance Hamlet: Issues and Responses in 1600*, Princeton, 1984, Chapter V, 'The deliberate Prince', section II, 'The ideal: Mars and Mercury'. Working on the evidence of half/half figures such as Mars/Mercury or Soldier/Scholar in the Emblem Book, *The Mirror of Majesty* (1618), Figs V, 2 and V, 3, Frye presents Horatio as a devotee of Mercury and Fortinbras as a devotee of Mars (p.175). The ideal was to unite the Mercurian character (defined by the emblematist as 'coward') with the follower of Mars (characterized as 'blunt') so as to achieve rational and proportioned action: an ideal which can be said to be represented by the Hamlet of the final scenes.

86 The underlining in the passage is mine. It is interesting to note the terms in which this particular passage is quoted by E Garin in a seminal essay on Renaissance concepts of history: 'La storia nel pensiero del rinascimento', Bari, 1954 (now in the series Universali Laterza, pp.179–95). Garin sees the Renaissance as divided between two contrasting concepts of history, one of which, in coherently humanist terms, underlines the human will as the effective creative force of the historical process, while the other, conceding more space to the play of fortune and eternal vicissitude, annuls all possibility of progress in a naturalistic vision of continual mutation which determines the life of man and the universe. Garin shows how two of the greatest thinkers of the Renaissance, Machiavelli and Bruno himself, expressed in different moments both these concepts of man's relation to history. As far as Bruno's historical thought is concerned, he sees the *Spaccio* as the work which shows Bruno in his most optimistic, humanist spirit, proposing a vision of man controlling history with the force of his will and his hands. On the other hand, the *Candelaio* passage cannot be seen simply as an early statement of an opposite vision which Bruno will later repudiate, for, as Garin points out, he was known at Wittemberg, after his departure from England, for his insistent

repetition of the words of Ecclesiastes: 'Quid est quod est? ipsum quod fuit. Quid est quod fuit? ipsum quod est. Nihil sub sole novum'.

87 *Hamlet*, V. ii. 216–18.
88 ibid., 382–5.
89 Bruno's presence within the culture of the Enlightenment has been the subject of numerous Italian studies: see in particular N. Badaloni, 'Appunti intorno alla fama del Bruno nei secoli XVII e XVIII', *Società*, 14 (3), 1958, pp.487–519. In England, the subject has been studied above all by Margaret Jacobs in a development of Frances Yates's work on the Rosicrucian Enlightenment: see *The Newtonians and the English Revolution (1689–1720)*, Hassocks, 1976, and *The Radical Enlightenment: Pantheists, Freemasons and Republicans*, London, 1981. Athough in these and other studies, the Enlightenment reading of Bruno is generally acknowledged to have been partial in its selection of his rationalist and encyclopedic motives and its indifference to his use of myth and his appeal to the imagination, this awareness has not led to a sufficiently widespread reappraisal of Bruno's presence within the Romantic movement, which begins with the work of F.H. Jacobi and continues in Schelling, with Coleridge in England as a participant in this new phase of Bruno's fortune. (F.W.J.Schelling, *Bruno oder über das göttliche und natürliche Prinzip der Dinge*, Berlin, 1802. F.H. Jacobi, *Ueber die Lehre des Spinoza in Briefen au den Hernn Moses Mendelsshon. . .*, Breslau, 1789; reference to Bruno above all in the preface and in the first appendix, pp. 261–77. S.T. Coleridge, *Notebooks*, vol. I (1794–1804), London, 1957. See, for Bruno, nos. 927–28–29 dated April, 1801, and the remarks on these entries by Coleridge's editor, Kathleen Coburn, in the accompanying volume of *Notes*.) It is at the culmination of this Romantic phase that the first modern editions of his works are published: the Italian works in Leipzig (1829) and the Latin works in Stuttgart (1836). Later, in a post-Romantic, and at times anti-Romantic, positivist climate of opinion and debate, the initiative is taken in Italy of organizing the preparation of a more complete and reliable edition of the Latin works, financed by the new Italian state (1879–91); while at the beginning of the twentieth century, Giovanni Gentile prepares his authoritative edition of the Italian works. Apart from some isolated studies of particular aspects of Bruno's reputation in this period, the exact terms and full extent of his presence in the mainstream of Romantic and post-Romantic European culture still have to be fully explored.

INDEX

INDEX

224